~ A ~ Pianist's Landscape

A Pianist's

Landscape

by Carol Montparker

Amadeus Press
Portland, Oregon

Earlier versions of parts of this work originally appeared in *Clavier* magazine, which is published by The Instrumentalist Publishing Company, 200 Northfield Road, Northfield, Illinois 60093. Used by permission.

All illustrations by Carol Montparker.

Paperback edition printed 2002.

Library of Congress Cataloging-in-Publication Data

Montparker, Carol.
A pianist's landscape / by Carol Montparker.
p. cm.
Includes bibliographical references and index.
ISBN 1-57467-073-5 (paperback)
1. Montparker, Carol. 2. Pianists—United States—Biography.
I. Title.
ML417.M849A3 1998
786.2'092—dc21 97-49643
[B] CIP
MN

AMADEUS PRESS
(an imprint of Timber Press, Inc.)
The Haseltine Building
133 S.W. Second Avenue, Suite 450
Portland, Oregon 97204 USA

Printed in Hong Kong
Designed by Susan Applegate

Some reviews of the hardcover edition of *A Pianist's Landscape*

"In *A Pianist's Landscape* she has woven a garland out of meditations on various aspects of a musician's life, sharing her experiences as well as her inner thoughts on what goes into the making of music and the making of musicians....Musicians very often have a difficult time putting into words what it is they do. Not Montparker. One of the chief delights of this book is that it is so engagingly well written; it opens things up to the lay reader without the slightest hint of awkwardness or pretension. Montparker talks about what musicians think, how they interact, their foibles, joys and fears, with the ease of someone talking about what's growing in her garden. The writing is direct, the expression of thoughts and feelings remarkably concrete." —Ted Libbey, *Washington Post Book World*

"Montparker, senior editor of *Clavier* magazine, pianist, teacher, writer, and painter, relates her experiences with music and people in a thoroughly engaging way. . . . Her essays will be enjoyed not by musicians only, but by all music lovers who want to be swept away by an honest and warm description of an artist's life and its trials and rewards." — *Booklist*

"Montparker's appealing account of her life as a concert pianist—practicing, performing, teaching—contains insights that will enrich practitioners in all the creative arts. Her sense of music as a spontaneous adventure and her reverence for the piano as a link to one's inner life show through in this variegated collection of essays."
— *Publishers Weekly*

This book is for Ernest

Contents

Foreword *by Jerome Lowenthal* / 9
Acknowledgments / 11
Preface / 13

AT HOME

1 Nature and Music / 17
2 Working and Concentrating at Home / 25
3 An Artistically Nourishing Environment / 34
4 Music-Making *en Famille* / 41
5 Pianos as Furniture and as Souls / 49
6 Old Music, Music Cabinets, and Tapes / 57
7 The Piano as Comfort in Times of Stress / 66
8 Letters and Mementos / 71
9 A Toast to Fine Technicians and Tuners / 86
10 The Creative Impulse / 89

ON STAGE

11 The Love-Hate Paradox of Performing / 97
12 On Being a Woman Pianist / 107
13 Memory Lapses and Other Mishaps / 116
14 Remembering Carnegie, Criticism, and Green Rooms / 125
15 Partner-Pianists / 135
16 On Playing Chamber Music and Concertos / 141

17 Some Privileged Coachings / 147
18 Early Pianist Jobs / 152
19 The Art of Programming / 159
20 The Essential Ego / 169

IN THE STUDIO
21 Why Teach? / 177
22 Playing Classes, Recitals, and Auditions / 186
23 Students I've Known and What They've Taught Me / 198
24 Teaching the Nitty-Gritties, Marking the Music, the Human Factor / 210
25 Leopold Mittman: A Memoir / 218
26 On Being Respected and Loved as a Teacher / 227
27 One Door Closes and Another Opens / 232

IN THE FIELD
28 In the Field / 243
29 That Infernal Little Machine / 252
30 The Most Jazzy Encounters / 260
31 Coping with the Extraordinary / 267
32 Away From Home / 278
33 Home Again: Some Final Thoughts / 283

Notes / 287
Bibliography / 292
Index / 293

Foreword

THOSE who deplore the tendency of pianists to be "fortists" will particularly enjoy Carol Montparker's collection of essays. For although as a performer Ms. Montparker is capable of the greatest range of expressive dynamics, as a writer she specializes in the art of soft suggestion, Chopinesque in its nuanced delicacy. Her interviews are dialogue-impromptus in which the form seems organically related to the person being interviewed, whether through motifs of psyche or art or even hair color (vermilion in the case of Tagliaferro).

Her explorations of the pianist's predicament are like variegated preludes in such keys as memorizing, practicing, choice of instrument, performing, teaching, and child-rearing. At first one is most charmed by the fantasy of her ornamentation, then by the consistency of developed melodic thought, and finally by the underlying structure of allusive form-types.

As with the great cycles of Bach and Chopin, each essay is a building block in the architecture of key-inclusiveness. Although an enormous number of questions are posed in these essays, the whole collection asks one great question: "What is a pianist?" To find the answer, read the book.

JEROME LOWENTHAL

Jerome Lowenthal, concert pianist and faculty member at the Juilliard School, has also served as chairman of Juilliard's piano department.

Acknowledgments

I WOULD like to give special thanks to my kind publisher at The Instrumentalist Company, James T. Rohner, who has been my boss at *Clavier* for almost twenty years. He has generously allowed me to use material from my "Carillon" columns along with excerpts from articles that have appeared in the magazine.

I wish to express my appreciation to the Glenn Gould Foundation in Toronto, Ontario; to Mrs. Arthur Rubinstein; to the family of Gerald Moore; to Horacio Gutiérrez; and to Donal Henahan, all for their kind permission to include material from their letters.

My most special thanks go to three great concert artists for taking time midst their unbelievably busy schedules to read my manuscript: Jerome Lowenthal for the Foreword for this book, Alfred Brendel for his time and words of encouragement, and André Watts for his abiding friendship and support.

To Eve Goodman, my dream editor, go my gratitude and thanks for her initial enthusiasm, her understanding, her commitment to excellence, and the pleasure of working with her.

. . .

I want to thank my wonderful husband and best friend, Ernest Taub, for *everything*, including a large measure of love and belief, his keen intelligence, expert advice and editing of these essays before anyone else saw them, and willingness to shoulder the lion's share during the course of this book. Ernie has an elegant way of placing a fresh cup of tea quietly beside me with a little kiss, and then leaving me to work for long hours, rescuing me when enough's enough.

I also wish to thank my loving parents: Grace Mont, particularly for her legacy of intellectual curiosity and action, and Edward Mont for his intuition and humor.

I send affectionate thanks to my friends whose enthusiasm and support were vital; special thanks to Judith Moshan for her "quirky reading" and fine suggestions, and to Andrea Klepetar-Fallek, whose multilingual skills helped to polish my spellings.

To all my students past and present, whose individuality, hard work, and affections helped shape this book, thank you.

Preface

THE essays in this book describe my life as a pianist—practicing, performing, teaching, and writing. Many were developed from the columns entitled "Carillon" which I have been writing for *Clavier* magazine for about seven years.

I have organized the pieces loosely into settings: home, stage, studio, and field, the various arenas of my musical activities, but in fact each piece of the landscape overlaps and touches the others. For example, if I have interviewed a famous artist (In the Field) for a feature article on Tuesday, chances are on Wednesday I will apply insights I have garnered from that privileged conversation directly into a student's lesson (In the Studio) or into my own practicing (At Home). If new and exciting revelations come to light while I am teaching a masterwork, as soon as possible I will be at work at my own piano, reexamining that work, probably with a view to performing it (On Stage).

My tangential career as journalist emerged as a by-product of my Carnegie Recital Hall debut in 1976. I kept a journal of the whole process—emotional, technical, artistic, and psychological—that ultimately became a little book, *The Anatomy of a New York Debut Recital: A Chronicle*,[1] and that, along with freelance pieces for various publications, led to my appointment as senior editor at *Clavier*. The exciting work I have been lucky to do for the magazine—interviewing, reviewing books and concerts, and doing research—has fed right back into my own playing.

A day doesn't go by without an idea striking and begging to be jotted down. My students are quite used to my scribblings if we hit upon something important that I do not want to lose. I have often wanted to borrow back their notebooks into which I have scrawled key instructions and guidance that might, by this time, comprise a useful compendium. I keep a pad on my piano for similar "light bulbs" going off while I practice, and I always have paper in my purse. I write backstage, in the darkness of the night in the pad on the night table, in airplanes, on concert programs, and even in the car at a stop light. Those fragments, which I have somehow kept for years, have seemed to jump together into essays, almost as bits of colored glass scramble and coalesce into designs inside a kaleidoscope. The resulting collection of essays describes the beautiful landscape of my pianist life.

~ AT HOME ~

O may she live like some green laurel
Rooted in one dear perpetual place.

WILLIAM BUTLER YEATS

~ 1 ~

Nature and Music

I HAVE come to think of myself as both naturalist and musician. Certainly I have found a great source of spiritual strength in both realms, and probing the relationship between the two has been an ongoing preoccupation and pleasure for as long as I can remember. Apparently even as an infant, I looked up into trees and murmured to the rustling leaves. Now, my first love, nature, can subvert my work at the piano, for example, when a red fox emerges from the woods and catches the corner of my eye, or a bird song seems more beautiful than anything I could ever play.

I have sometimes transcribed an interview with a legal pad on my lap, the tape recorder in one hand and a pair of binoculars in the other, while sitting right in my garden; that's my idea of the perfect work environment. During the warmer months, I have to leave extra time before I teach to transform my hands from a gardener's to a piano teacher's.

On our screened porch, we have a rule: no radios, tapes, or other distractions—only the sounds that nature dishes up. It has become a sort of Zen retreat: nourishing, restorative, and ultimately inspiring to transform that beauty into various creative channels. The French have an expression for what I do out there: *laisser l'esprit vaguer,* to let the spirit wander. I call it *vaguer*ing, and May is probably when I *vaguer* the most.

The thrush, in particular, has a song that moves me as much or more than any music. He had been missing from our property for a few years, although he stopped to sing and forage en route to more densely forested areas. Of late we have left our wooded tracts alone, neither tended nor pruned, and it is almost too wild to walk there; the overgrown thicket not only attracted the fox, but brought back the thrush, and I take it as a compliment and a blessing. More often heard than seen, he is relatively plain, with speckled breast and umber plumage. But his full-throated, intermittent phrases, delicately ornamented, slightly and infinitely varied, render me a captive audience; I stand motionless wherever I am while his song reaches me over the trees and across the green expanse of lawn from his podium branch. No mere grackling, clucking, chirping, or whistling of ordinary birds, this fluting is what many years ago I told my little girl, Kim, to strive for in her music-making. She knew what I meant and has since become a beautiful, mature flutist.

On one particular morning of the thrush's return, I was in such a state of reverie that I couldn't bring myself to practice. It seemed almost sacrilegious so I kept the doors wide open during all my lessons that day; our mortal endeavors were punctuated by the unattainable, and the lines by Robert Browning, who was a trained musician, came to mind:

> That's the wise thrush: he sings his song twice over
> Lest you think he never could recapture
> The first fine careless rapture![1]

Wordsworth, Keats, Tennyson, and Shakespeare similarly immortalized the bird. William Morris wrote, "O Thrush, your song is passing sweet," and Thomas Hardy noted its "fullthroated evensong of joy illimited."

I don't need poets' words to authenticate my response to the thrush's song. I have accompanied menial chores around the house with a Mozart piano concerto or a Beethoven symphony, but I can barely get a thing done for listening to this refrain. I feel like the daughter to whom Yeats wrote his "Prayer"—"O may she live like some green laurel, / Rooted in one dear perpetual place"—because of the infinite beauty in our modest piece of land, and not the least of the beauty comes from the music in nature.

We have all enjoyed the music of nature in a chorus of insects on a summer night, wind rustling through trees, a rippling brook, a torrent of rain, bird songs; what we are not so aware of is the extent to which music is a language that derives from the sounds of nature. The solo piano literature is rich with examples of compositions clearly inspired by nature. Brahms was asked about a certain Andante from his intermezzos, "How did you dream up that beautiful theme?" He replied "A lot of walking in the woods." Of course Andante comes from *andare,* the Italian verb, to walk. There are many works that are clearly called "Spring Song," or "The Butterfly," conscious references by the composer to a particular experience in nature. But most music is absolute, and then the sources of inspiration are not as accessible to us. However, even in the most abstract music, there are hundreds of stylized imitations or references to natural phenomena. Moreover, music, of all the arts, parallels the basic rhythms of life with its patterns of ebb and flow. It is so related to our systems that it has been proven to affect our blood pressure, metabolism, and pulse. Music makes us want to dance and makes our bodies try and match its tempo, while having a potent effect on our emotions. The reason is that music is closely related to the very thing from which it comes: music is an extension of nature.

The inspiration that composers have drawn directly from nature has been well documented. I heard the late Japanese composer, Toru Takemitsu, speak about the connection between the music he wrote and the elements of time and space represented in Japanese gardens. He said, "I try to work the elements of time and change represented by plants, and the permanence that rocks convey, into my orchestrations. You might say I design gardens with music."

In my work as a music journalist, many performing artists have told me of the repose, solace, energy, and inspiration they get from direct communion with nature. Andras Schiff told me that for many years he chose to live in Austria to be close to the countryside that inspired Mozart, Schubert, and Beethoven (despite the enduring presence of Nazism which ravaged his family during the war). Pianist Krystian Zimerman told me that when he is nervous backstage he tells himself to "think of a beautiful tree": with that image before him, he gathers strength and calm.

When I play Bach, I am reminded of nature on a universal, cosmic plane. The Greek philosopher and mathematician Pythagoras wrote about "the harmony of the spheres," believing that a kind of primordial music soared throughout the universe. Bach's music is like the "harmony of the spheres," order-giving, perfectly proportioned, infinitely varied, heavenly, and uplifting. The idea of a mighty music reverberating to the largest laws of nature was also described by the late great conductor, Bruno Walter.

No one said it better than Beethoven in letter after letter, reconfirming Nature as his source. He never walked in the woods without his notebook. He knew the brooks and trees and birds would speak to him, and it was his refuge where he was naively happy, whereas with men, his rage about his increasing deafness would come to the fore. He chose his rooms in Vienna specifically because they were situated just at the city gates and he could walk in the parkland. In a letter to a friend, he wrote:

> You will ask me where I get my ideas. That I cannot tell you with certainty; they come unsummoned, directly, indirectly. I

> could seize them with my hands in the open air . . . in the woods, while walking in the silence of the nights . . . incited by moods that are translated . . . by me into tones that roar and storm about me until I have set them down into notes.[2]

Beethoven wrote musical shrines to his beloved countryside in many compositions, most notably the Pastoral Symphony, where he noted his intentions by writing right into the score: "Awakenings of happy feelings on arriving in the country." You can hear him taking that first deep breath of fresh air in the opening bar's rest. Beethoven spoke of nature as "a glorious school for the heart" where he would be a scholar and learn its wisdoms. Every time I play the Sonata, Opus 79, in G major (a key that many musicians associate with a purifying and uplifting quality), I feel Beethoven's exultation in the natural world. He wrote the call of the cuckoo right into the score: the first movement becomes almost a fantasia around that call. It is full of the gladness of nature and the spirit of unabashed joy felt by the great master as he notated his musical ideas, all of which we can experience if we allow the music to wash over us.

Several years ago I spent many happy hours at home preparing a solo lecture-recital on the subject of nature and music, which I have since presented several times. The most difficult thing was choosing among the myriad possibilities for the program. I had to forego programming Schubert, whose songs describe every natural delight, with the piano accompaniments translating natural effects into music. I would have loved to play some of Liszt's sketches from *Années de pèlerinage* after his travels in Italy and Switzerland. But the program I finally decided upon was filled with glorious examples: along with Bach and Beethoven, I included Mendelssohn, who was intensely moved by his natural surroundings and who expressed his enthusiasm, as I also love to do, in watercolors as well as in music.

Chopin was also on the program. George Sand wrote about him,

"His genius is full of the mysterious harmonies of nature," and indeed, the cascading showers of notes and violent winds are clear testimony to his sensitivity to nature. The painter Eugène Delacroix described the pastoral setting of Nohant, Sand's country estate:

> This is a delightful place. Every now and then there blows in through your window opening onto the garden, a breath of the music of Chopin who is at work in his room, and it mingles with the song of the nightingales and the scent of roses.[3]

Similar sensations have made me grateful to have a view of the garden and woods from my piano which likewise brings energy from the out-of-doors directly into my music-making. Just substitute my thrush for Chopin's nightingale.

As no recital about nature and music would be complete without the Impressionists, I programmed Debussy's *Reflets dans l'eau*. The Impressionist painters translated nature into light and color, and the composers responded sensuously with tone paintings. There was great camaraderie and cross-pollination between the artists in all genres—so much so that they borrowed from each other to describe their work, crossing boundaries into what the English novelist George Moore called "audible color and visible sound." Debussy created evocative pictures from what he called "atmospheric vibrations," and in his work, water seems to play the most significant role, as in *Jardins sous la pluie, La cathédrale engloutie*, and others. In *Reflets dans l'eau* we are transported to Monet's gardens at Giverny where the *nymphéas* (water lilies) pop right off the page, where a pebble tossed into the ponds causes concentric circles to ripple and swirl, where raindrops fall gently, turning into cascades and torrents of wind. It is all there in the music, and although I am highly visual, I find that the best approach to playing it is not to "copy" nature but to become infused with the feelings that nature evokes.

Because of my interest in birds, I worked at putting together a grouping of music inspired by bird songs. The list is endless, from Couperin's *Le coucou* to Liszt's *Prédication des oiseaux*, Ravel's *Oiseaux tristes*, Bartók's *Musiques nocturnes,* and Messiaen's *Catalogue des oiseaux*. Messiaen was, as I am, an amateur birdwatcher, but he took courses in ornithology until he could recognize the calls of more than five hundred species. Early in his career, his teacher Paul Dukas told him, "Listen to the birds; they are great masters." Messiaen tried to notate the complex trillings, rhythms, and melodies. But bird songs are often extremely fast, with infinitesimal intervals, closer than our scale tones. What matters to us is not his naive struggle to reproduce the songs, nor the authenticity of his results, but rather that the music is a product of that process of its coming through the prism of his imagination. He wrote, "The melodic contours, those of merles (blackbirds) particularly, surpass the human imagination in fantasy."

I called Patelson's Music House in Manhattan to order the *Catalogue des oiseaux* only to find, to my amazement, that there were seven volumes, averaging $30 apiece! So I ordered a volume that had "L'alouette" (Skylark), one of his favorites, and found that these catalogs are not concert music but rather compendiums—episodic, strange, and very complicated with diarylike entries about the terrain sporadically appearing throughout the score. It is clear that birds were his passion:

> Birdsong is my refuge. In dark hours when my uselessness is brutally revealed to me and all the musical language in the world seems to be an effort of patient research, without there being anything behind the notes to justify so much work, I go into the forest, into fields, into mountains, by the sea, among birds . . . it is there that music dwells for me: free anonymous music, improvised for pleasure.[4]

I heard a lovely story from a friend, Arbie Orenstein, who has written books on another composer who notated bird songs and incorporated them into his symphonic works: Maurice Ravel. While Orenstein was standing on the balcony of Ravel's home near Paris at Montfort l'Amaury, overlooking the Rambouillet woods and hills, he heard a bird sing a phrase that astonished him by its similarity to the famous flute theme from Ravel's *Daphnis and Chloe*. One can imagine Ravel on his balcony, jotting down the song of this bird's ancestors.

. . .

I included in the plan for my "Nature and Music" program "The Bird as Prophet" from *Waldscenen* by Schumann. The bird that inspired Schumann must have had a similar episodic and rhapsodic song to that of my thrush, singing from a branch, as from a pulpit, deep in the shrouded refuge of the woods.

~ 2 ~

Working and Concentrating at Home

DID you ever notice that the outside world (and even friends and family) do not always truly respect the work one does at home *as work?* All my work—practicing, teaching, writing, and painting—is based at home, yet the mere fact that I answer the telephone makes me fair game to anyone who feels like talking. Unfortunately I am too curious to let the answering machine take calls when I am home.

"Are you teaching?" a well-meaning acquaintance might ask. "No, but—" I begin to answer. I was practicing, but that's the end of that, as the person, pleased at being so clever as to call during a nonteaching slot, assumes I am free. Even if I respond, "No, I was working at the piano," or "No, I was writing," only my close friends have ever offered to call back. Playing the piano must seem such an agreeable pastime to others; it all sounds so frivolous—not like a real nine-to-five job. It reminds me of something I heard the writer Eudora Welty tell in an interview: a neighbor of hers called on her, remarking in a charming Southern drawl, "I knew you weren't busy, because I could see you writin' through the window."

The problem is mine, not anyone else's. First of all, there are ways of communicating that I have not yet tapped; I have a close friend whose several books have been written under strict regimens at home. When you call her during her prescribed hours of work, you know it by her clipped, terse tone. Anyone with a fairly sensitive ear receives a clear message of intrusion and gets right off. I don't think I could learn to use that voice technique to my advantage, though I respect her for the sincere and jealous guarding of her time, as well as for her clear sense of priorities. I'll have to learn how to say, "I cannot talk now," and try to get on with the fascinating and complex phenomenon called concentration.

Concentration is as much a talent, I am convinced, as anything else. It is an illusory thing that cannot be taught, yet can possibly be copied if perceived in others. I have students who can sit through a sibling's lesson in the same room and read a book or do their homework. I could not. I cannot read with music playing, nor can I read at the beach or in the garden, because invariably I find I'd rather be contemplating the sky, water, or trees.

When I sit down to work at the piano, I must have certain prerequisites before I can begin to concentrate. Unlike Saul Bellow who said "I like to think of writing as an achievement of stillness in the middle of chaos," if there is the slightest disorder in my work space, I go about the room straightening it out. Unfinished business or unresolved issues interject themselves as well; my mind must be as clear as the workspace, or the feeling of unrest subverts the concentration. Call it a ritual rather than a compulsion.

. . .

Years ago I had a New York recital scheduled and had put a substantial down payment on the hall. Then I found myself in the middle of a divorce (although the situation leading up to it was chronic, the culmination came suddenly). There was no way I could prepare sufficiently for a recital because there was no repose in my life that would permit concentration. I had to claim a physical illness (not too far from the truth) in order to be able to disengage myself from the commitment and retrieve my money. I didn't feel good about it, and

I would have loved to be able to restore myself with good work and ultimate success, but that was not meant to be. Around that time I had lunch with the great pianist Radu Lupu, who was in New York for a concert, and as I was expressing these feelings of disappointment to him, he generously shared the fact that there were times in his life when he, too, could not concentrate because of inner turmoil.

"What—do you think I always want to practice? I do not! Do you think I can always concentrate? I cannot!" he insisted with an emphatic sympathy. It was a great comfort at the time. Yet there are artists who can stay at the piano eight to ten hours daily, no matter what. They can obviate all else, apparently, and if they can escape the physical abuse to their bodies, that gives them a great advantage. Some artists need more time than others; their physical apparatus requires more repetition to absorb new patterns. I have heard stories of pianists who practiced a thorny passage hundreds of times while reading a novel propped up on the piano. That would never work for me. Neither would the novel be savored, nor would I notice the little threadbare places that needed technical reweaving here and there; the alternate fingering or approach that might suggest itself with full devotion to the task, would all be lost. I have never practiced more than three or four hours in a day. My heart and mind might want it, but my neck and back say "No!" Besides, I strongly feel that you get diminishing returns after four hours, and that relates to how much one's body and mind can absorb. (Incidentally, listening to music requires great concentration, too, and one may not always be in the right frame of mind to listen to a concert, even when one finds oneself in a concert hall!)

. . .

The presence of another pair of ears is likely to transform true practicing into "playing." Arthur Rubinstein once declared that the arrival of a chambermaid in the hotel room where he was practicing instantly changed his focus; from that moment he was playing to her. I have, for that reason, done some of my best work in the silence of the night.

Most of the time I spend at the piano is in preparation for a concert. It is pure work, under pressure of time, but it is not without its deep satisfactions: the sense of workmanship and problem-solving, the tangible development of technical facility, and the exploratory passage down deep through the strata of work-levels from the purely physical to the moment of striking gold at the core. If anyone were around, he or she would think I was nuts. I might shout an angry imperative out loud—"Oh, c'mon!"—when I fail to grab a difficult bunch of notes, or an annoyed observation—"You're kidding!"—when something stupid happens. I haven't figured out who I'm shouting at: my hands? the muses? God?

When I do find the rare entire day to work at the piano without a concert pending, a quirky, evasive mechanism sometimes occurs: the sense of luxury renders me inert until I can decide how to spend the precious hours. Deciding how to spend found time is as hard as finding the time! Occasionally I have a fifteen-minute hiatus between lessons, and even that takes on a precious quality, particularly if I sit down at the piano. It makes one wish to be stranded on that proverbial desert island.

During those rare times when I "just play," I may either indulge in some new music or reacquaint myself with old repertoire. One day I might choose to play through the entire volume of Chopin nocturnes, or spend three hours purifying myself with a Mozart sonata marathon. Soon I might finally get to the Bartók suite that's been on my piano for a year; and finally last summer I learned the Schumann *Kreisleriana* after yearning to for ages. A lifelong project with a high priority is my pilgrimage through the two books of preludes and fugues of Bach's *Well-Tempered Clavier*. I find it incredibly and continually daunting that Bach created a second book of his twenty-four preludes and fugues in every key, twenty-two years after the first volume of masterpieces, and that each one is distinctly different from its predecessor in the same key. Of all music, Bach requires supreme concentration, not only for the initial learning but also for the process of peeling off layer upon layer to get to the deepest level. Slowly, phrases in the form of posed questions, and then answers, pop off the page like so many holograms, hitherto hidden from one's vision; wit, sadness, elation, all emotions are "colored in" (with as much delight as a child confronting a fresh page in a coloring book) with a variety of touch, dynamics, stretto, rubato, voicing, and so on. Given ample time, I can get myself into a possessed state, replaying a hundred times, making musical decisions, until all the symbolism, passion, and spirituality make their way from the dots on the page into my heart and soul.

A friend asked me, "Is it a lonely experience to make these discoveries? Don't you feel you have to share them with someone?"

The answer is, unequivocally, "No." First of all, there are no words that could describe the experience. Secondly, there is no one available that could share it exactly as I would need to at that moment. Although I know many fine musicians and people who like to try to verbalize abstract ideas, it is not a megaphone type of phenomenon; it is an inner matter, and one has to feel content and whole unto oneself. Most importantly, there are no absolute truths, and my convictions might not hold for the next musician. I was hard at work to "do right by" Beethoven's Opus 109; it felt better and better, yet I kept questioning myself as to whether I had unearthed the true meaning of the great late-Beethoven. Just at that moment I read Mitsuko Uchida's honest and wry admission: "I haven't a clue about late Beethoven. . . . But then, who does?" So much of how we work is thoroughly subjective, based on our personal experience, with high hopes of coming close to Beethoven's. These are the purest moments in music—much more so than performances.

. . .

When I am entirely relaxed, I can savor every aspect of being a pianist and of the instrument's charms, along with the sense of the pair of us together. In order to accomplish that, I push the music desk back or open the lid so that the full nuance of the sound gets to me. If I watch the furry white hammers through the strings, there's a strange sense of the randomness of their pop-ups, as they are so removed from my fingers through all the mechanical elements of the action; if I watch my hands, they too seem to have a mission of their own. I try to divest myself of any awareness of the components of the act to achieve a kind of weightlessness, and finally of oneness with the piano and the music. Playing in this state is, I believe, a form of meditation, because if I manage to achieve it, I come away restored and deeply grateful. Sometimes the word *revelation* might apply, because I have allowed myself to concentrate to the point of clear insight, becoming truly swept up as if in a spell, until thoroughly exhausted. That kind of experience is cleansing and illuminating, but rare.

The works with which I have become intimate over the years, those that do not require devotion to either page or keyboard, may be summoned directly from deep inside of me; I don't just play them, I play *with* them, or they play me. The music fills the chambers of my being, the piano, the room, the house, and, if I am looking out the window to my woodland muses, I feel thoroughly connected to every living thing: trees, flowers, birds, foxes, rabbits; then I am only another of God's creatures, species: musician.

. . .

As a pianist who also writes, I find it interesting that the same rules for concentration do not apply to my writing. I can and do write anywhere, it seems. I can tune out conversations, activities, airport announcements, whatever, when internal monologues need to be recorded. If I am both performing and writing about the same piece of music, invariably I have played it first. My relationships with works of music always go from physical attraction to deeper levels. Then as my emotional and intellectual involvement gels, I sometimes feel the need to record whatever insights accrue. I also like to ferret out odd fragments of information from the wonderful library we have collected at home that might enhance the excitement of the discoveries. The curiosity to explore and then the impulse to share (with readers or with an audience) have led to the engaging format of the lecture-recital; not only are listeners interested in knowing more about the music, so am I. The writer E. B. White complained, "My mind is too much of a busybody to suit me." I like to have a busy mind. Each precious day is, at once, twice as long and never long enough, especially when I am engaged in preparing a program. Each facet enhances and subtracts from the other, and I always feel a tug-of-war between practicing and writing, simply because of the limits of time and energy.

It is much easier to write: it is not the physical labor that playing is, and words are not the evasive, abstract expressers of feelings that notes are. Moreover, what we write is, and ought to be, truly of us: original and creative, whereas when we play, we are what one of my teachers, Josef Fidelman, used to call "middlemen." Granted that a lot of ourselves goes into it, but we have to tread within certain valid confines of expression that are as true to the composer as to ourselves.

My new computer and I are still getting acquainted. It's an instrument without a soul, beyond question. It is powerful and opinionated, but not at all cultured. I had to turn off the "Spellcheck" tool because when I typed "Poulenc," it asked me if I didn't really mean "opulence," and when I typed "Brahms," it asked, "Brahma?" (And I am not about to type in every composer's and performer's name into the computer's memory.) Having given up the cozy corner of my couch, yellow legal pad, and pen for a glaring screen and a little mouse, I am still determined not to become a "techie." I wasn't even curious about computers and had hoped, one day, to have a distinguishing epitaph: "Here lies the last manual writer," but well-meaning friends and up-to-date publishers conspired. I admit that the luminous, otherworldly little screen has a commanding presence like a beacon of light calling me to it from wherever I might be, but my piano has a patient, even more potent attraction.

The piano is linked to one's inner life, is an extension of oneself, while the computer seems lying in wait to invade one's privacy. All I want to be able to do is to Write, Save, and Print. I am going to resist with all my might E-mail, surfing the Net, cyber this and that, viruses, scams. Maybe in my old age I'll get more adventurous. Right now I am happy to be writing in an upstairs bedroom which I have converted into "a room of my own," to borrow a phrase from Virginia Woolf. (My husband putters around in his own room, and we have "our" own room as well.) There are no rules about admission to my inner sanctum, in fact anyone I love can come in any time. It's a beautiful room, Edwardian-style—the floral linen spread on the daybed, burly maple bureau, oriental rug, art supplies, all *except* the computer, which, however, is at a wide window that looks out into a great old tree. The keyboard is so silent that sometimes my husband comes in and reads a book while I am writing. That is idyllic: the combination of working hard at something one loves, and being, at the same time, close to someone one loves.

The only concern is to find the most innocuous positioning of the hands to avoid the danger of a tendonitis that would impinge upon my work at the piano. The first week of computing led to a slight tendonitis of the right index finger that operates the mouse. I was quite worried about it, but mercifully it went away. (I confess to treating the two instruments differently: I am thoughtful about my fingering on the piano and thoughtless on the computer.)

• • •

The last significant difference between writing and performing, and the one for which I am most grateful, is that the ability to edit and rewrite enables us to have an end-product for all time which represents our true intention, whereas it's a one-shot-deal with performance and therefore infinitely more demanding.

The problem is maintaining a delicate balance: I don't ever want to go over the deep end and write myself into the realm of—dare I utter it?—*musicology*. I read somewhere a quotation from the painter Barnett Newman, "Writing about music is for musicians, what ornithology is for birds." I wish I know who said, "Writing about music is like dancing about architecture." Yet we do it anyway, and for good reasons. Alfred Brendel told me that he writes to contribute to an understanding of such questions as "What is a masterpiece?" and "How does the mind of a composer work?" My goals are more modest. I am trying to probe the depth and density of a pianist's experience, and with the encouragement of many readers over the years, I persist.

~ 3 ~

An Artistically Nourishing Environment

EVER since I took my first piano lessons in Leopold Mittman's garret studio, surrounded by beautiful paintings, easels with works-in-progress, and shelves upon shelves of art books, I have been keenly aware of a kind of cross-pollination and *synesthesia* that exists between music and the other arts. The dictionary defines synesthesia as "a process in which one type of stimulus produces a secondary, subjective sensation, as when a specific color evokes a specific smell sensation." For me, the connections occur most frequently between my auditory and visual senses. I might simply be inspired by the beauty of a painting or landscape and, nourished by that beauty, feel motivated to make music. Or, more specifically, visual imagery will give me a handle on some music that might otherwise have evaded me. For example, in Chopin's B minor sonata, the E major triplet section of the third movement didn't "click" until I beheld a painting by an artist-friend, Stan Brodsky. His beautiful work depicted the water's edge and tidal flows, and the painting uncannily cast light on the music. Similarly, as so much of music derives from sounds of nature, visualizing water, clouds, fog, wind, or turbulence might help to capture those effects in music. In Chopin's Barcarolle, I utilized the visual memory of our time in Venice to help create the atmosphere. Connecting painters or paintings with musical masterworks or styles occurs subconsciously within me, but I have shared those notions at appropriate times with my students.

I know painters who use music when they paint, for similar reasons. Some years ago I interviewed the painter Robert Dash, who trained as a pianist before being swept up in the ferment of the art world in the 1950s. He is a painter who likes to play and who for years was an art critic, and I am a pianist who loves to paint. Together we agreed that talking about music or art is a vain pursuit, and that the analogy between piano and paint fails by the same small edge as the anagram. But that did not stop us from enthusiastically engaging in the subject anyway. There were many tempting questions on the relative tensions and joys of painter and pianist. Dash has created an utopian enclave for living and working on the east end of Long Island. He is also an award-winning gardener whose glorious horticultural creations are juxtaposed against farmland and then the ocean. He has one of the most enviable work spaces I have ever seen.

We spoke about the many creative artists whose gifts extend beyond their chosen field: Leonardo, Klee, Sargent, and Schoenberg came to mind. Dash said:

> These days undue emphasis is put on having to focus for fear of being diffuse, but I don't care what art you choose, all arts enter into it, and you have to know everything. I don't find this overlapping or fertilization odd at all, but at the moment you paint or play or dance, instinct takes over.[1]

I couldn't agree more. I have always felt self-conscious talking about my love of painting, even though for a long time painting has been among my most ardent preoccupations. I grow a garden, of course for the restorative smell of the soil, the pleasure of nurturing plants, and the challenge of blocking out a palette of colors from growing things, but primarily to have an unlimited supply of flowers to paint. And one of my favorite things about travel is keeping a journal containing watercolor sketches (that in the end mean more than snapshots), along with a written diary. Yet most folks' reaction is that if you splinter creative energies between art and music, or between music and writing, you will never do anything as well as you might if you had only one focus. Certainly in terms of time spent, that theory holds a grain of truth. But the crux of the matter for me is that the more the juices flow—in any direction—the more there is to express, and there is a constant flow of energy from one medium to the other. I asked Dash to try to identify the common elements between music and art.

> The closest element is the blocking stage, the sensing of the various forces, plotting your way through a work at first go. You plan your elevations, in musical phrases or shapes in the painting's composition, rapidly establishing the territory of the thing, orchestrating it.

My friend Sol Berkowitz, who is a composer and orchestrator, uses the language of art and architecture ("palette of colors," "materials like stone and brick and cement") to describe how he might orchestrate musical lines. As Dash put it with his wry wit: "You can use the language of any of the arts to speak about the others. These words have entered the language and so are easily transferable, albeit often abused, especially in the field of restaurant criticism: a pizzicato of anchovies."

Dash said he withdrew from the music world because he did not have the stomach for it. He spoke of the touring and concertizing tensions with disdain and pity but acknowledged that the piano taught him a great deal: "The tolerance for long hours of hard work, for solitude, an appreciation for refining the details, the trills and embellishments, and even my wrist, which I can say was developed on the piano." This last remark was uttered as he flung an imaginary glob of paint from an imaginary brush with a violent flick of the wrist.

Both arts offer up hard surfaces: the canvas is an obdurate thing, and the piano keys are also hard. The energy that goes toward transforming the hard surfaces into soft, round tones or strokes can be exasperating, and therein lies the challenge.

We agreed that there are tensions in all the arts, but Dash defines those of a painter as "private tensions." If the tensions of the pianist are oppressively public, is there anything in the painter's lot to compare with the exhilaration of having performed a successful concert? "Maybe a nine-second elation when you finish and you like it, but immediately it becomes a part of what you were, a thing of the past." We agreed that both are lonely ventures and both deplete energy, and that above all, any artist must allow the world to enter into him instead of staying insulated, coddled, suffocated, cosseted. There are artists for whom the moment is never "right" enough to begin. They go into a kind of aesthetic catatonia instead of experiencing the life around them. Dash likens the artist to a bit of litmus paper floating through the world. "You make your own academy, taking a little from here and there, sorting through principles that could be taught in a few sentences in a conservatory or an art school but are better learned in an individual way."

. . .

It seems to me that artists are more isolated now than they were, for example, during the Romantic and Impressionist periods, when dialogues and friendships between poets, painters, and musicians ignited the transference of ideas from one art to another. In our own home, my husband, Ernest, whose expertise lies mainly in literature and films, and I treasure our evenings with other creative artists; abstract ideas fly back and forth with no boundaries or barriers between forms or mediums.

A few years ago one of my adult students, a professional painter, asked me whether I would consider swapping a month's worth of lessons for a portrait of myself. The idea intrigued me, and so I sat (and wrote) after each of four lessons while she sketched. It was a happy trade-off.

Another time my close friend Mary Abrams, who is a fine artist, came over and sketched while I practiced. Mary and I have shared our artistic responses for many years; as she painted and I played, an aura of creative energy floated over us, intensifying and in a strange way supporting the impulse to work.

During the past several years great museums, such as the Metropolitan Museum in New York, have filled every available space with fine, live music, perhaps in an attempt to bring the arts closer together (while also attracting visitors). Many museums have lovely recital halls, but I am referring to unconventional spaces: a Renaissance courtyard filled with a consort of authentic Renaissance instrumentalists, a string quartet on the balcony overlooking the Great Hall, and to everyone's delight, a pianist playing light classical music in the museum cafeteria.

For some the art most closely allied to music is not the visual but the literary. The concert pianist Jerome Lowenthal, for whom literature is as much a passion as music, once told me, "To understand one art, understanding others is basic. Literature, with its wide-ranging possibilities, is the art that casts the most direct light on other arts, in particular music. Similarly, I think that music, by its purity, illuminates aspects of literature that are often ignored."[2]

Our conversation led to a discussion of Robert Schumann and Robert Browning, and to what Lowenthal described as a need "to be aware of the spiritual nuances of a chord—not the harmonic name, but what the use and sound suggest." He recalled the poem "A Toccata of Galuppi's," in which Browning refers to the interval of a diminished sixth in Schumann's music. Galuppi, an eighteenth-century Venetian composer, may be an obscure name for many of us, but in that poem Lowenthal found a reference point, the diminished sixth, that became pivotal for his understanding of Schumann's Fantasy in C major, Opus 17, and even that work's derivation from a Beethoven song, "An die ferne Geliebte" (To the Distant Beloved). Lowenthal is not a "visualizer." He would rather call himself a "conceptualizer." He draws from his connection to literature: "The subtlety with which a great writer moves from phrase to phrase, building his structure, helps me to understand the real structure—as opposed to textbook structure—of a musical composition."

. . .

In my own studio, within arm's reach are art books and music reference books of any given period or subject that will enhance my understanding of music literature; I also read from certain collections of composers' letters if I think they will serve to enlighten. I have gone about the business, over the past many years, of consciously surrounding myself with paintings, pottery, and books that help to put me (and I hope my students) in a sensitized, peaceful, receptive, and fertile state of mind. What seems to count a lot to me is not only the availability of reference material, but a harmonious space, with every corner balanced in form, color, design.

The act of creating this environment is an art form in itself. The great Japanese potter Yanagi suggested that art's prime function might be to provide a kind of religion based on the worship of beauty.[3] He believed in art as an instrument of order and peace, and a direct link to the human heart. The objects with which I have surrounded myself transcend the material and enter into a realm where each has properties of beauty and meaning integral to the whole place. There is a beautiful Japanese word, *shibui*, which describes the kind of subtle plain harmony of an environment for which I strive. It is never cluttered. (Clutter is close to chaos and nothing disturbs me more than that.) People have a natural instinct to adorn themselves or their environment, and like magpies, we collect and stow things.

Every now and then I have to step back and ask myself, "Do I really love and want this object, or can I live without it?" Then comes the process of paring down to the essentials of utility and beauty: a wedding present of a native American earthen bowl puts me in touch with the potter's hand, cupped around it; a portrait of my husband reading poetry to me, painted by a close friend, records an intimate moment in our lives; my daughter's paintings add accents of expressiveness and sensuous chromaticism here and there; a music stand carved for me by my son is as witty and wonderful as it is useful; an excellent pastel portrait my sister did of me, my daughter-in-law's fine collages, a custom-made music cabinet, a Shaker-inspired stereo cabinet expertly built for us by a close friend, my own favorite watercolors of my garden, my father's Calder-like wire sculptures, my two big black beautiful pianos—all these "things" resonate together: *Home.*

~ 4 ~

Music-Making en Famille

MAKING music *en famille* can be deeply fulfilling, but in my experience "folks who play together stay together" is little more than myth.

I know a few good two-musician marriages, but I must say most marriages between two musicians are not the idyll people might think, with sweet music-making all the way into the sunset. The reason may be that spouses do not have that genetic connection; moreover, music is a huge realm, with plenty of room for disparate personal tastes, temperaments, and styles.

One partner might love Italian opera at 100,000 decibels; the other might loathe it, preferring German lieder, much to the dismay of her spouse. One partner might have a chamber music temperament, the other a soloist's; the chamber music type's idea of a heavenly violin and piano duo might be the Mozart sonatas, while the soloist prefers a Wieniawski concerto. The twain do not easily meet, and such collaborations might lead to a soloist-type bopping a chamber-type on the head with his bow! Listening to someone's practicing is more difficult for a musician than for a nonmusician. One musician-spouse might want to verbalize her responses to a concert (between compositions), or squeeze her partner's hand; the other musician-spouse might be locked into an insulated world of concentration and resent the intrusion. One musician-partner might revel in hearing young, talented performers despite occasional flaws in execution; her partner might be a perfectionist who angrily swears off live "flawed" concerts forever in favor of good-old historic recordings of acknowledged, dead greats. Any marriage can be vulnerable, but I might have foreseen that two musicians of such conflicting personalities would not be able to live in one house for more than twenty some-odd years.

. . .

Genetic musical connections are a different story. My son, Dennis, who teaches cello and chamber music at a large university, is one of my two favorite chamber music partners (the other being my daughter, Kim, a superb flutist). Over the years Dennis has participated in major events such as competitions and auditions, including his New York debut, all of which required a fine pianist. He did not ask me, nor did I volunteer, and I hasten to add that it had nothing to do with matters of competence. We have given many enjoyable joint recitals, and we might some day decide to do a CD together, but I have not chosen to play for him in the monumentally important events for the same sorts of reasons a surgeon might refuse to operate on members of his or her family. The tensions for performing artists are awesome enough without adding extra familial baggage.

Yet the special way we have in ensemble transcends the nitty-gritties of interpretive decisions, and instincts and intuitions make the collaboration organic and integrated. No doubt genes play a huge role. I recall the evening before my son's departure for college when we played Beethoven's Sonata for Cello and Piano in A major, Opus 69, with a resonance and meaning that words could never have conveyed in saying goodbye. To this day, the rare opportunities I have to play something with him, or for him, are of great importance to me. I value his ear and intellect enormously, but alas, when families are separated by half a country, there is never enough time for the exchange that I would cherish.

Still, music has served us well; indeed I am certain that its presence in the house from the time my children were born combined with genetics to shape their lives. Their little cribs were steps away from the living room in the modest studio apartment of early married life, and in that small space we crammed chamber ensembles of every permutation, masterworks mingling with the very air they breathed.

. . .

With the birth of my first grandchild I found myself musing about how it is that children are born or become musical. Certainly this baby boy was loaded with musical genes from both sides of the family. If it is true that Glenn Gould's mother played classical piano recordings during her pregnancy, perhaps this baby's listening to cello music helped to cultivate musical sensibilities, shape his tastes, and give him a prenatal headstart in musical development. None of us would ever have contemplated trying to shape a little person's future, but there is always the temptation to look for signs: will he dance or move responsively when he hears music? Will he sing on pitch? Will he toddle over to a keyboard and pick out tunes? When this child was an infant and my son held him on top of the piano as I played, we watched his face as the vibrations of music permeated his tiny self, and we knew there was music in him. We have photos of Rollie strapped in a sling on my son's back, peering over his shoulder as his dad practiced the cello. Not only did this arrangement keep him out of mischief, but the music was most assuredly being absorbed deep in his cells. My little grandson "conducts," "choreographs," and generally rejoices wherever there is music. Other traits are equally telling about a young child's musicality. Our second grandson, Steven, who has two musical parents, is quite an active little tyke, but it amazes me that no matter how wild his game, whenever I play within his hearing, he sits as though transfixed and asks me, "Play it again, Grandma." I am certain that music will be an important element in his life.

I remember the thrill of recognizing those gifts in my own children. *Gifts* is exactly the word, because musical talent is a bonus beyond being open and responsive to the world in all its beauty, that which all of us wish for our children. When a musician recognizes musicality in an offspring and knows he or she will have an extra, rarefied language with which to communicate—that is an especially magical moment.

Yet this is also one of many paradoxes in a musician's life. For those of us who know what an arduous struggle it can be to make music one's life's work, it might be easier to forego the magical moment and welcome the relief of a not particularly musical child who is headed for a more conventional life. Studies have revealed that not every person who has musical talent is grateful for it. And not all parents are thrilled for their child. We all had an extremely hearty laugh when Rollie exhibited a bit of hard evidence of his musicality at my piano; my son's eyes rolled skyward as if to say, "Oh no! Better if he were a scientist." The bottom line is that there is no choice. What is meant to be will prevail, and prodigious talent is not only obviously a great responsibility for parents, it is downright dangerous. The care and handling of real talent is as sensitive as it might be with any "abnormality." The parents had better make sure that their agenda is the success and happiness of their child, and not success for themselves through their child. Most importantly, children should have childhoods. We may feel we are doing a tightrope act to maintain a balance between responsibility to a talent and obsessiveness which leads to burnout.

As there is, I feel, the right instrument for the right person, allowing a young child to choose the instrument to which he or she feels chemically attracted is a good way to start. Both my children absolutely yearned to play the instruments they chose. Consequently it seemed as though the instruments became like appendages to their bodies. My son wrapped himself around his first small cello as though he were born to play it, and my daughter's lithesome way with her flute was equally spontaneous and natural. (As pianists we are more distanced from our instruments than anybody. The violinist tucks his under his chin, the cellist's entire body is in contact with his, a stream of air directly connects the wind instruments to their players, but we have to strike a block of wood, and that impulse must go through a fairly complex mechanism before contact is made to the source of sound.)

Yet the piano is arguably the most attractive instrument of all, and I can remember my first feelings of fascination. But I know only a bit about my own musical background. I know from what my mother has told me that I toddled over to my grandfather's piano at about age three and started picking out tunes. I remember always feeling imbued with something special and recently read a lovely passage that resonated with my own early recollections. In her beautiful book *The Song of the Lark*, Willa Cather delicately describes an early awareness of budding talent:

> She knew, of course, that there was something about her that was different. But it was more like a friendly spirit than like anything that was a part of herself. She brought everything to it, and it answered her; happiness consisted of that backward and forward movement of herself. The something came and went, she never knew how. Sometimes she hunted for it and could not find it; again, she lifted her eyes from a book, or stepped out-of-doors, or wakened in the morning, and it was there—under her cheek, it usually seemed to be, or over her breast—a kind of warm sureness. And when it

was there, everything was more interesting and beautiful, even people.

. . .

Quite recently, because I probed him about it, my father told me that when he was a boy he heard a violin concert and "carried on" until his parents took him to buy one. The most amusing part about the tale is how his teacher eventually gave up on him because he continually preferred playing by ear to reading the notes (endearing in a father, exasperating in a student!). My mother is also somewhat musical, and with her rudimentary knowledge of the piano, she was able to give me a loving start at home until I went to a "real" teacher at age five.

. . .

I think it is very important for siblings to study different instruments so that the normal amount of sibling rivalry that exists in most families is not exacerbated. If two siblings study the piano, for example, the less successful one might well feel frustrated and possibly even jealous of the more advanced one; what is not as obvious, but equally damaging, is when well-meaning parents oversensitize the more successful child about the competitive and unhappy feelings of the other.

. . .

Pondering the nature of musical talent is irresistible: genetic studies abound on the subject of perfect pitch. The mystique surrounding it exists more for those who do not have it than for those of us who do. In fact, perfect pitch can be as much a bane as a boon. For example, playing on a piano tuned one-half step off becomes nearly impossible unless you do a temporary lobotomy on your auditory brain cells. Admittedly the games of identifying quartets or symphonies in the instant it takes to identify the key are amusing. Although my grandson has a very good chance of developing perfect pitch, that in itself means little. There are documented cases of individuals who could identify the pitch of a train whistle yet cared not a whit for music as an art, while many others who are tone deaf are passionately involved with music.

Talent is ephemeral and may imply a composite of emotions, perceptual skills, intellect, aesthetic sensibilities, and motor skills. Though we speak of it as inherent, as eye color, is it inborn or a function of culture? Children's sense of tonality may relate to differences in basic tonal patterns and modes in their mothers' lullabies. Influences from the cradle have been proven to shape musical preferences.

Perhaps musical talent is only one facet of an umbrella-like aptitude for several arts in one individual. My daughter, Kim, was so prodigiously talented on the flute that Jean-Pierre Rampal once told her in amazement in a master class, "When I was your age I could barely blow my nose!" She went on to win some Young People's competitions, and then to major in music at Oberlin College. Yet she has found her niche and success as a painter of large abstract canvases and as a textile designer. There are many unanswered questions about the nature of talent, including the relationship of personality and intelligence to musicality. Recent studies show clear correlations between the early exposure to and study of music and intellectual capacity. Attempting to reduce the elements of talent to components and statistics may be a fascinating folly. I prefer for it all to remain a wonderful mystery.

. . .

My idea of a perfect marriage is a mixed one: a musician and a musical nonmusician. My nonmusician husband has sometimes pulled up a chair close to the piano when I practice, as though by being close he would absorb the music through osmosis and somehow come to a deeper understanding of it. His aesthetic response and curiosity mean more to me than if he had had a formal music education. I find it thoroughly endearing when he goes around the house whistling his slightly skewed version of a theme from a piece I've been working on or teaching. When he sings along with the strains of a mighty Brahms symphony on the car radio, it touches me more than if he were the maestro on the podium.

These mixed marriages can have their humorous aspects. I remember the first time my husband came to pick me up for one of my recitals before we were married. There he stood at the door with a flotilla of multicolored balloons looking like an escapee from a carnival, and there I stood, nerves in full bloom, beholding what seemed to me bizarre, perhaps inappropriate. I thought, "Oh boy, this man has no notion of what I'm going through, no idea of protocol." Once inside, he let go of the bunch of balloons, one of which had "Superwoman" written all over it. A very curious thing happened as they wafted to the ceiling: every stitch of nervous tension was lifted clean out of me with the delight of that colorful bouquet of balloons. I was buoyed up and out of myself, and what is more, I stayed relaxed even while waiting backstage before the concert. Unwittingly, my nonmusician fiancé had hit upon a more effective cure than any musician or manual had ever come up with!

After the concert, there he was with a most appropriate and beautiful bouquet of flowers.

5

Pianos as Furniture and as Souls

I HAVE written exultant paeans to my piano—human loves aside, it is my dearest treasure. I haven't played a piano anywhere that I could love as much. Since my first proud moments of ownership, I have jealously guarded my beautiful Steinway A, vintage 1924, from harm by careless guests with drinks or other hazards, or abusive pianists (who one of my teachers, Josef Fidelman, would have called "fortists"). The scratches on the fallboard borne of my own good hard work enhance the beauty for me.

My second piano, a Steinway grand, model M, was a gift from a dear old man who came into my life serendipitously twenty years ago. I was in line in the green room at Avery Fisher Hall after an André Watts concert, when a tiny bird of a woman asked me how I knew the pianist. I explained that I had written the interview of Watts that had appeared that Sunday in *The New York Times,* whereupon she stood on her tiptoes to kiss me, exclaiming in a charming Viennese accent, "You wrote that? I love you!" In the strange and funny way that things happen in New York, she and her elegant Hungarian husband, who watched his wife with wonder and amusement, became good friends of mine. She had been a concert pianist in her younger days, and her husband was an art historian and collector. Together they led a rich cultural life that I was delighted to become a part of.

After her death, her husband continued to be a distinguished presence at musical events, causing people to whisper and wonder about this man walking down the aisle with two canes. His mane of white hair and strong profile reminded us of his compatriot, Franz Liszt.

When Mocsi (short for his surname, Mocsanyi) moved to a smaller apartment, he offered to let me use his wife's piano for teaching, as he understood my misgivings about the wear and tear of many students each week on my own instrument. I countered by offering to pay a monthly fee, which he accepted with grace, and I imagine used in ways befitting an old bon vivant and connoisseur. After two years of this arrangement, he put up his hand signifying "enough" and said, "I am happy that Dita's piano has such a good home." Mocsi was born in 1900 and died close to his birthday in April 1994. Besides his generous gifts, I have many rich memories and colorful anecdotes and letters including a love note he dared to pass me in a restaurant, right under my husband's nose. It was a joke, of course, just as life was a big joke for him. The piano is a magnificent gift and quite a fine instrument; the scratches on its finish now bear witness to the good hard work of my students.

Not everyone feels the way I do about scratches and scuffs. A friend of mine got one of the great bargains of the century when he purchased a gorgeous concert grand that had been used as a bar. Finally its owners decided the instrument had too many scratches and circlets from wet glasses embedded in its finish. The hammers appeared to be spanking new, and the deal was closed for a song. The notion of pianos as furniture, the graceful curves enhancing a professionally decorated living room, strikes me as ludicrous on one hand and understandable on the other.

The curvaceous contours of a piano suggest a mystique that connects nonmusicians to a world otherwise unattainable. I, too, love the graceful lines and stodgy presence of my two big black instruments with their gleaming white keys, golden harps, and red felts, and there must certainly be something aesthetically pleasing about the form itself if folks are building piano-shaped swimming pools and patios, according to popular decorating magazines!

But apparently some other folks are designing pianos in the shape of swimming pools. An architect named John Diebboll has decided that as "the piano stopped evolving 100 years ago," it is high time to change that course.[1] He has decided that pianos should be adapted to their surroundings, and for those who can afford them, he has designed rustic log-cabin pianos for Montana lodges, Guggenheim Museum–shaped pianos for art collectors, and even a Murphy-bed piano that folds up into a wall for a man who wanted the space to double as an exercise room. Art cases for the privileged. Lest the reader think this is all just folly, the architect assures us that his goal was "to make each piano fit for performance." The question is, what self-respecting pianist would be caught dead sitting on those benches?

. . .

The oldest uprights also have a kind of beauty. There are two forlorn spinets, sometimes used to accompany dance sessions, at the Y where I attend exercise class. They look pitifully derelict and abandoned in a corner of the gym; yet as I jog by, a little voice from within these distant relatives calls to me. The other day I stepped in on behalf of an old beat-up black upright about to be consigned by my friends to the curbside. They were moving in a few weeks and were unable to take it along, and I happened to be there just before it was carried outside. A quick chromatic scale revealed all eighty-eight keys to be in working order, albeit quite rinky-dink. I couldn't help thinking there must be some child who wanted lessons but whose parents could not afford to buy an instrument. Suddenly it became my mission to rescue this poor old thing. With my friends looking on helplessly, I sent the garbage pickup men away, tipping them for their futile trip. I gave the piano a reassuring pat, as though to acknowledge its embarrassment of having been considered little more than trash, and started calling music stores. All the proprietors agreed to post a sign: "Free piano. Just cart it away." I also phoned a few teachers with beginning students, and within hours the piano had a home.

There are those of us who even talk to pianos as though they had feelings. My student Alison, who has become a piano technician, called me in ecstasy, "Ms. Montparker, I just played such a beautiful seven-foot-four Knabe piano in the shop today that I felt like a queen and should have been wearing a gown! Then I came home and said to my old Wurlitzer, 'I hate you, you wimp! Nothing personal, but you sound rotten!'"

. . .

When I was a child my parents were concerned that I had no instrument to play at our summer cottage. My mother put an ad in the local newspaper offering to trade a TV for a piano. In no time we had a choice of three pianos. I ended up with a well-built upright that had mysterious trap-doors, chambers, and levers from its days as a player-piano. It also had genuine ivory keys, fanciful carving, and a fine tone.

My parents still own the Knabe baby grand they bought for me when I was a teenager. Responding to an ad for a used piano in *The New York Times,* my father and I went to see the instrument and I fell in love with it. Alas, that piano has seen better days, but my parents' sacrifice to buy it for me so many years ago transformed my daily practice into sheer pleasure.

In my early married years I rented a vertical piano. Although there was nothing enchanting about it, the technician who came to tune and to service it was Avner Carmi, the man who discovered the Siena Pianoforte and with his wife wrote *The Immortal Piano*. The book is about a remarkable antique instrument, purported to have been played by Liszt, himself; it survived mummification in an African desert when it was stolen and then plastered up by German soldiers.

In a rescue operation that dwarfs any efforts I could ever make, Carmi restored the piano to its former glory and went on tour to promote its virtues. To support this cause he worked as a piano technician, and fortuitously arrived in my home. Subsequently he invited me to enjoy an intriguing session with the Siena piano. This instrument had the uncanny quality of changing its timbre to suit whatever music was being played on it: if I played Albéniz's *Leyenda,* it sounded like a guitar; with Bach it took on qualities of a harpsichord; and Chopin or Liszt sounded harplike.

Unusual pianos keep turning up here and there. In an old estate I played a lovely square concert grand built in the 1880s, and though the action was flabby with age, the tone was pretty. Recently, while browsing with my son and his family through antique shops in New Orleans, lo and behold, I stumbled upon an old Broadwood piano, gorgeously embellished and carved, and in beautiful shape. The name Broadwood conjures up so much history. The company was founded in the 1700s in London, and its instruments were owned by and associated with such giants as Beethoven. For a mere $10,000 (actually quite a good price), I could have owned this relic, which needed very little rebuilding. I walked away from it quite reluctantly.

I do have another instrument in my home, a relic with no soul at all. It is a "silent keyboard" which I inherited from my Hungarian friend along with the piano. It has no soul because it has no hammers, strings, or soundboard. It was built by a company named Schauffele in Stuttgart in the 1880s when these contrivances were developed as learning aids, concurrent with the piano's rise in popularity. My keyboard has three octaves and is not at all the fancy eighty-eight-key Virgil silent clavier I saw in Claudio Arrau's home when I went there to interview him. (He was a silent keyboard enthusiast, as were Moritz Rosenthal and Rafael Joseffy.) Aside from not disturbing others, silent practice was supposed to develop the imagination and memory while exercising the hands. The mechanism has a knob to adjust the action, and indeed, it quite resembles the feel of a good sturdy piano. I do not consider myself deficient in the imagination department, but it has been useful backstage when I desperately want to have a keyboard under my fingers. (It is extremely heavy, however, and unless I had help getting it to the concert hall, my hand would be wrecked before the concert!) Believe it or not, I have a second silent keyboard: a crazy little one-octave job, "and what could be the use of it, is more than I can see" (to paraphrase Robert Louis Stevenson). I suppose it could keep my fingers busy backstage, too, but I am using it for a bookend.

. . .

There is one more " piano" in my home without a soundboard, hammers, or strings, but nevertheless with soul. It was fashioned by my son, whose hobby is woodworking and who presented it to me at the holidays to serve as a kind of mailbox. It opens at the fallboard to reveal the interior space, and it even has a lid to prop open as a signal to a mailman. In the past, folks have brought me all manner of piano gifts, but this special handcrafted piece, a product of hours of loving work, is mounted on my front porch for an occasional note.

. . .

In my town there is a secondhand furniture store that buys estates. I enjoy browsing there, and occasionally the owner notifies me when a piano comes in. I have made some happy love-matches between used instruments and my students. It is amusing how the owners got to know me. I sauntered in one day many years ago and spied a wonderful old oak dining room table; it was exactly what I'd been looking for, but priced way beyond my reach. Just as I told the dealer I would have to live without it, I spotted a grand piano in another corner of the store. I played a scale on it and asked the owner what he wanted for it, just to get a sense of his pricing policy. When he told me, I replied, "That's quite a bit overpriced." (This predates the skyrocketing cost of pianos by many years.)

"Oh yeah?" he replied defensively. "What do you know about pianos?"

"It's my profession," I responded quietly.

"O.K. Prove it. Play something," he challenged.

Rarely have I refused to play when asked, so I sat down and played the flashiest piece I could think of, Chopin's Polonaise in A-flat major, Opus 53, in a truncated version. As I played, customers gathered round, and still others came in from the street. After the final heroic chords, the flabbergasted merchant said, "You know that oak table you want? Take it at half price."

That table, which I have enjoyed for many years, represents the highest fee I've ever been paid for playing a single piece—actually half of a piece! The poor fellow even offered me a job playing there on Saturdays, but sitting in his musty shop amidst overstuffed furniture, oriental rugs, and collectibles somehow did not appeal to me; even I have my limits. I politely declined, but whenever I walk in, I know I will get a more-than-fair price on anything I hanker for.

. . .

I love to perform in traditional recital halls, but my favorite setting of all is at home on my own dear piano, for a handful of choice listeners. A few years ago I had a broken leg, so to cheer myself up I put a long, elegant, black velvet skirt over my full-length inelegant white plaster cast and gave a gala concert and dinner party for a wonderful gathering of people, among whom was my orthopedist. Aside from the fact that I could not use the *una corda* it went beautifully. (That, incidentally, is an excellent exercise in tone control. Every pianist should have to play without the *una corda* once in a lifetime, preferably without breaking a leg.)

Since that time, I realize I do not need a broken leg to justify the urge to have a *soirée musicale* at home. It's a heavenly idea any time, and the best reason is my piano. I have met many a piano I could love, but I have formed a special partnership with my instrument.

Something feels as though it comes alive in my hands, almost as though the piano knows what it is supposed to do. I have heard carpenters speak about a well-worn and well-balanced tool that has been fine-tuned over time, that contains in its design a wealth of experience from which the hand of the user can draw. In that sense, if I pay particular attention to my piano, let it guide me a bit, from its wellspring it has much to teach me.

6

Old Music, Music Cabinets, and Tapes

OLD music has sensual delights: the sandy texture of the fragile dried paper, flaking like toast crumbs all over the keyboard, and that wonderful smell, faintly reminiscent of used-book shops—the redolence of the past. The tinted aging pages barely hold together, and the flaking, especially of the French editions, produces a most lovely litter; I almost hate to trim the edges off the tattered pages, and I love the way the paper turns to an oatmeal-like granulation. (Regrettably the sensations associated with old books are increasingly rare in the modern world, as students seeking information in great libraries no longer come into contact with the volumes themselves, but rather with excerpts radiating from illuminated computer screens.) Thank goodness there's no way—yet—that the computer can impose itself between the pianist and her music library.

I seem to have amassed truckloads of music over the years, and, of course, the music with the most meaning to me has the scribblings of my teachers, unfortunately fading into oblivion. Leopold Mittman, with whom I studied for most of the twenty-three years from age eleven, never hesitated to mark my music whenever he thought it necessary, and I was always grateful for his suggestions. His garret doubled as a painting studio, so that he might grab whatever was at hand—even a blunted crayon or a piece of pastel chalk if no pencil was handy. This is the stuff that transforms a new copy into one that has been lived with and worked over. I have even enjoyed buying used music just for the chance to consider other musicians' views. In a way, it is a form of voyeurism, because if it comes from someone like me, it is freely and liberally marked with broad gestural strokes which, upon analysis, might reveal one's deepest insecurities, frustrations, even anger. I love to read the fingering, comments, and other markings of those whose hands have traversed the same pathways and whose teachers shared their now-faded wisdom. Just recently I was working on Ravel's *Jeux d'eau* and decided to compare a detail from my Kalmus edition with an ancient, inherited French edition. Scribbled on top of the cascading cadenza a couple of pages from the end, by some other pianist or her teacher, I found "like Eden." It was moving to share with that unknown pianist a passage that I thought of as sheer bliss.

My music has been adorned with such novelties as a note from my little daughter with her naive and wonder-filled response to a particular piece, placed silently upon the piano so as not to disturb me, or, in my copy of *Pictures at an Exhibition,* with a reproduction of the great Ilya Repin portrait of Mussorgsky, given to me by Mittman. One of my Chopin volumes has a photo taken when I was at his grave in Père Lachaise cemetery. It fills me with the same reverential feeling I experienced there. If I happen upon a particularly useful article about a piece, I generally stick it into the music for future reference. My Chopin Barcarolle music has, pasted permanently into the back cover, my article of many years ago, in which I interviewed seven great pianists about that work, and enclosed in Chopin's Ballade No. 4 is a similar project I did with that piece.[1]

. . .

Aside from music I purchased myself, I inherited trunks and wilting cartons of music from friends who either moved or passed away, and even from strangers in the community who call me before they dispose of boxes of music. Few things are as much fun as the sense of imminent discovery while I leaf through unsorted stacks of music and the thrill of finding a rare edition or fine hardbound albums. I felt blessed to find amidst one such windfall two pristine hardcover volumes of the Henle-Verlag *Well-Tempered Clavier*. I already had the Kalmus, Schirmer, and Breitkopf and Härtel editions, all in varying stages of decay, but these new ones I keep permanently on my piano.

The same inheritance included hardcover albums of all the Gershwin songs arranged for piano solo quite faithfully to his own recorded improvisations, and Russian editions of both Tchaikovsky's *Nutcracker* and Prokofiev's *Romeo and Juliet* in the composers' original piano transcriptions. These are treasures I probably would not have bought for myself, assuming they were even available. After covering them in clear Contac to preserve them (a habit I learned from Josef Fidelman) I could hardly resist sitting down at the piano to read through some of the music, leaving piles of unsorted compositions all over the floor. It is a luxury to have duplicate copies, not only to lend to students until they get their own, but to be able to compare several editions of the same work. Even with the extra copies, I still find myself searching in vain for music which I am sure walked away with some student or other, and nothing is more exasperating than that! (During a recent interview, Alicia de Larrocha showed me her New York set of piano literature beautifully housed in custom cabinets in her west side apartment. She told me she became so frustrated each time she reached for something and realized that it was in Barcelona or Switzerland that she instituted near-complete libraries in each of her homes.)

Where does one put it all? Chaos reigned for years, no matter how many attempts I made to organize. Invariably the stacks got rescrambled so that it took too long to put my hands on a particular piece of music. Finally a few years ago we paid a carpenter about

$50 to slap up some plain shelves on my office wall. He rigged up a grid of about eighteen capacious cubbyholes, each designated for a specific composer. The music lies horizontally, which was already a big improvement, as years of vertical shelving had contributed to the chipping away of old dry pages. Although this new system worked wonders, it still wasn't enough. In a junkshop I found a crummy, peeling music cabinet with six narrow shelves to hold work in progress and alleviate the pileup on my piano. I stood the cabinet on the grass, sprayed it with black enamel, and got myself a good case of tendonitis from pressing the spray button. Now I had a lustrous black cabinet alongside my piano into which I placed the Bach and Beethoven albums I must have near me. However it was weeks before my right hand and arm recovered sufficiently to play anything. Organization had its price.

My favorite cabinet came to me fortuitously on my birthday a few years ago. The widower of a piano teacher in the community called to ask me if I would be interested in a cabinet that had been made for his wife. I politely explained that I would not be interested in investing in a music cabinet at that point, but I offered to make some inquiries for him. "Oh no, you misunderstand me," he explained. " I would like you to have this as a gift in return for the pleasure I have had in attending your concerts. It would make me happy to give back something to you." He didn't even know it was my birthday. My husband and I went to his home that very day not knowing what to expect, especially as he had described it so modestly. There stood a lovely chest of drawers, custom-made in a mellow, honey-colored hardwood, with round wooden pull-knobs, each drawer designed for music. Transcending mere utility, this fine specimen of furniture now sits proudly in our living room not far from the pianos. It holds my most frequently used volumes, and I never open a drawer without feeling warmed by the generous gesture of a music-loving friend I barely knew. It is quite the nicest chest for music I have ever seen.

In my music library are several facsimiles of original manuscripts, including a wonderful one of the complete Beethoven sonatas in their first edition (published by Tecla) reproduced from the Hoboken Collection in the Austrian National Library. It is a thrill to see the ornate title pages, to read from horizontal text in wide, expansive print with notes and stems hand-drawn by expert copyists, and to whittle the music down to bare essentials without the pomposity of editors' touches. If I want editorial comments I have the wonderful Donald Francis Tovey edition with his insights placed in essays before each sonata.

I have two handwritten manuscripts from Löli Mittman, as we fondly called him, in my cabinet. One is his gorgeous transcription for solo piano of the slow movement of Rachmaninoff's Sonata for Cello and Piano, Opus 19. The other is a little Sarabande he wrote and presented to me after a lesson many years ago. I have always meant to program those pieces at least as encores, and one day I will.

My husband and I like to sing old tunes from Gilbert and Sullivan operettas or Broadway shows, and so I have accumulated volumes of songbooks—you should hear our rendition of Irving Berlin's "I Love a Piano." From my days as choral accompanist at Queens College, I have the scores to every choral masterpiece from Bach's *St. Matthew Passion* to Stravinsky's *Symphony of Psalms*. Then when no one is around, I sing those arias and choruses on high, as though I were still under the excellent direction of professors John Castellini or Sol Berkowitz.

A quite major portion of my music is for chamber ensembles of every shape and size. The collection started with music for violin, cello, flute, and piano, which were played, *en famille*, for many years. Now I enjoy trios, quartets, and quintets with friends and colleagues, and when there is a chamber masterpiece I cannot play in the original, such as Beethoven's Septet, Opus 20, written for violin, viola, cello, bass, clarinet, horn, and bassoon, but no piano, then I play it in the transcription for solo piano by Gustav Rösler. This version would sound thoroughly unsatisfying to anyone but myself, so I reserve the delightful indulgence for moments of solitude, as I do with my closet readings of Schubert lieder. In the same category are the Beethoven symphony arrangements for either solo piano or piano four-hands. Radu Lupu once confided his secret urge to program the Liszt transcriptions of the symphonies, but I cannot help thinking it was just a folly. Such transcriptions certainly are the only way we pianists can dig into those works and steep ourselves in the great literature that orchestra members are so lucky to experience. The duo versions have two drawbacks, however: first is the need to find an equal partner both in sight-reading and intimacy with the works; and second is the abuse they may wreak upon one's piano when one tries to become an orchestra or, even worse, when *two* enthusiastic pianists try to be an orchestra! Among my most amusing four-hand experiences was an impromptu session with André Watts, reading Tchaikovsky's "Pathétique" Symphony. The transcription is pretty thorny terrain, and we were both struggling.

During a recent evening at my pianist-friend Joan Horn's house, she brought out a book of transcriptions of Beethoven's String Quartets, Opus 18, for piano four-hands. Her background is as steeped in chamber music as mine, she knows the literature intimately, and as a pianist she has pined as I have for the pieces we cannot play. (Truly it is the ungrateful pianist who would complain about anything at all, with the bounty of music written for our instrument.) Yet we laced into those quartets with *mucho gusto*—I in the treble as the first and second violins, she in the bass as viola and cello. Honestly, we phrased, gesticulated, and breathed like string players, and for several hours we were in heaven, playing what we both experienced as the most elevated, intimate music ever written. Mercifully our husbands were busy watching a football game, and no one was around to hear us.

. . .

Inside yet another important piece of furniture, an old oak filing cabinet, I keep hundreds of cassette tapes of interviews I have been privileged to have with world-renowned concert artists, and countless tapes of past concerts, some of which I barely recall giving. This cabinet contains a veritable treasure trove of wit, wisdom, and memories, and I worry about their ultimate preservation. Originally Löli Mittman gave me a fine Ampex reel-to-reel recorder along with a professional mike. About ten years ago I figured out the complicated jacks involved in transferring the recorded reels to cassettes, and began the laborious task of rerecording memorable moments in my life, including my performance of Brahms' Piano Concerto No. 1 in D minor as a result of a concerto competition I won at Queens College when I was nineteen. Imagine my dismay when I recently tried to play the tape for a friend, only to find it utterly deteriorated. It is horrible to ponder precious musical mementos insidiously slipping away.

I called Max Wilcox, the superlative sound engineer behind most of Arthur Rubinstein's oeuvre and of so many of the best recordings around. I had interviewed him some fifteen years earlier as "Rubinstein's Alter Ego."[2] I asked, "Max, how does one go about getting a CD made?"

"Well, you call me and ask me to help you," he blithely replied. I was too stunned to respond. He continued, "Are you interested in doing this on an established label, or is this a personal project?" As he and I well knew, unless these were world premieres, long-lost manuscripts, or some other similar angle, and without a manager or a million-dollar name, no big companies would be that anxious to have my CD. I decided a long time ago which route I would take, and what I have now is my ability to play the piano and quite a few creditable tapes to prove it.

An overwhelming sense of not wanting those tapes to decay merged with the need to leave some trace of my pianist-self behind. Max guided me along, and we selected from tapes of two special recitals: from my recent return to Queens College on its Alumni Series (Four Fantasies from Opus 116 by Brahms, the Sonata "quasi una fantasia," Opus 27, No. 1, in E-flat major by Beethoven, a Chopin group of three mazurkas and the Fantaisie in F minor, Opus 49) and from my debut recital at Carnegie Recital Hall in 1976 (Bach's Partita No. 1 in B-flat major).

For this personal project, to use Max's euphemism, I could not afford the luxury of studio takes and hours of editing, nor did I need or want that; on the other hand, I hoped the recording would capture that electricity and immediacy inherent only in live concert performances. When I received the cassette back from the company that transferred the tapes from my performances to the CD master, I was quite apprehensive. Upon playing it I was a bit dismayed by some audience sounds and a trace of the air-vent system at Carnegie Recital Hall. A few tiny flaws popped out and poked me in the ear.

Then I remembered the book *The Unknown Craftsman,*[3] which André Watts had given to me as a birthday gift years earlier. His inscription to me is as beautiful and generous as the gift itself: "From one craftsman to another. For Carol—with all affectionate greetings—André." The book explains the Zen worship of beauty as Art, and the ideal of beauty as exemplified in the humanness that may appear in irregularities, whether in an uneven glaze on a piece of pottery or a slightly imperfect interpretation of a musical work. After rereading the book, I felt pleased and comfortable that the CD is an honest representation of my intentions and the love I have for the music. It also faithfully conveys the excitement and spontaneity of my live performances which could not have been duplicated in a studio. The personal label for my work is Pianogarden, a name I came up with for a watercolor that has had a lot of mileage as a *Clavier* cover, a poster, and the jacket for the disk. The recording project brings my personal history home to stay—*Pianogarden* exactly describes the way I feel about the place where I live.

~ 7 ~

The Piano as Comfort in Times of Stress

SOME of our most challenging and rewarding moments in music occur far from the concert stage. After my friend Margaret died, her husband asked me to play at her funeral. I could scarcely refuse but found the request overwhelming. That night I lay awake contemplating hundreds of pieces in search of something appropriate, not knowing whether I could contain my grief sufficiently to play at all. I wanted a piece that communicated sadness without morbidity, that was profound yet not obscure, uplifting yet not lightweight. The piece should express not only my feelings but also those of the congregation, saying what I wanted without seeming self-serving. I wondered how to express what I knew about my friend through musical symbolism. I wondered what music Margaret would have wanted and conversely whether the music should be chosen to serve the survivors. Such philosophical questions plagued and obsessed me, displacing all work for an upcoming recital.

I received an onslaught of suggestions from friends and colleagues who knew of my dilemma, but the selection had to seem right to me and to Margaret's family. No one else could help me decide.

Margaret had been a cheery, positive soul who as a nurse ministered to friends in need and volunteered in clinics serving the underprivileged. An Englishwoman and an avid gardener, she generously shared her beautiful roses every year from a garden that rivaled Monet's Giverny. First I looked for flower pieces, as in *Blumenstücke* of Robert Schumann. While the naiveté and simplicity of MacDowell's "To a Wild Rose" offered the pure and tender sentiment I was looking for, it felt too thin. From Bach's *Goldberg Variations* I played the Aria over and over, ultimately rejecting it as too weighty. I played Schumann's *Warum?* (Why?), the million-dollar question, but in this context the title seemed almost gimmicky. Two Chopin nocturnes, shorn of passionate middle sections, seemed to offer the beauty, delicacy, and uplifting quality I sought, but ultimately I kept coming back to Schubert, whose music transports the listener to a kind of never-never land (someone once called it "Schubertland") where the mixture of bitter and sweet plucks all the right heartstrings. I finally chose the Impromptu in G-flat major, Opus 90, No. 3.

My musical offering unfolded traumatically. I had thought myself reasonably composed when I sat down to play, but somewhere in the middle, the solemnity of the atmosphere, the stony silence, and a floodgate of memories all subverted my concentration, and I struggled to play as I sobbed and trembled. I doubt that I will ever put myself in such a vulnerable position again.

I have had similarly poignant moments, both happy and sad, enhanced or exacerbated by music. I remember my ninety-one-year-old mother-in-law almost rising from her wheelchair, clapping her hands and stamping her feet in glee when I played Chopin mazurkas on the piano in her convalescent home as she recalled her girlhood in Poland. I remember a dying Scotsman in the bedroom of a Tuscan villa, feebly singing and laughing through tears of nostalgia and melancholy as I played Scottish folk songs.

But it is in the most private moments of unhappiness that those of us who have resources may draw strength. T. S. Eliot once wrote "Poetry is not an expression of emotion, but an escape from emotion." For me, music has been both a channel through which to express *and* to escape. At those times of crisis or unresolvable conflict the piano has been like a best friend to help me regain my equilibrium. Yet one might easily take its huge presence for granted or, in a perverse state, reject and shut it out. The piano makes great physical demands, and if one is already emotionally or physically exhausted, one is less inclined to expend more energy. In those moments, I have found that playing *sotto voce*, or in the darkness, can be very comforting. Then the music seems to return, to ricochet back into oneself, rather than dissipating outwardly.

Although the piano has come through for me when I am sad, I have found I cannot play if I am angry. I do not associate anger with music-making. Indeed, any negative state of mind is likely to affect the work I do. Nowhere is that more obvious than when one is asked to play ensemble with a person or persons with whom one experiences tension or antipathy. Love is what one ought to take to the piano, and I have a loving relationship with mine. When I am feeling agitated or stressed, I am much better off throwing myself into a purely physical, unintellectual pursuit (like scrubbing the floor or building a stone wall around my garden) with no emotional associations.

It is ironic that some of the greatest loneliness can come from the very fact of being an artist in any field and feeling unproductive or unappreciated and isolated, and the best source of restoration and renewal can be found at the heart of our art. The piano is where I am reminded of the rewards that have been bestowed upon me, and at the piano is where I can reharmonize my spirit. Some artists' best work is borne of tension rather than peace and serenity; each person knows his or her ideal creative climate. Oftentimes we simply have to fall back on the underlying discipline and training, so that even when there is no inspiration, a fallow period, we can most quickly get back on track by keeping our "apparatus" busy—the painter may doodle, and we may too. I often wish I were freer in the jazz mode. I watch my son-in-law, David, who is quite a gifted improviser, as he unwinds, "doodling" around on the piano, and I can almost see the tension vaporizing into thin air. Whichever mode one chooses, the quickest way back to productivity is anything but avoidance.

At times even the physical aspect of our art may fail us. Illness is certainly a form of stress, and it may either visit us with insurmountable obstacles or lend unexpected new dimensions and perspectives. I was moved to read of Byron Janis' fight with his chronic arthritis, and how for years he managed to play and conceal the fact from his audiences. He said about his illness, "During the first year when I didn't play at all, I had no idea who I was. I was really upset. I was frightened to go out. Then I found I was using some of the things I learned about life from my music. I think I learned a lot about breathing during those years. Before that I was very much a virtuoso . . . and now the 'singing passages' are coming from a place I am not sure I touched before."[1]

For years I suffered with Lyme disease, a pretty insidious illness that frequently defies diagnosis, taking hold of the entire organism until it is essentially beyond complete "cure." I was misdiagnosed for five years and felt myself falling more and more victim to it; even after I was finally able to convince physicians that I had an infectious disease and not "just stress" (which they kept on reiterating), the illness kept worsening. Not even intravenous antibiotics would reverse the arthritic pain in neck and limbs, the severe headaches and the trembling. During that awful period of my life (not so long ago), I kept on playing with an obstinate will (the illness did not affect my hands, thank goodness); I think that the piano, along with the love of those close to me, kept me from losing my hope of recovery.

This would be the moment to thank my wonderful homeopath and friend, Sylvia Faddis, for bringing me back to health. I was never so grateful to feel the sense of power and possibility returning in myself, to rise to new challenges in music, along with everything else, as when good health began to retake me. I believe the physical struggle brought me closer to composers' struggles; during that time I learned how to concentrate more fully, because I had to harness my energies as I had never done before. I also think I became more spiritual. With renewed awareness and a heightened appreciation of the moment, I learned how to allow the music to take me completely out of myself to somewhere else.

~ 8 ~

Letters and Mementos

FOR as long as I can remember letters have been like windows in my life. I seem to throw out missives much like a spider throws out spinnerets, and the daily mail is always an event. Letters are my favorite genre; our private library contains some of the great correspondences, for example between Ellen Terry and George Bernard Shaw, between Elizabeth Barrett and Robert Browning, and whole anthologies of composers' letters. They give an intimate and privileged glimpse into the psyche and are often a valuable resource in the study of great music.

I have kept packets of letters from memorable correspondences and have wondered what it would be like to have my own back, to trace the metamorphosis from one phase of my life to the next in all its varied aspects. Glenn Gould, a compulsive letter writer, kept copies of all his own letters as well as of those he received. Imagine my surprise to stumble upon one he wrote to me in a book containing 184 of his letters released some time after his death! (All 2030 of his letters were filed in the National Library of Canada.)

The inveterate correspondent knows that you don't *get* interesting letters unless you *write* them, but the "getting" is only a part of it: the mere act of writing the letter is, in itself, a joy to me. A great part of the pleasure is related to the act of communicating exactly, economically, and hopefully beautifully, with a special individual. A dear friend who lived right in my own town and I preferred to correspond by letter rather than by phone because we both loved that mode of communication; now she lives in Italy, and our letters are a vital link. I still do my letter-writing in longhand in a cozy corner of a couch with a view of the garden, and the pleasure is there with or without the prospect of getting one in return—children write to Santa Claus, and I once wrote to Beethoven; I was simply overwhelmed by a sense of gratitude, debt, and love, and I had to say thank you.

I have unearthed copies of letters I wrote to Arthur Rubinstein that classify me as a groupie. He was one of my prime teachers, just through his concerts and recordings. Let's face it—I loved him: his playing, his wonderful old face, his magnificent heart and hands. Relatively few people follow through on feelings and record their thoughts, so that letters expressing awestruck admiration are not as common as one might think. Rubinstein once asked me, "Are you the lady who wrote me that letter about my *Carnaval*? I loved that letter and saved it!" Rubinstein was one of the music world's liveliest presences, and though he has been dead for many years, there is still a void. Aside from his supreme artistry, what was unique to him was his *joie de vivre*, reflected in every note he struck. He once said he was never a pianist "who kept his nose buried in the keyboard. I'd rather have been a dishwasher than not to experience life. Everything I played was singing to me from my heart."

I have cherished my many letters from readers of *Clavier* over the years and have tried to be punctilious about answering each one, including the few dissentient ones. Some letters have even led to friendships. After I reviewed the late Mildred Portney Chase's poetic book, *Just Being at the Piano*, she wrote to me that she never expected to have her book reviewed by someone she felt to be "her soulmate." Naturally I wrote her back directly, and our letters grew into a loving friendship that lasted until her untimely death a few years ago. A fellow named Brent Johnston in Alpine, Wyoming, wrote me in response to a column on nature. The "cowboy" turned out to be a fine pianist who ultimately came to New York for a coaching at my home. Now this is an annual ritual with a good friend, and we finally visited his inn and restaurant, called Brenthoven, during a breathtaking trip to the Grand Tetons.

Over the years I have accumulated so many letters and photos of great musicians that I finally instituted a huge album to accommodate the collection. It is barely portable, filled with the extraordinary and charming letters that are among my most precious belongings. I have a friend whose sense of history and love of music have led him to collect letters of the great composers, and of course some collectors are driven by the hope of market value and appreciation over time. For me no such larger purposes are needed. Yet lately I have come to feel that these treasures have lain hidden between my album covers for too long. Beyond their personal meaning (in some instances they also bestow generous praise for my work, for which I am grateful beyond words), they may hold pleasures for a wider audience. I trust that these mementos of gifted writers will delight and inspire others as they have me. There is a special tale to tell behind each one.

. . .

The opening pages of my album contain photos of me with Rubinstein when I was a younger woman. They were snapped backstage after a concert on Long Island. He is wearing a greatcoat with a shawl fur collar and effecting a theatrical pose. I am wearing a silly grin. Prior to the concert, he had requested that I stay with him in the dressing room before he went on stage. I requested the photo in return for a kiss he decided to bestow upon me in his inimitable puckish style. Then on the next page is a telegram he sent me (in November 1972 from Chicago) thanking me for a watercolor of a cat—he adored cats and I love to paint them—which I sent him as a get-well greeting when he had shingles. Among my proudest letters is a note from Aniela (Mrs. Arthur) Rubinstein, dated 18 February 1987, regarding an article entitled "Life With Father" that I did with their son, John, the actor:

> The article of yours about John's reminiscences and opinions about his father is probably the best I ever read—and I congratulate you and Johnny— You, for not distorting what he said, and him for his loving and lucid opinion of his father. We are so used to journalists usually writing what they want to say, with preconceived ideas about people, so reading your text, was a most refreshing experience, because every word was true—and gave a genuine portrait of my husband. Thank you again,
>
> Cordially yours,
> Aniela Rubinstein

Then she requested permission to reprint the article in several different languages for her husband's posthumous one-hundredth birthday celebrations being held in countries around the world.

. . .

In my album are two letters from Rudolf Serkin: one referring to my "Chronicle," as it was titled when it first appeared in *The Piano Quarterly* in Vermont near where he lived, and one declining to be interviewed. (In addition, there is a little note scribbled by my son many years ago: "Rudolf Serkin called person to person. Will call later. NO JOKE!")

A journalist routinely receives refusals for interviews, but some are more elegant than others. For example, in the mid 1980s I wanted very much to interview Donal Henahan, who was then chief music critic of *The New York Times*. Years earlier, in 1976, he had reviewed my own debut program at Carnegie Recital Hall. I was planning a piece on music criticism, and I thought talking to my own critic would be fun. His reply (January 1985) exhibits the droll wit that personified his writing at the *Times*.

> I've been away from the office, and have not been able to burrow from under the office trash that piles up when I am not on hand to sweep it off my desk onto the floor on a daily basis. . . . I know *Clavier,* of course, and I believe I was once a subscriber until I dropped a number of periodicals as a result of a momentary paralysis of my check-writing hand. I believe I also know you, if only tangentially, from the days nearly ten years ago when you were known as Mont Parker.[1] I greatly admired your "Anatomy" when it first came out and just now have hunted it down in my library and found it to be as good as I remembered it. That I figured in it willy-nilly, colors my judgment, of course, but rereading it gave me a flush of satisfaction anyway: even if your career has developed in a different direction than I might have expected, I don't believe I did it any serious harm. That may strike you as a weak sort of boast, but I am content with it.
>
> Over the years I have noticed other articles by you, and have always been impressed by your direct and thoughtful approach. So, if it were possible to persuade me to sit for an interview, Carol Montparker would be able to do so. But, please, I must ask that you let this cup pass from me. The music world is full of creative people who have stimulating things to say and both want and need the exposure you can give them. I am a dull talker who craves nothing but peaceful obscurity. If you will forgive me for turning you down, then, you will forever be the friend of
>
> Donal Henahan

Not only was the rejection worth it for this delightful letter, but it also led to further communication and a subsequent informal meeting. I had requested his permission to quote from his letter for publicity for my little book, *The Anatomy of a New York Debut Recital: A Chronicle*, and I mentioned that I would fill in the whole title lest his shortened version be misunderstood. He wrote: "Now that I reread what I wrote in haste, it does seem that my words of appreciation for your *Anatomy* might easily be misconstrued. Everyone needs an editor for just such missteps." He wished me good luck for an upcoming concert entitled "Felix and Frederic"[2] and asked that I let him know when my article about former pianists would be published:

> Such a great idea. All of us apostates will read it with rueful understanding, though the world of active pianists may scorn us. We are a universal, silent brotherhood.
>
> Tacitly yours,
> Donal Henahan

. . .

In 1987 I wrote to the great "unashamed" and unparalleled accompanist Gerald Moore in England (his wonderful book is titled *The Unashamed Accompanist*) to ask if he would agree to do an interview with me by either mail or tape, as I had done with his frequent partner, the renowned baritone Dietrich Fischer-Dieskau. According to a subsequent letter from his wife, his letter dated 24 January 1987 from his home in Buckinghamshire was the last he wrote before his death. I am so very proud to have it.

> I can sum up the pleasure your book gave me in one phrase: I wish I had written it. . . . Yes, I should enjoy an interview, but I am pushing 88 and would do so only if it were conducted by mail. (Airmail, naturally. Your letter arrived Jan. 22—written on Dec. 1st it might have arrived sooner had you swum the Atlantic with the precious cargo gripped in your teeth.) As for your avoidance of mundane issues, this

possibility is not within your province. You see, my friend, having read you—I know you.

I look forward to hearing from you.

Yours, with warmest regards,
Gerald Moore

. . .

Among my favorite letters is a rare one from Radu Lupu, whose artistry and character I consider to be at the highest level. Of great importance to me are his kind words regarding the interview we had just had (especially in light of all his reticence beforehand) and his thoughtful reconsideration of several points he had made in the discussion. He writes about Beethoven's sketch of a descending scale for the third movement of the First Piano Concerto which we had been discussing and his views of Beethoven's attempts to unify the entire work. He expresses some self-criticism about previously stated views on Chopin and, last, retracts with good humor some remarks regarding French music. His modest and good-natured review of my manuscript for the article, signed with thanks and love, is in stark contrast to some rather egotistical returns and emendations I have received in the past. The friendship that evolved from our first interview and this letter mean the world to me.

. . .

There are five notes from Vladimir Ashkenazy, all related to the several interviews I did with him. Written in a small, fine hand, they are kind, formal, and explicit, expressing gratitude for the "faithfulness" to what he said. In sharp contrast are the many informal greetings and notes from André Watts, scrawled in his large, open handwriting that exactly reflects his warm, generous, and openhearted character. Stuck here and there throughout the pages are snapshots taken with these artists at lunch or backstage, juxtaposed on their professional glossies sent in press kits by their managements. Several amusing shots show André and me at my piano furiously sight-reading transcriptions. Neither of us knew they were being snapped, and they reveal our frenetic concentration along with good fun.

Two pages are devoted to the late pianist and teacher William Masselos, whom I interviewed when he was already suffering from a debilitating illness which made it trying for him to speak. His expressive handwriting and comments make interesting documents and are amazing in light of his physical affliction. In the photos he is showing me original manuscripts of Erik Satie's music embellished by beautiful art nouveau plates by the French artist Charles Martin. The late pianist Rudolf Firkušny wrote me two notes, saved in my album alongside wonderful photos taken of us, during the interview, by Laura Lynn Miner, whose photography of performing artists ranks with the best.

Jerry Lowenthal's letters are literary jewels. It is difficult to imagine his writing a dull or mundane word; I could read or listen to him with rapt attention for hours. The letters from Peter Frankl exude the same warmth and hospitality that he and his lovely wife, Annie, treated us to when they invited my husband and me to lunch at their home in London during our honeymoon in England.

Among the most thoughtful letters I have ever received is one from Horacio Gutiérrez, (November 1982) after he read my first little book. I will include an excerpt because it reveals great truths for all pianists:

> You know, we concert artists are not always in a state of inspiration. Traveling, jet lag, time changes, hotels, different pianos, different halls, etc., all take their toll on what should be that fresh encounter with great music. Besides, sometimes not having enough quiet time before a concert in which to think and experiment with the music, can all add to the burden for the upcoming concert.

Last month I was on my way to a recital on the West Coast feeling some of the above, and I began to read your book. Seeing what it meant to you to have the privilege of playing these great works, sharing the miracle of their creation with your public, and your humility throughout, awoke in me that which was temporarily dormant in seat 4-B of the nonsmoking section: my own feeling of being privileged to be a concert pianist.

I believe I played a very good recital the next day. Thank you for your inspiring book.

With warmest best wishes,
Horacio Gutiérrez

Among my many letters about *Clavier* interviews over the years are one in French from the already ancient Magda Tagliaferro (whom I had had to interview in French), a funny one from Peter Schickele, alias PDQ Bach, annotated with a self-caricature), some serious ones from Gary Graffman (related to articles), and charming notes from Evgeny Kissin, Vladimir Feltsman, and Ruth Laredo. I treasure the good wishes written by Claude Frank on the occasion of my marriage, along with all his good-natured missives.

. . .

The wonderful letter from Alfred Brendel is especially appreciated in view of his first sentence: "I am the world's worst correspondent." He wrote some kind words about both my books and the article resulting from our interview, and suggested that I look at Weber's Sonata, Opus 39, which he was "playing with affection." Then he said that he would call the New York office of Philip's Classics and request that they send me a set of his complete Mozart concerto CDs as a token of his gratitude. This generous request set off a comedy of errors. A few weeks later a huge box appeared on my front porch from the Philips warehouse. Mozart wrote a lot of concertos, but not *that* many! Inside were *ten* complete sets of the Brendel-Mozart concertos. I must admit to a moment of sheer fantasy that I would give my kids and a few close friends each a set, but that dark thought was quickly undone as my husband and I reckoned that my reputation was worth more than a few boxes of CDs. As it turned out, the warehouse mistook me for a distributor, and they ended up having to send an independent trucker to pick up the remaining sets, which cost them more than the sets themselves, they later told me.

. . .

I got to know the great cellist Janós Starker during the years that my son studied with him at Indiana University, and I was also fortunate to attend some of his master classes during which I learned a lot. Over the years we have exchanged letters, I have interviewed him, and he wrote a fine piece at *Clavier* on "partner-pianists" which I edited. A quite charming note has the economical greeting: "I'll be thinking of your Schumann concerto while I'm doing Lalo in Texas. See you in NY!" One afternoon, before a solo engagement with the Long Island Philharmonic, he came over to play Bach sonatas with me, a highlight of my musical life. After the session, the extremely fastidious, well-dressed Hungarian cellist reached into the pocket of his tweed sportsjacket and fished out a hunk of Hungarian salami (admittedly among the tastiest in the world) and asked, "Would you make me an omelet with this?"

. . .

The three letters from Glenn Gould are the only ones about which I have received queries concerning my willingness to sell them. Gould is as close to a cult figure as a classical artist can get, and I imagine his letters have taken on another aspect in that light. The publisher of the now-defunct *Piano Quarterly,* Bob Silverman, once told me that Gould had been planning to write a "sequel" to my debut book. He did write me a wonderful note about my book, calling it "one of the most un-put-downable pieces of music journalism I have come across in many years," and he called me up during one of his nocturnal telephone marathons, in the wee hours of the morning, to discuss the video of the Bach *Goldberg Variations* that he was making with the filmmaker Bruno Monsaigneon. The phone rang at about 5:30 A.M. in a hotel room in Chicago where my husband and I were staying during a visit to *Clavier.*[3] My husband answered the phone and turned to me mumbling, "Some guy says he's Glenn Gould." Needless to say, I awoke with a start and cleared my head of sawdust to be able to converse with him. As it turned out, however, Gould did ninety percent of the talking, and I just kept marveling that it was I he had chosen to talk "at."

The most fascinating letter he wrote me was in September 1979 in response to my query about his boast that the Steinway piano in his Toronto apartment never went out of tune.

> I wish I had a simple explanation—or indeed, any kind of an explanation—to account for this rather unusual phenomenon (if I did, I'd patent it.) The fact is, however, that it's as much a mystery to me as to anyone else who has heard it, or, indeed, has heard it described. I am, by the way, quite used to skeptical glances and suggestions from friends that I have simply invented this improbable story and am probably smuggling in tuners under cover of darkness; needless to say, no one has ever explained why that would be a useful or sensible thing to do, but the passing reference to it in the Times was the first occasion on which I've gone 'public' with a mention of it. I recall that approximately a year after its last tuning—i.e. some time in 1964—Emil Gilels practised at my apartment before a Toronto concert, made some appropriately pleasant sounds (in German) about what a fine instrument this was, and, when told that it had not been tuned for more than 12 months, (at that time) gave me a look

which suggested that something had been lost in the translation.

The piano, moreover, sits more or less in front of a radiator and, with no humidifier in sight, and, though the odd unison does go astray from time to time, it seems to have a self-correcting capacity in that regard. It is, as I said above, a mystery, and I really can't shed any appropriate amount of light on the subject, and, as with most mysteries, it's perhaps best not to try.

All best wishes.

Sincerely,
Glenn Gould

. . .

A few photos record the pleasure of my interview with Leon Fleisher in New York in 1986. It was after he lost the use of his right hand, and one meeting with this upbeat, energetic artist confirmed that his resilience and creative energies would always be in full use, whether it be as pianist, conductor, teacher, or administrator. He was open, engaging, philosophical, and witty. We discussed the importance of ego and self-doubt, and Fleisher said:

> Very often the teacher has to remind the student that although Mozart and Beethoven were great composers, they were also human beings. What they experienced, all of us are capable of experiencing and communicating. I have to remind my students not to be in such awe—the great composers and performers were people who got angry, crazy, wild—and their humanity ought to be allowed to come out. So depending on who the students are, and whether they need toning down or firing up, you give them what they need.[4]

Fleisher described how he became quite adept at playing right-hand passages with his left hand, as he sat at the right of his students. With that left hand he carved out of the music a monumental sculpture of sound, with a grandeur that convinced the listener he made no compromises in tone, phrasing, or territory. He was, however, candid about the despair and desperation that led to a two-year depression before his optimism could take over and redirect his energies. "In fact," he reflected, "looking back, and having been as active as I am, I think that in certain ways only being a soloist can be a rather limited and limiting way to spend your whole life."

Fleisher has since resumed his life as a two-handed performing pianist. If, as it is said, the man and the artist cannot be separated, in Leon Fleisher the greatness of spirit evidenced in his playing and described by his students is mirrored in the ways he seems to live his life. I asked him to prophesy about the future for all the wonderfully gifted young artists on the horizon. "As they say, there's always room for greatness," he stated, but then he added wryly, "but the level of mediocrity is continually rising, which makes life more and more tantalizing."

. . .

On a much lighter note are a letter from the Prince of Wales (typed by the Equerry to H.R.H.) in response to one I wrote in appreciation of Prince Charles' beautiful book of watercolors, and a note from Shirley MacLaine, signed "Love, Shirley," expressing her enjoyment of my article on the film *Madame Sousatzka* in which she portrays an eccentric Russian émigrée piano teacher.

I treasure two letters from the late composer William Gillock, written on delicate Japanese rice paper, which reflected his love of Japanese art and artifacts. He wrote many kind words to me about my work at *Clavier*, and still managed some wry humor on the subject of the terrible disease that claimed his life.

. . .

This chapter is incomplete due to the copiousness of the letter collection. One final letter, however, stands out among the many that arrived after my *Chronicle* was published. It was written by my fourteen-year-old daughter (now a lovely woman)—her teenage idea of a joke:

> Dear Mrs. M.,
>
> I read your Chronicle last night and I couldn't put it down for one second! There's a lot I want to discuss with you. If you will meet me at my hotel I will be overjoyed! I only wish I were much younger and could marry you! I just can't tell you how much you and I are alike! I'll be looking forward to seeing you.
>
> Sincerely,
> Arthur Rubinstein

It is nearly as priceless as the authentic Rubinstein letter.

. . .

In various drawers I have also kept ancient relics—programs, photos, and tapes from my girlhood. A group photo celebrates the class of my first piano teacher, Miss Esther R. Bernstein, who, incredibly, is still teaching in Brooklyn, New York. Some twenty piano students up to about eighteen years of age pose on a stage alongside a grand piano. The younger ones are sitting in front on the floor, including one very small child of six, face resting indifferently in palms of hands, looking like the least likely to make the piano a career: me. Programs from those early days reveal that I played Grieg's *Vöglein*, Schubert's Scherzo in B-flat major, MacDowell's *Shadow Dance*, and Bach Two-Part Inventions in those recitals. Another photo shows a bunch of important-looking gentlemen, including Henry Morgenthau, Jr., secretary of treasury under Franklin Delano Roosevelt, and George Kleinsinger, the composer, with whom I played the Haydn "Kinder" Concerto in D major at some public event. I have 78 rpm records crudely made by my father with an old wire recorder, taken off the television or radio, including one from the "Ted Mack Original Amateur Hour" when I was eight. Until recently, I would never have admitted to being on such a silly program, but a friend who is a sound technician converted the old record to a cassette for me so that I could hear it for the first time since I was a child. Apparently I played Chopin's "Minute Waltz" pretty fast and clean, won the contest, and got some money that ultimately was used for my orthodontia some years later! (I was happy to learn from Mr. Mack's introduction to me on the air that the fine pianist Abbey Simon was also "an alumnus" of the program, a fact that he, too, might find a dubious distinction.)

In my little office which is more like a rabbit warren, I am surrounded by shelves of music and photos. I made a pastiche of snapshots from interviews and of special people in my life that looks like a rogues gallery; my sketches and paintings of musicians hang alongside posters from memorable musical events in my life, including the big one from the front showcase at Carnegie Recital Hall. The letter album, no longer portable, occupies an entire shelf; a boxful of unfiled letters and a carton of concert programs from my past wait to be put in chronological order, perhaps in another heavy album. My office is a cozy place to visit, but you wouldn't want to work there.

~ 9 ~

A Toast to Fine Technicians and Tuners

IF THERE is anything as essential as having a fine piano, it is having fine piano caretakers. A long time ago there was Wally Schreiber. He was a rare bird because tuners and technicians are usually two different species, and he was great at both. He understood my instrument, and he understood me. His generous and thoughtful ministerings are sacred memories; when he died I mourned the loss of a dear friend and an indispensable person.

Now I am blessed again to have both Joe Bisceglie and Craig Ryder in my life. Joe was the top voicing man at Steinway for many years and the manager of technical services. He joined Steinway in 1947, and like many of the senior craftsmen and technicians, he worked up through the ranks to become a supervisor. Although officially semiretired, he still comes over to tap and tinker on my piano. He slides the heavy action out and lugs it to a table across the room. I have even seen him get underneath the instrument and lift the two-ton babe with his back to slide a caster under a leg. One day while Joe was at my house, he noticed a split in the seat of an old oak kitchen chair. He turned the seat upside down to explain how I could reinforce it with another piece of wood adding, "Never mind, I'll do it next time I'm out."

Joe is a genius at diagnosing problems; he can change a maladjusted instrument into a dreamboat, also transforming its unhappy owner into an ecstatic one. For years at Steinway, he enchanted and inspired concert pianists with his ministrations, going over the entire keyboard, note by note, until it was beautifully voiced. He strikes each key several times, writing hieroglyphics with chalk on the wooden shafts to indicate exactly what to do with the felt on each hammer when he removes it from the case. He listens for minute gradations of sound, from the most strident and shrill to the dull and lifeless, then proceeds to stab and prick or file the woolly felts as he deems necessary.

Next he goes over the whole action to attain just the right amount of resistance, eliminate wobbles, and establish equal spacing between the keys. He repairs cracks in the shanks, hammers loose pins, and uses mysterious little jars of parts and magic potions. He keeps dozens of tools in his bag, but my favorite is a brass alcohol burner with a long spout that he calls his "Aladdin's lamp." He perches it precariously inside the instrument, its blue flame glimmering all too close for my comfort. In fact much of what he does is either frightening to watch or jolting to listen to. But I trust him implicitly. Even when I argue with him because I fear he is mellowing out the piano's brightness, he is always right. Perhaps it was his experience in World War II as a sonar operator for the Navy that helped his ability to make delicate distinctions between tones.

Even though I describe his work in terms of its mystique, he teaches me the physics and engineering behind his machinations to the extent that one of my adult students quipped that we feel as though we have earned college credits by the time he leaves. He certainly knows every nook and cranny of the instrument, and his instincts and intuitions are what make him an artist-technician. When faced with a perplexing problem, as he once was with my teaching piano, he offered to take the action home during the summer to tinker with it until he found a solution. Another time, he carried the innards of the piano out onto the screened porch where I was writing some letters, and there he worked quietly while the birds chirped an accompaniment for both of us.

. . .

I am a nut about the tuning of my piano, and as far as that goes, Craig Ryder is the man. I think there is a dearth of skilled tuners, although to look in the local *Pennysaver* ads, you'd think there were one on every block. Having an instrument in perfect tune is a luxury that string players can have every time they go to play. A fine tuner must have a keen ear, although it is not necessary for him to be a musician. He must have mechanical ability and an education about the piano's construction; Craig is also a terrific technician and an expert in rebuilding pianos. He has the instinct, patience, and understanding of the artistic psyche: he can deal with his more finicky clients and has generously appeared on weekends at recital places to give the final once-over to instruments I am about to play.

Then there is that extra little *quelque chose*, a little squiggle of the wrist, a little worming in of the pin, a deft play with the tuning wrench—whatever it is, after Craig is done (and this includes his fastidious vacuuming of the instruments and removal of the dust and flakes of sheet music), I sit down to play and I cannot drag myself away. Not too many pleasures compare with playing on a freshly tuned, beautiful instrument. Craig gets a big kick out of my response to his work, but not nearly as much as I do at that moment. Not only is my piano as perfectly aligned and in tune as it can be, so am I!

~ 10 ~

The Creative Impulse

THE re-creative musician can find plenty of room for creativity. I have never had the urge to compose and squeaked through my composition courses in college with no great surges of inspiration. But I have satisfied my impulses to create something from scratch with paints on paper and by writing; and performing artists certainly have a wide enough margin in which to flex their creativity.

The most wonderful aspect of performance is the special chemistry each artist brings to a composition. In two separate projects for *Clavier*, I explored the varied responses of seven great pianists to a single work, Chopin's Barcarolle, Opus 60, then some years later, Chopin's Ballade No. 4 in F minor, Opus 52, with another group of pianists. I approached the projects with a sense of excitement for the potential revelations about those intangible creative qualities that distinguish one artist from the next, tinged with apprehension that I'd end up with a conglomeration of cursory or redundant observations. No matter what my doubts, there were constant reminders that the gifts and communicative powers of artists do not stop at their instruments. Most artists of my acquaintance think and live creatively and are generally eager to accept the challenge of defining and sharing their insights. In our conversations they expressed views that could be, amusingly, diametrically opposed, but they were always marvelously original and inventive.

The Barcarolle is the Chopin composition to which I feel the closest. Many would say it is his finest. Certainly it is a difficult, enigmatic, and highly personal work. Whether the pianist secretly harbors a personal set of images or approaches it more abstractly, no two pianists will play it exactly alike; it is the kind of piece that makes a pianist feel as though she owns it, and that it was written for her to play. It is exactly this provocative element that made it excellent material for analysis. I spent a good piece of time with pianists Rudolf Firkušny, Claude Frank, David Bar-Illan, Gary Graffman, James Tocco, Byron Janis, and Nadia Reisenberg. Their ideas came together as a richly textured collage, now pasted into my music. As this is not a book on musical analysis, I will not include the copious examinations of the piece by each pianist. More valuable than any single interpretation is the overall conclusion that we may, and do, each offer our singular and unique perspective, within the bounds of fidelity to the composer's intentions and good taste, *as we see it.* When I go to hear a concert, half the joy comes from hearing a great masterwork, and the other half comes from listening to what that artist has to say about the work. There is something to love in every performance; certainly as much as there might be to criticize.

How do we know the composer's intentions? The million-dollar question. It reminds me of something I heard many years ago that I never forgot. The pianist Lorin Hollander was describing, on TV, how he somehow put a piano on a street in Harlem in New York City and proceeded to sell his wares. That is, he began to play—to an accompaniment of a Softee ice cream truck jingling across the street and a rock record joint blasting nearby. He didn't exactly play to a full house, but a few curious passersby hung around, especially one little boy of about seven who snuggled close to his leg on the sidewalk.

After Hollander had finished one of his offerings, the child asked, "Is the man who wrote that alive?"

Hollander answered that the composer was named Schubert and that he was dead.

"Then how do you know what to do?"

"Well, the composer wrote it down on paper," whereupon Hollander showed the child the system of lines and dots which comprises musical notation.

The child studied the lines and dots, and then, "Does that tell you *exactly* what he meant?"

A fine reward, indeed, for Hollander's efforts, and a heavy question no matter who asks it.

. . .

There is something deeply stirring about confronting the raw stuff of a great manuscript and trying to project oneself back to the act of creation: an angry impulse that caused a careless blot of ink to fall on the paper of a Beethoven score, a scribbled *rinsforzando* in the Liszt sonata, or an exquisitely etched sea spray of a scale dabbed in by Chopin in a polonaise. The J. P. Morgan Library in New York has an extensive collection of more than three thousand manuscripts, an embarrassment of riches, through which I have browsed on several occasions.

As one saunters reverently from one showcase to the next, from Mozart's elegant hand all the way across time to Webern's unexpressive and stodgy notations, the temptation might be to draw conclusions about temperament and mood from the style of script, in a sort of graphological analysis. Although one might find conveniently credible correlations to support such conjecture, there are even more surprising contradictions. Beethoven, who was known to have carefully formulated rational schemes in his head before putting them down on paper, had a crazily impetuous hand; and Mozart, from whom the music poured almost faster than he could jot it down with hardly an imperfection to emend, notated in rational and consistent penmanship. Moreover, what might seem to represent a certain trait to one viewer comes across entirely different to another. I remember thinking, after an exhibit years ago, that Brahms' manuscript seemed to reveal an unpolished, peasantlike side, and then reading Donal Henahan's description of the same score as frivolous and charming. In short, such explicit deductions, while an amusing pastime, are probably sheer folly.

Yet the serious student or fancier of memorabilia can learn many things from these wondrous pages. Sometimes there are clear changes, neatly, even artistically, cross-hatched out as by Chopin, for example. Some of his refined writing is polished enough to go straight to his engraver, and some is in varying stages of alteration reflecting his constantly restless dissatisfaction that caused him to make changes even after a piece was published. Some tracts of writing are hastily rejected, as by Liszt in his indecision about the slow introduction to his B minor sonata. These changes yield clear insights into the mechanism of the creative impulse and make a pianist grateful for what was mercifully omitted (as in some almost impossible passages from Liszt's *Mephisto Waltz*. His pages, with their many revisions and deletions, are among the most revelatory, especially in his great sonata.

Sometimes the ink is entirely different halfway through the page, from which one might deduce a flagging of the imagination or a distraction. Often the very strokes of the pen recreate the natural flow of the music as in Debussy's tiny cascading dots in the rough, preparatory draft for his *Étude pour les arpèges composés,* which surely only he, or perhaps the most astute of copiers, could decipher. In the score to Ravel's *Jeux d'eau*, the fountains and cascades of water can be conjured from the graphic splashes of the notations. The pianist who beholds the original score to Ravel's Piano Concerto for the Left Hand will clearly, viscerally, experience a renewed appreciation for the singular demands of its acrobatic leaps for the left hand from deepest bass to high treble.

It is a delightful bonus when the composer has scribbled words as well as notes—as with the loving inscriptions in the margins of the *Fantasiestücke* from both Robert and Clara Schumann to their friend, Becker, who was the best man at their wedding; or on the pages of *Images oublieés,* of 1894, by Debussy:

> may these inscriptions be accepted by Mlle Yvonne Lerolle with a little of the joy that I have in dedicating them to her. These pieces would fare poorly in the "brightly lit salons" where people who do not like music congregate. They are rather "conversations" between the piano and oneself; it is not forbidden, furthermore, to apply one's small sensibility to them on nice rainy days.

The manuscript belonged to Alfred Cortot who recorded the *Images oublieés,* which were somehow not published as a set until 1977.

. . .

It is almost impossible to browse through these manuscripts without at least a glimpse of the surly Beethoven scribbling passionately into the night in the flickering candlelight, or the frail, consumptive Chopin at Nohant. The material may sometimes be seen with special permission even without a public exhibit. Anyone who has never experienced the primal feeling of connection with the composer by gazing down at a sheet from the past has a remarkable encounter in store. The manuscript pages veritably ignite the imagination.

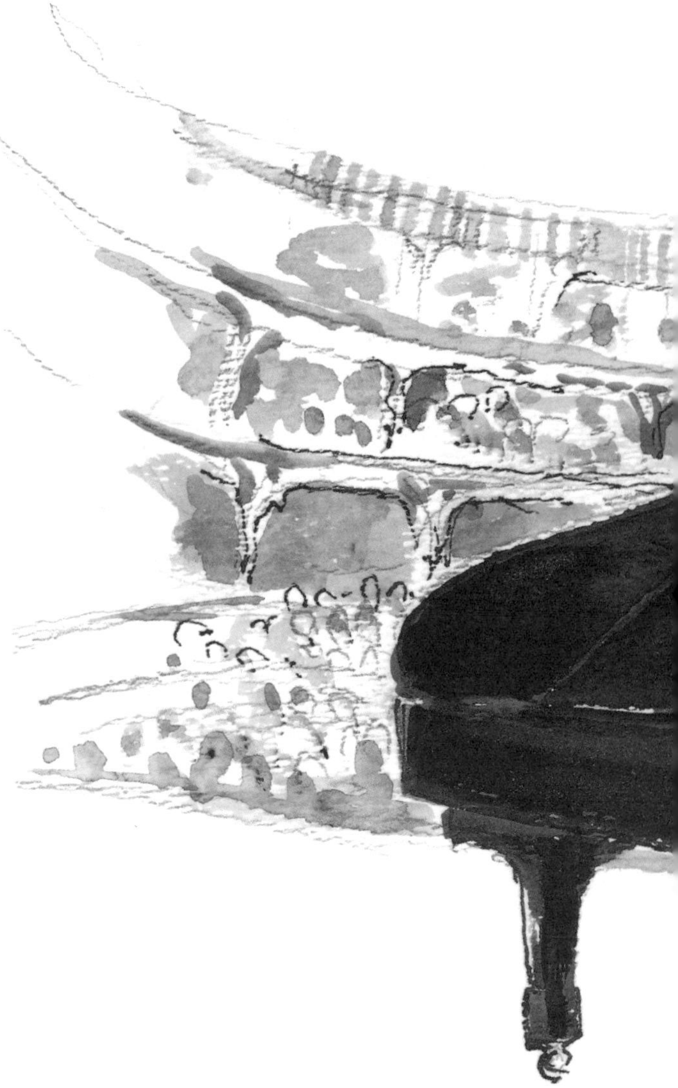

~ ON STAGE ~

All thro' my keys that gave their sounds to a wish of my soul,
All thro' my soul that praised, as its wish flowed visibly forth,
All thro' music and me!

ROBERT BROWNING

~ 11 ~

The Love-Hate Paradox of Performing

OVER the years, anything that could happen to subvert the enjoyment of concertizing has happened to me, and for that reason I have continually resolved never to perform publicly again. But even the most adamant decision to make the next scheduled concert a farewell event will vaporize when "that old feeling" starts to rumble within me and an attractive and challenging invitation is extended that I cannot resist.

Inside even the most renowned and seasoned concert artists is an ongoing dialogue that comes from a classic love-hate relationship with the stage. André Watts once sent me a telling cartoon from somewhere on tour that depicts Santa Claus, in full December regalia, lolling in a grass hut in Hawaii surrounded by hula lovelies. The caption reads: "I was halfway down a chimney in Des Moines, when I suddenly thought, 'Who needs this?'" The joy of communicating great music to a live audience is juxtaposed against the pain of anxiety, leading to heavy self-questioning as to why one is doing this: Does the world really need yet another pianist performing? The realistic answer may be a resounding "No!"—yet we persist with the rationalization, "Yes. I have a unique voice and am therefore justified," followed by the granting of permission to oneself to keep on going.

Pianists speak of talent, technique, timing, luck, and even political connections as factors essential to success, but few acknowledge or address the importance of having the right *constitution*. Traveling long distances, scurrying across the globe, racing for planes and taxis, living out of suitcases, being separated from family, engaging in small talk with concert organizers when one would rather be resting or practicing, performing despite illness, having little or no time for a personal life, all make the late Glenn Gould's decision to quit the stage and confine himself to recording seem utterly rational.

Most performing artists detest the traveling they have to do. When Radu Lupu played in New York this past season he arrived at 2 A.M., gave his concert that afternoon, and left for Europe, all within twenty-four hours. Backstage, he lamented the fierce struggle to concentrate with such fatigue and an audience that seemed to have a collective paroxysm of coughing. It reconfirmed how abhorrent that life would be to me. Jerry Lowenthal, in contrast, loves his travel time. "For me," he has said, "reading is one of the major things in life. Of course, for the performing artist, there is all the time in the world. And then there is the extra good fortune that pianists do not have to carry around their instruments on their backs. I go to my hotel and don't feel guilty that I cannot practice, because I have no piano. So this life works out very pleasantly for me."[1] Lowenthal *has* the right constitution for it.

One does not have to be a globetrotter to experience the insidious hold performing can have on one's entire life. Long ago I decided to limit my concerts geographically within a reasonable distance of New York, and to play only as frequently as I could do in balance with my family life and teaching. Still, it is astonishing how a concert looming large on the horizon can dwarf everything else by the time and energy it voraciously consumes. Yet—and this is the powerful ballast—what can be compared to the moments when the composer verily speaks through us and we hold an audience in the palms of our hands?

We have all read books on coping with stress through yoga, Zen, relaxation techniques, imaging, nutrition, and so on. Peter Serkin related to me that when he is practicing at home, he tries to conjure up the tense atmosphere of the stage, and when he is on stage, he tries to place himself mentally in the comfort of his studio.[2] Rubinstein consciously chose a particular person to focus on and play to, not uncommonly a woman he found attractive. In the countless interviews I have been fortunate to have, I've almost giggled aloud a hundred times out of a kind of nervous empathy when a famous artist like Peter Frankl, for example, admitted that he sometimes "perishes with fear" when he is backstage.[3] I overheard Martha Argerich say that the reason she rarely plays solo anymore is that "It is so lonely." When asked why she didn't travel with someone, she hastened to clarify, "Not the travel! It's the stage that is so lonely."

Some artists have even gone so far as to develop physical handicaps that defy medical diagnosis, but which nevertheless prevent them from playing, perhaps as an acceptable means of escape.

So we are in good company with all our anxieties. One morning, on the day of a concert, I tried to analyze my particular variety of nerves and found myself writing on a scrap of paper:

> it is one of the most unpleasant sensations, originating with subconscious brain waves that transmit their bilious chemicals to the pit of the gut, and from there permeate the entire system. It is a state of being that begets the question "is it worth it?" and readily answers itself in the negative, measuring days of anxiety, at least at the subliminal level, against moments of pleasure. The applause is not the high point; it is the relief. The greatest moments are actually in the prepa-

ration, and the projection of an imagined audience (that often surpasses the real one.)

If you are lucky, you have those exquisite experiences of actual communication with a real, rapt audience.

Finding myself backstage at the real event, with the soundtrack of my heartbeat pounding an accompaniment to the murmurs of the audience, I have developed my own little techniques to relax—visualizing scenes of nature, or even puppies playing! (Pets have been proven to lower blood pressure and generally help to regulate our metabolism, and, oddly, I find they even serve in fantasy.) I use my silent keyboard to keep my fingers busy; when you think of how a violinist can tuck his own instrument under his chin and fiddle around, or a cellist wrap himself around his, or any other recitalist under the sun for that matter, except for us, the presence of a facsimile keyboard is some scant comfort. At a recent trio concert, both instrumentalists were blithely warming up while I was about to go out on stage to play some solo piano pieces to open the program. I did not have any keyboard, not even a mute one, and I could barely concentrate on my music for all the diddling, sawing, and tooting that was going on; both players bridled at my timid suggestion that they desist even for those few moments.

At one engagement, I inadvertently underwent the perfect cure for nerves. While I was warming up on the piano in the gracious large salon of an old Victorian mansion before the audience began to arrive, just behind me there was an ear-splitting explosion. A bullet, fired through the glass from outside, shattered the floor-to-ceiling window and whizzed right by me as I sat at the piano. It could have been all over: no pianist, no concert! But as it was not all over, I still had a recital to give. Police came by and concluded that it had been a drive-by shooting (the historic mansion had recently been restored after a period of rundown neglect when it had served as a temporary refuge for derelicts and addicts). I tried to regain my equilibrium, and somehow my *constitution* allowed me to land on my feet. Playing that evening seemed less intimidating after surviving that incident.

Another bizarre and less threatening recital experience took place in a small hall that doubles as an art gallery. I usually love the juxtaposition of art with music, but the exhibit running concurrently with this concert consisted of basketry and extravagant sculptures fashioned out of vines, rushes, and cane. Although they were stunning visually, when the reeds and cane began to vibrate sympathetically with certain tones, I knew I was in for trouble. Worse yet, exotic insects native to the materials had incubated prematurely in the warm room, appearing on the keys and on the music. I remembered a quip from a friend in the Chicago Symphony regarding the sheet music at outdoor concerts: "If it moves, don't play it!" My excellent clarinet partner, Gene Keyes, commented wryly that he would not have to worry about running out of reeds in that room, but it was no joking matter. For someone as phobic about insects as I am, here we had another situation where distraction by external circumstances served to reduce normal performance tensions. However, I would have preferred my own cozy jitters to either of these "cures" any day.

The truth is that anxiety is far from the only deterrent. The quality of the pianos we are expected to play ranks equally high. I cannot imagine why any self-respecting pianist would care to give a recital on a "P.S.O." (piano-shaped-object), and yet that is exactly what we are expected to do. If the whole point is to communicate, then we need an instrument that will speak and sing with us. I am not a prima-donna type. I have played for benefits, charities, and educational institutions without getting paid. I have played more than my share of rinky-dinks with a sporting attitude and suffered all the indignities—including whispering, coughing, squirming children in the first row, crackling cellophane, and slamming doors. But there is one thing I know: to play without an excellent piano is no longer worth it to me. I have heard pianists beat the daylights out of an unyielding instrument. The results were so excruciating to hear that I winced in pain. Sometimes even with such a piano, you can "talk" to it—coax *something* out of it—try to counter the piano's brittleness. For the concert in that old Victorian mansion I had been warned about the "gorgeous-looking rosewood piano, like three separate instruments: rich bass, dead middle, brittle treble." In fact, what I found was a charming turn-of-the-century, eight-foot square grand with an action flabby with age; yet one could still coax a beautiful tone out of it, and in that reverberant chamber, the sound was quite pleasing.

I have gladly waived a part of my fee when it was necessary to provide a good piano for myself, because the only pleasure and purpose I feel from performing comes from having an instrument that will respond to what I am trying to say: not the applause, certainly not the physical or emotional toll, and not the money. I have ceased to expect to get rich on music-making and even if I am a victim of my own high standards, I am determined that if and when I do perform, it will be on my own terms.

It took me a long time to come to that conviction. Some years ago Krystian Zimerman told me that is why he takes one of his own six pianos on tour with him, underscoring the important connection between his tone and the voice of the piano. He spoke of his disappointment with an instrument on which he was to play Brahms' Second Piano Concerto: "It was a fine piano, but I couldn't find the sound. Before it is possible to get a deep tone, one must establish a sensitive connection with the piano. I couldn't talk to it. It wasn't beautiful."[4] This artist regrets the high expense involved in transporting his own instruments, even with fees that he could not complain about, but still considers having the right instrument an essential factor, even if he breaks even. (When taking his final bows at the end of a successful concert, Zimerman has acknowledged his fine piano as a jockey would do his prize horse, or a singer his or her accompanist.)

I have accepted several invitations to play for a wonderful organization called Ridotto in the town where I live. The audiences are warm, receptive, and educated, and the spirit of the *ridotti* (artists committed to creative freedom and unrestrained exploration and diversity) prevails. The programs combine music, theater, poetry, and dance, and the format appeals to me greatly. The director, Margarethe Maimone, is a fount of ideas, and the events are well-publicized. Everything adds up to an attractive prospect but for one factor: the piano in the hall does not have the capacity for *cantabile* or *sostenuto*.

They have assured me that I can go to a local piano dealer and select any instrument that I like, which in most instances would be a fine solution. Even a decent piano sounds good there because of the lively acoustics. However, for one of their concerts, problems arose. After several hours of trying to settle on a good piano, I left the store utterly dispirited. I had already committed to the concert, and not a single instrument had a compatible action or lovely tone. I was preparing myself to waive my fee and rent a piano from Steinway when a former student and friend offered to allow his concert grand to be moved from his home to the hall. Overcome by the generosity of his gesture, I accepted his offer even before getting to know the instrument. After spending some time at his home, however, I found that although the piano unquestionably had the character I was searching for, it was in desperate need of voicing and regulation. Moreover, the *una corda* wasn't functioning correctly. These realizations became apparent to me two weeks before the concert, and simultaneously (yes, this began to feel like a soap opera) I came down with a devastating case of the flu.

For six days of the remaining time, I had a high fever and neither a grain of energy nor any interest in getting out of bed and carrying on. After two attempts to try the program, I became depressed. Visions of canceling a most enjoyable concert experience (all Chopin) interrupted the mental run-throughs of the program that were turning like broken records in my head. My homeopath prescribed special remedies, and I patiently trusted and waited for my energy to return. Finally I could stagger down to the piano to comfort myself with a *sotto voce, meno mosso* trial, and found that as weak as I still was, I had enough principal in the technique bank to draw from.

During the next few days of slow recovery, I realized that every nerve and muscle would have to be focused on the job if I were to get through it creditably. I had not yet solved the piano problem, but when I tried my friend's piano again and found that in addition to all the other problems some notes were sticking, I knew I still had to find an instrument, and fast! As a last resort I could move my own wonderful piano to the hall, but then I would have to drag my pillow and blanket and sleep underneath it until it would be safely back at home where it belonged.

I called the piano store again, and miraculously several new pianos had been delivered to the warehouse in the interim. Three days to go, and after an arduous search, a fine instrument turned up and would be sent to the hall for me. I could devote whatever strength I had left to practicing; it wasn't much.

. . .

Not all directors and administrators of concert series are as sympathetic to artists as Ridotto's. Folks who go into arts-related fields ought to have more than just administrative skills. They ought to have at least an inkling about the nature of an artist and the act of making music. I was invited to give my "Nature and Music" lecture-recital for a renowned scientific institution on Long Island, because the program related the humanities with science. The dame who is the director of programming, whose office doubles as an artists' dressing room, greeted me as I arrived about three-quarters of an hour before concert time:

"Oh, you can't stay in here. I have work to do."

"Then would you just lead me to a quiet place somewhere so that I can concentrate and relax?" I asked.

"Why are you so nervous, sweetie?" she asked with a vinegary tone of voice. Then she complained that I had "audaciously" asked an audio engineer to tape my concert without her permission, and she generally tried to subvert the peace with similar negative jibes to add to the normal amount of nervous tension. By the time I walked into the hall, trying to look radiantly happy and confident, the audience by contrast was a balm for my ruffled spirits.

A big draw for me was the glorious piano, a Hamburg Steinway, rented from Pro Pianos in New York for this event. But ironically the so-called recital hall was an acoustically dead lecture hall. There is an old saying in gardening lore: a fifty-cent plant in a four-dollar hole will do better than a four-dollar plant in a fifty-cent hole. The same goes for pianos. This hall had no resonance and I had to overplay to project, but the concert went well (in spite of the murmuring of someone on the phone in the sound booth, entirely audible to me throughout).

For this event there was also a very nice fee. Usually the "honoraria" are a joke, and the preparation time figures out to be a nickel an hour. But money cannot be a prime motivator, although in this case I took the money and ran, having well-earned every farthing. (Sherrill Milnes has been quoted as saying that his fees were ninety-nine percent for nerves and one percent for singing, because he would gladly sing for nothing.) That is essentially how I feel—that is, *when* all the extramusical considerations do not conspire against the music.

. . .

So why play? I haven't asked myself that question point-blank until now; nor, strangely, have I posed it to any artist I have interviewed. But I have thought about it a lot. At the crux of the matter is that once one has achieved a certain level, there is no turning back or away from it. The art and the individual are like two separate entities, and the art has an insatiable life of its own. Almost like a tapeworm, it inhabits you, controls you, and takes away your prerogative to make choices. The artist who is sometimes perceived as an essentially egocentric, selfish creature is really quite the converse: the true artist is a nurturer and a *giver*. The artist is not nurturing himself or herself, but the gift. It is almost as though the gift were leased, and once having been bestowed must then be shared with others. Who would consciously choose to keep experiencing the preconcert stress that spreads and manifests its unpleasant sensations in many of us? But the music wants *out*, and I, for one, must yield to it.

Then—after decisions and preparations have been made, and you are ready to make that musical offering, when all the elements go right: the hall, the piano, your concentration, and your audience—you feel that by the grace of God, you have had a kind of visitation and you have been brought outside of yourself; that you have joined forces with the composer to bring his music to life, and you are playing as though there is no tomorrow.

12

On Being a Woman Pianist

AT TIMES I am keenly aware of belonging to the species *homo pianisticus*, a peculiar strain of creative humans distinguished by a deep attachment to their great instrument. At other times I am less identified with that specification, but then a nonmusician, such as my husband, drops a comment about what an enviable thing it is to be a musician and reminds me that musicians are among the privileged few to have an outlet for their feelings that is both satisfying and productive.

The subspecies, which might be called *femina pianistica*, may encounter inner conflicts between domestic and professional life. The women I know who are professional pianists have had to make clear-cut choices between both facets of their lives, choices that may be more traumatic than male performing artists have had to make. I enjoyed meeting and interviewing Madame Alicia de Larrocha and developed an affection for her and a feeling of kinship, especially when she spoke of the conflict between her performing career and her desire to spend more time with her daughter and grandchild. There she was, the grande dame of the piano, surrounded by extravagant bouquets of roses from her concert the previous evening at Avery Fisher Hall in New York, wanting more than anything to be relaxing with her family in Barcelona—and her tour was only half over. While he was alive her late husband, the pianist Juan Torra, fortunately took over the domestic responsibilities along with managerial details of her career so that she could pursue her international concert life. De Larrocha spoke about the burdens of organizing and maintaining her residences in Barcelona, New York, and Switzerland, yet for her this was better than bouncing from one hotel room to the next with no home base in this country or on the European continent. Since the loss of her husband, she has been even more beleaguered by the extramusical considerations of her career.

The happiest musician will still suffer pangs of loneliness while on the road for months away from family. Many women with a career on the concert stage decided not to have children or delegated their upbringing to someone else. Waking up in Gopher Prairie one day and Timbuktu the next is scant recompense. For the superstar women pianists the notion of struggle is paramount. Consider Martha Argerich, for whom concerts are such an emotional upheaval that she frequently has had to cancel. Certainly stage fright is experienced by both sexes, but she has been articulate about the loneliness and anxieties of a woman on tour. When I listen to Mitsuko Uchida's fiercely concentrated and illuminating recitals I understand why this great artist has decided not to have children in order to focus so intensely on her musical explorations.

Ruth Laredo raised a daughter primarily alone in New York while building her career, accepting only those engagements that would not separate them for more than a few days. For years my friend Rita Bouboulidi, the Greek pianist, put her career on hold while she devoted herself to caring for her late husband during his protracted illness. Such domestic restrictions sorely limit the availability and flexibility crucial to establishing or sustaining a major career. I know of few relationships in which the roles were reversed as they were with Madame de Larrocha and her husband. Most male concert artists I know have spouses devoted to "the care and feeding" of their famous artist-husbands. (Naomi Graffman wrote a wonderful article entitled "The Care and Feeding of Pianists" for *Clavier*, July/August 1986.) I also know quite a few marriages between two pianists wherein the wife has given over all her original plans or hopes of her own career to nurture her husband's.

I often wonder about all the great women of whom we have not heard who chose the quiet realms of home life with the inner knowledge of their talents to keep them warm, and only occasional twinges of regret for what might have been.

• • •

Maintaining a teaching studio in one's home presents relatively few juggling problems; in fact it is the lucky mother who can work on the same premises as her family and be available should emergencies arise. Yet a career in teaching will not assuage the yearnings of a person who wants to perform. Fortunately I stumbled upon the perfect formula that kept me happy and fulfilled while raising a family. Because I had children when I was young and fresh out of school, any thoughts of a concert career were shelved. I never experienced a moment of resentment because my children learned early to respect my serious work at the piano and to occupy themselves creatively. Limited teaching and occasional recitals in the New York area were always a lovely balance to my home life.

I feel strongly that audiences are basically the same everywhere. The mix in big cities is much the same as it is in suburban or rural areas, with the *cognoscenti* seated right alongside the occasional concertgoer. For me the perfect audience has always been a select group of listeners in a salon-like setting, a situation I can create for myself any time the spirit moves me. That is the ultimate concert experience for effective communication and pleasure with a minimum of anxiety, and a format that I plan to pursue more as I gradually retreat from public appearances.

Many a summer my garden and my household called to me, but

I had to put everything on hold until the last of a cluster of recitals was over. I have often overextended myself, accepting too many invitations for concerts or lecture-recitals, and have had to admit that I would have preferred to be digging around in my flower beds and fixing my closets than spending all those hours at the piano. Part of the problem is that I inherited a philosophy from a dear old friend: I never regret anything I do, only the things I didn't do. The trouble with this credo is that one slowly loses the ability to say "No" and pass up an attractive opportunity.

One tries to have it all: performing, teaching, writing, personal life. But playing publicly while keeping a full studio and a happy home is trying to be Superwoman. In an interview the late great conductor Sir Georg Solti, who was trained as a pianist, was asked why he had waited twenty-five years without playing the piano publicly. "Are you kidding?" he replied. "Do you know what it takes to give a piano recital? You do nothing else but practice for several months. I haven't had the time." Doing nothing but practice for several months is a luxury I have never enjoyed.

But I am not the only woman-pianist I know who has done that juggling act. I have quite a few friends who have raised families and kept active to some degree with concert work. In fact, for about twenty-five years I have belonged to an unusual piano workshop group, which consists of eight women pianists, all but a couple of whom are the original members. Although we are as different from each other as eight people can be—stylistically, culturally, emotionally—a bonding has taken place over the years that we have been meeting every month, most of us playing each time. Our meetings are as much support groups as they are musical discussions; we often have to cut off our gab-fests to get back to the music, which is important to all of us. Oddly this is the place where I am the most nervous to play. We all usually know every note of what is being played. We all know each person's potential and are familiar with each other's idiosyncratic behavior, which may include the occasional use of undignified expletives when matters fail to run as smoothly as planned. Some meetings are better than others: sometimes we go home with an earful of terrific playing; other times the sessions evolve into an airing of our various and sundry impedimenta—from muscle spasms to marathon house guests.

An especially stimulating function of the workshop has been to whet our appetites to study compositions performed by another member of the group. In this manner many a sonata has been passed from hand to hand as several of us took a crack at it. Never are the dynamics of personalization more dramatic and fascinating than when this happens. We have all grown considerably, of course, over this amazing number of years. Some whose careers were more active years ago have settled more into domesticity with only occasional sorties into the concert arena. Others have only recently ventured out finally to realize long-postponed plans. The group has been a most valuable resource, not only for trying out programs beforehand, but for emotional support.

. . .

None of the women pianists I know personally or have met professionally have had to struggle as did the high priestess of the piano in the nineteenth century, Clara Schumann. Without doubt she is among the most fascinating women in history. Her life and art, while seeming highly romantic, were a triumph of her will over adversity of epic proportions.

In Nancy B. Reich's excellent book, *Clara Schumann: The Artist and the Woman*, we can read astute and sensitive interpretations of countless letters and documents from Clara and Robert, Johannes Brahms, Clara's father Friedrich Wieck, and others. Clara Schumann owed everything to her own determination first to break free from the hideously controlling father who made her an instrument of his own ambitions from her early childhood (yet whom she loved as a grateful child) and then to continue to pursue her career after her marriage in September 1840 to an equally controlling husband. Outwardly, a career in which she was continually introducing works written for her by her great husband, as well as by Brahms, Mendelssohn, and others, would seem an ideal lot, but the life of this consummate artist and composer in her own right was anything but enviable.

The story of Clara and Robert is fraught with conflict and contradiction. Yes, Robert continued to write noble piano music for her to perform, but at the same time he was keeping her "barefoot and pregnant" and writing unbelievably restricting letters. On 9 September 1838:

> My Clara will be a happy wife, a contented, beloved wife. I consider your art great and holy. I hardly dare think of the happiness you will give me with it, but if we don't consider it necessary, you won't lift a finger if you don't want to, for people who aren't even worth playing scales for, isn't that true my girl? . . . I believe you can preserve art without having to make great concert tours.

And in 1839:

> I am musing about our first summer in Zwicken as married folks. First (another kiss), young wives must be able to cook and to keep house, if they want satisfied husbands, . . . and then young wives may not make long journeys right away.

Two days later he wrote:

> you shall forget the artist, you shall live only for yourself and your home and your husband—just see how I will make you forget the artist—because the wife stands higher than the artist, and if I only achieve this much—that you will have

> nothing further to do with the public—I will have achieved my deepest wish. Yet you still remain an artist. The bit of fame in the contemptible paper. I despise it.

And then:

> Trust me and obey me, after all men are above women.[1]

As shocking to our twentieth century ears as these pleas sound, that is what Clara had to surmount in order to survive as an artist. And she married him knowing he felt that way! Yet somehow their art and their marriage flourished because, first of all, they passionately adored each other. Their artistic needs interlocked, and they shared both a musical and emotional interdependence.

Her life story is daunting. She could not practice when he was composing; their modest apartments were never big enough, and she would always yield to his work. She was so entirely human in certain ways: she suffered mental anguish before concerts like any of us; she had physical symptoms such as pain in her fingers, shoulders, and arms, apparently caused by stress; she had depression, fainting spells, neuralgia; and yet there are the superhuman facts that she bore eight children (she was continually pregnant) and performed, at times, in her ninth month of pregnancy as well as one month postpartum. She toured alone (although Robert sometimes accompanied her) at a time when women did not travel without an escort, and she thought nothing of her public appearances in late pregnancy, despite societal attitudes about women hiding themselves during those months. She hired wetnurses one month after delivery and saw to the details of her household before she left to go on tour, or long distance by letter. She had three house-servants, and friends who, in effect, acted as *her* "wife" when she was on tour (including Brahms, who had become a beloved friend of both Clara and Robert). As Robert's mental illness increased—it was apparent that he had episodes of instability early in their marriage—she suffered sincere anguish and concern. But she could point to her earning power, which in several weeks equaled his in a year, as a prime argument in favor of her continuing concerts.

In 1840, the year of their marriage, Robert Schumann openly declared his love for Clara in an ecstatic deluge of lieder in which his emotional outpourings no longer masqueraded behind such pseudonyms as Eusebius or Florestan. Although many biographers think that he reached his peak of creativity with the vocal writing, the melodic lines in his piano music during the happy periods of his life are every bit as lyrical. Only with Clara's urging was he induced to write larger works, among them the Piano Concerto in A minor, Opus 54. By the time he completed the work with the addition in 1845 of the last two movements, Intermezzo and Finale, his health was already declining. The work has been criticized for a lack of unity, but it *is* unified by the imagination and spirit that thread through the entire concerto, creating a metamorphosis from pain to joy, emotions that always tug at each other in his music. From the impetuous opening throughout the work, there is a successful interplay of moods, roguishly deceptive meters, repartée between piano and orchestra, and the great lyricism of the songs. Clara wrote of her pleasure in studying and playing it. After Robert's death she played the concerto at a benefit concert to raise money for a grander graveside memorial for him.

Her daughter Eugenie's loving account of the concert inspired me at a time of major change in my own life. I was invited to perform a solo concerto with an orchestra on Long Island, and I chose the Schumann concerto not only because I loved it but because it was so apt: the A minor yearnings of the first movement, the ponderings of the colloquy of the Intermezzo, and the final Allegro vivace with its ebullient arrival to A major in a sort of Dance of Life all seemed to depict my own concurrent passage, uncannily so. Clara's life story stands as a bulwark for any pianist, male or female. But in the end, it is the artist's own experience which yields substantive clues for performance.

~ 13 ~

Memory Lapses and Other Mishaps

I HAVE read exasperating articles on the merits of playing from memory, written by prominent critics. What always strikes me is the tone of reprimand and the sense of indignation toward artists who dare to appear in public with music. Of course they speak of pianists who, of all musicians, have the most to memorize: polyphonies, clotted chords, and fistfuls of notes. The pianist is the one instrumentalist plagued and persecuted by this taboo, thanks to dear old Clara, who decided to play from memory and thus spoiled things for the rest of us. (It never bothered anybody when the great virtuosos who preceded her, including Beethoven, Clementi, Mozart, and others, had their scores in front of them.)

Who among us hasn't had the near-death experience, the feeling of entering an altered state, of temporal displacement, with a flickering concentration teetering on the edge of blackout; when even for a split second the audience's presence, as a sea of pointillist speckles, threatens to submerge us, and the keyboard becomes a black and white striped yardstick by which to measure our survival skills; when the sounds coming from the piano seem disembodied, other-worldly and not *of* us, and the hands seem to belong to someone else because the axons that tie them to our brain are momentarily severed? While that split second seems of interminable length to us, it may be barely perceptible to others. We have some choices during that fleeting interval: we can acknowledge the mishap and let everyone in on our emergency, or we can try to mask it to save our souls. Even what seems like the worst scenario may be handled with humor and grace —if one can make it through the guck of that moment. When we hear a tale of a concert disaster, especially stories involving famous artists, whether apocryphal or not, it is like the fascination of the abomination because it embodies our own worst fears. (My pianist-friend Christine once responded to the question, "Do you compose?" with "Only when I have a memory lapse.") A famous pianist on the Juilliard faculty once had a memory slip during a performance, stopped, turned to the audience, and with deadpan delivery quipped, "You wouldn't believe how well this went at home!" I was there and inwardly murmured, "Bravo!" for his aplomb. He started again and gave a moving performance. Instead of fearing and rejecting our humanness, we ought to cultivate it; instead of expecting ourselves to be as infallible as computers, we ought only to strive to fulfill our highest potentials. This is what I tell my students before they participate in recitals.

I have never had to stop, but I have sat through other pianists' emergencies, and although they did not seem earth-shattering to me, as a pianist in the audience I suffered vicariously. I have only three nasty recollections from my years of playing publicly, when I had to improvise a sequence or a modulation to get myself back on track without stopping. I heard the tape where I "made up" half a bar of Brahms. It sounded a bit more like Schoenberg, I must admit, but I didn't miss a beat! Another time I had to play the rhythmic introduction to *Alborada del gracioso* by Ravel twice through before the missing link to the opening theme came to me. In the dressing room I had tried to "play it on the table" (mistake number one), and reaching an impasse, I had no music to refer to, having left it at home (mistake number two). I knew I'd have trouble as I walked out on stage, and

I did. I recall a third instance when I was about sixteen: I was performing the Toccata and Fugue in D minor and had to fugue my way through the circle of fifths until the dang thing went back on track. Something about Bach can make you feel as though you are in a private struggle with the devil until you land on your feet at the end. That devil made the King of Bach, Glenn Gould, retire from the stage.

Although I have never used music in a formal solo recital or concerto performance, I have at times had the score during my lecture-recitals and in ensemble concerts where convention permits its use. I would have played much more frequently in recent years if using the score had not always been such a controversial issue; the time consumed in memorization becomes a problem for those of us who do not have six to eight hours a day to commit to a program. For this reason I have begun to trailblaze by occasionally using the music, for example in Bach. Why not? Harpsichordists and organists blithely do it.

I have found a great solution, courtesy of cellist Janós Starker, whom I saw on a New York stage brandishing his music to the Bach solo cello suites, music he has recorded and played countless times. With typical droll humor, Starker addressed the audience, "For my friends who are wondering why I am using music after playing these suites thousands of times, I can answer that each time I behold the score I see something new." This may indeed be true, but Starker's tongue was most definitely in cheek; he had found an elegant rationalization for indulging in the comforts of the score. Backstage he showed me his ingenious invention, which I now pass along: he makes reduced photocopies of the entire Bach suite and pastes up all the movements on two oversized sheets. This eliminates page-turning but requires a good pair of eyes. Let's face it; we know the work ninety-nine percent securely, but it is that one percent that threatens to subvert the rest of it by standing between us and the liberated feeling so necessary for making music. These ministats will only work if one is already intimate, not only with the music, but with the topography of each page—the look of it—so that the eyes can catch hold of a passage at a glance if necessary.

Even during ensemble concerts I would rather eliminate the need for a page-turner if at all possible. I have been sabotaged by even the most experienced readers who accidentally grabbed two pages at once, or forgot to return to the start of a Menuet movement after the Trio, or obliterated half the page preparing to turn, or did not read at my exact pace (a bar ahead of the music), or who simply vagued out and forgot to turn at all! So "Trust myself" is my motto, but this can present logistical problems of the first order in a Brahms sonata or chamberwork, for example. Therefore I also photocopy and paste up portions of pages so that I can turn conveniently when there are rests. I write directions to myself in red in open bars, such as "Dog-ear page," where I can easily grab the corner of the page when I need to; I draw a pair of eyeballs when there is a swift turn with lots of action on the following page, and so on. I seem to have it down to a science, unless the music falls on the floor, which it once did while I was playing on the radio. Mercifully it landed open to the right page and I cranked my neck to read it off the floor until the final bars. (Not a technician in sight to pick it up for me and replace it on the piano.) At times I have had to yield to a page turner, for example when the air-vent system started blowing pages closed.

• • •

One might ask what memorization has to do with the music. "Is it a parlor trick, a minor sideshow, or something more?" asked music journalist Will Crutchfield. Or as Bernard Holland wrote: "Surely the immersion required to make a piece of music one's own will naturally result in memorization, or something so close that a decent amount of drill work will do the rest. Clinging to the printed music, it seems to me, can be a kind of shield between the performer and full entry into the act of performance, a security blanket against the risk of abandon."[1] The truth is the opposite: a reduced copy on the music stand provides a psychological safety net and thus allows the player to take risks. In one *coup d'oeil* we can see the familiar topography of the musical line. That's all we need. No one is talking about being glued to a printed page for minutiae.

Crutchfield: "It seems to me that the musical community is right to insist . . . that soloists perform 'off the book.'" As a pianist he must understand the hours upon hours of hard work and repetition that memorization demands, not to mention the stresses it puts upon the artist. It does *not* get easier the longer you do it. Two of my favorite pianists, who perform more than one hundred concerts annually, suffer from backstage nerves each time, and it is precisely the fear of memory lapse that haunts them.

Bernard Holland wrote about memory: "having the music in front of you can be an act of courage, an acknowledgment that musicians are in the service of something other than themselves. Written music becomes censor and conscience, a brake applied to freelancing egos."[2] Well, that is another nice rationalization, but not one I feel the need to use as fodder.

My teacher once shouted at me, "You want to memorize this? Then you must suffer for it!" I don't want to suffer, but I do want to play. So, for the occasional evasive passage, I'll continue to put my minicopy on the piano, even if it only consists of three thorny bars, enjoy my concert, and hope that no one will bat an eye about it.

. . .

I think an essential mark of an artist is how he or she recovers from a mishap. While at the ballet, my husband and I witnessed a most incredible act of courage and inspiration. Even though it happened to a dancer, there is an important lesson in it for pianists—indeed any performing artist. A prima ballerina at the New York City Ballet was leaping gracefully and confidently across the stage when she tripped and fell flat on her face and stomach—splat! It was a surreal sight, and an awful, collective gasp of horror blew across the thousand-member audience, but in a moment, with the adroit help of her partner, she scrambled to her feet. Despite some apparent injury, she proceeded to dance again, beautifully, and at least to all outward appearances, with an air of self-assuredness.

What must it have taken, in terms of sheer courage, will, emotional energy, spirit, and ego, to overcome what must have been a recurrent refrain in her head—"Oh my God, what a dreadful fall I just took in front of all those people"—and to pull herself together to finish the ballet? Rubinstein once said, "If I play a wrong note, then I play the next one twice as beautifully." Indeed, the dancer did seem to end triumphantly, and her ovation reflected the audience's appreciation of her performance and of her remarkable recovery. The control and grace embodied in this incident are the highest measure of an artist. The dancer exemplified our humanness and she exhibited the resilience to rebound from error. Ultimately she was strengthened by it.

. . .

To be alone on stage with every eye and ear tuned to us is the most demanding art of all. Martha Argerich has been quoted as saying, "I love to play the piano, but I hate being a pianist." I have yet to meet the artist who did not admit to backstage nerves, and I think a lot of it has to do with the fear of losing one's concentration.

Which leads me to my number one pet peeve: bad audience behavior. This includes crackling wrappers, hacking coughers, beeping watches, bleeping hearing aids, snorers, rustlers, gabbers, fidgeters, latecomers, and early departers. How can anyone concentrate with all that going on? I once watched Radu Lupu—*as he was playing* a profound Adagio from a Beethoven sonata—stare down a boor in the first row who was peeling a cellophane wrapper from a candy. After the recital he moaned in amazement, "They think if they unwrap it slowly it is better! It seemed to last for half the movement!" I heard Lili Kraus stop in the middle of a Schubert sonata, glare at a woman who was coughing persistently, and sneer, "Madam, it is either you or I." Madam left. Kraus began again.

At a concert many years ago by the late great guitarist Andrés Segovia, the old maestro stopped because the intimate sounds of his instrument could not be heard above the noises of a disrespectful audience. How clearly I still remember his beseeching gesture and his pitiable plea, "Please—" He resumed and even offered an encore, but by then the race to the parking lot had begun, and the din of opening and shutting doors drowned out his music. I was so ashamed to be among that body of people, and wanted to vanish on the spot. Since then I have imagined inventing a blow-gun to shoot at offending audience members. The dart would inject a temporary but instantaneous tranquilizer, effective until the end of the concert.

Part of the problem, aside from the issue of basic manners, is a failure of perception. Most audience members have little sense of what it means to prepare and execute a solo recital, and there is really no way we can tell them. For one afternoon concert, I arrived an hour early to practice with my chamber partners in the hall. As we were going over a few spots, a couple barged in and started choosing seats. I stopped playing and said, "I beg your pardon, but the room is not open yet." The woman shrewishly retorted, "I'm sorry, but I didn't break my neck to get here an hour early to chance not getting a good seat!" I asked her again to wait outside, but she continued her stroll and placed her ostentatious fur coat across several seats before sauntering out.

When the time finally came for us to disappear backstage (in this case a euphemism for an unheated closet-sized storage area), we heard an enormous crash as a pile of stacked tables collapsed inside the door, blocking us from entering. We located a custodian who had to enter through the fire exit after deactivating an alarm that would have brought down the fire department. The heavy metal tables had fallen on top of the clarinetist's suit jacket, and it took ages to lift and remove them. My good-natured partner rescued his mashed jacket, but it was ten degrees Fahrenheit outdoors, and by now the long-open fire exit had made the room an icebox. As his reeds and instrument started to ice up, my colleague's good humor descended to the level of my ill temper, but being a veteran of refrigerated backstage cells, I had brought a little heater. Naturally there was no outlet in the closet. The custodian went on a safari for an extension cord, but when he returned, it was already curtain time.

The person taping the concert got sick and dashed out, leaving the machine with someone else who clicked around trying to figure it out throughout the first movement of the opening piece. The eyeglasses I had left alongside on the music desk turned up on the strings of the piano. The overflowing audience were seated practically at our elbows and breathing down our backs, making concentration a struggle.

Yet somehow we managed to make some beautiful music in spite of it all.

Then there was the time the piano began to roll away from me as I was playing because the movers had not locked the casters. My first panicky impulse was to grab the keyboard by the black notes and scoot myself forward with the bench to catch up to the new position of the piano on stage. Finally I had to acknowledge to myself and to the audience that I needed a custodian to help secure the wheels, and then to start again. I have arrived at halls where the piano was still backstage with no one in sight to roll it to center stage. So I donned the role of mover and did it myself. Another time, arriving at a hall I was told by the proud concert arranger that they had "fixed" the piano so that it was more beautiful. Apparently this meant that they had had it varnished, and some of the varnish had leaked inside onto a few hammers. I have also experienced a moment when the entire pedal mechanism dropped from the piano, and I once had to remove a broken string. These little mishaps oddly serve to relax and amuse me. They take the edge off the awesome solemnity of the moment and break the spell with some levity.

14

Remembering Carnegie, Criticism, and Green Rooms

CAN a building be beloved? To artists the world over, not only all New Yorkers, Carnegie Hall, and its littler sister, the Recital Hall, renamed Weill Hall at Carnegie, could certainly be described in such endearing terms. With legendary warm and near-perfect acoustics, both halls have been good friends to musicians who have performed there.

Situated on the southeast corner of 57th Street and 7th Avenue, the russet brick building represents the best of nineteenth-century architecture. It was declared a national and city landmark in 1964 and in 1986 was restored to even more than its past glamour. To think that in 1959 it was on the verge of being sold to a developer, razed, and replaced by a garish modernist tower makes the triumph of its survival and the story of its $50 million restoration all the sweeter. Thanks to the efforts of violinist Isaac Stern and financier James B. Wolfensohn, we can indulge in a celebration of good taste and cherished values, and continue to listen to great music in a most hallowed hall.

Fifty-seventh Street stretches from the East River to the Hudson River on the west side. For this native New Yorker it is among the most varied, colorful, and bustling streets of the city; on it one is likely to cross paths with anyone from André Watts to Woody Allen.

It is all elegance as it traverses Park Avenue at the exclusive Ritz Towers residential hotel, wherein lives my dear friend, Andrea—a devotée, collector, and patron of the arts, whom I first met on the streets of Manhattan on the way to do an interview. At the corners of 5th Avenue are Bergdorf Goodman and Tiffany's; then going west past piano showrooms, book shops, dance studios, and silk and woolen remnant outlets, the street assumes a seedier air past CBS-TV Studios down toward the river. Around 7th Avenue, though, the area is dotted with artist management offices, with the venerable little Patelson's Music House right across the street from the stage entrance on 56th Street. The Recital Hall sits like a miniature beside the magnificently refurbished Carnegie Hall, both visually stunning with Italianate campanile towers and Palladian windows all clean and rosy, as if in new ballgowns. A stone's throw from Carnegie Hall on 7th Avenue is an ornate building, Alwyn Court, wherein I enjoyed several valuable coachings from my generous friend, the ebullient Greek pianist Rita Bouboulidi.

I have had a fascination with the warren-like back stairways and rooms at Carnegie ever since I was a teenage pianist performing in the hall with a youth orchestra and wandered curiously up a staircase to try to view the hall from a high vantage point, becoming utterly lost. I should have (as I once heard the manager, Judith Arron, suggest) scattered a trail of breadcrumbs to find my way back through the complex of private studios and workshops. The balconies yield what is perhaps the grandest view of the stage and hall, but to be on that stage is to experience its awesome presence and glowing aura.

From all the history that has been made there, the name *Carnegie* has taken on magic of its own, and for years lesser-known artists who appeared at Carnegie Recital Hall have also been able to feel about them its special mystique and ambiance. Historic debuts, farewell concerts, indeed nightly events have made it a fabled place.

My debut recital was "historic" within the context of my life. I have presented many other important and fulfilling recitals since 1976, but in the most serendipitous ways that event has led me through a maze of corridors, not unlike those I explored at Carnegie, conveying me from one exciting episode in my life to the next. I have already fully documented the recital to the last detail, but I still smile whenever I pass by, remembering my dash across 57th Street, weaving in and out of stalled yellow taxicabs, with my black velvet gown flapping on its hanger, and all the expectation and high drama of the evening. That night all of New York City seemed to be illuminated and glittering, poised and waiting for Carol Montparker to play—at least that was my fantasy. I was not disappointed in any way. Even twenty years later, I view the whole thing with warm sentiment and gratitude.

The years that followed had a kind of momentum that was launched that night, and through those corridors I made my own way without managers or agents. I had no plan but to continue to play; and I knew I did not want to limit my musical life to performance alone. This is a factor that becomes so clear to me as time passes: that I love my concert work *all the more* because it has been in balance with my home life, teaching, and writing. Had I knocked on doors to be heard by managements, or they on mine, and had I committed myself to a touring life, I would have grown to resent its devouring nature.

The subject of managements, promotion, and publicity is a tricky one. For artists who want a performing career in the biggest way possible, those matters have to be tackled head on. Several years ago I read a distressing *New York Times* article from a journalist who purported to understand artists who buy advertising space in *Musical America*'s annual directory. He portrayed these musicians as pitiable creatures waiting to be hired by concert managers and derided them for placing vanity ads, which they pay for themselves. The journalist mentioned that by phoning the numbers in the ads, anyone can speak to Mrs. Basso, or even Mr. Basso, himself.

Let's get real. There are many gifted people in this world who struggle to be heard, and the directory is an advertising compendium in which unknowns appear side-by-side with world-renowned musicians. That delightful notion, in itself, gives the lesser-knowns an emotional lift, and democratizes a business wherein the good gigs seem to keep going to the same coterie of famous artists. Certainly some careers are waning and others are rising, but I doubt that readers would, as the author claimed, "put two and two together" and deduce from the ad sizes who is "in" and who is "out," and then gossip about it.

In one of the article's few unrepellent phrases, the journalist wrote "hearts full of hope, they want to tell us who they are." He prefaced the phrase, however, with "checkbooks in hand." Is it surprising that artists want to be heard? And what is wrong with someone who believes in his or her talent or has the ego to think he has something to say in music and goes after it? And yes, it costs money.

It is too bad when someone uses a podium as public as *The New York Times* to dismiss people as minor talents because they are "unknown" to the writer "who, after all, converses with the music business every day." He added that perhaps they are "truly important artists thwarted by a shrinking market, poor connections, short-sighted managers, and bad luck . . . virtuoso pianists pining for fame while teaching Cramer and Kuhlau to teenagers still sweaty from cheerleading practice."[1] These words may hold some painful truths, but why such contempt?

The journalist chalked off page after page of promotional photos as hype, and even when he suggested the tragic aspect of failed aspirations, there was a ring of mockery. For example, in citing the practice of taking blurbs out of context for quotes on a flyer, he never addresses the satisfaction an artist has from a favorable review, and the pride in being able to extract a meaningful phrase for quotation, or for that matter, the angst of trying to find a single usable phrase for quotation from an unfavorable review. Perhaps he has never had to sift through reviews from a long career in music, however fulfilled or unfulfilled, to compose a flyer, brochure, or advertisement. And he certainly doesn't seem to understand how difficult it is for most artists to promote themselves when they do not have a manager. It is no fun for them to pay high prices for these ads, so why poke fun at the basso "grinning out from behind his large bowtie"? I could write a whole book on critics who do damage. (It makes me all the more thankful for my own fair treatment and enthusiastic review.)

How well I remember buying a small ad for that debut concert. That postage-stamp-sized ad cost a fortune, but it was delightful to see my own obscure name on a page with Radu Lupu and Rudolf Serkin. At the time I wrote in my journal that the patchwork page of concert ads seemed to me to be "a joyous tintinnabulation of all the concerts being played at once, proclaiming themselves and clamoring to be heard."

Yes, we are all clamoring to be heard, and we do not need someone who is lucky enough to be widely read using the space to wield gratuitous jibes for sport. I once interviewed Harold Schonberg on the subject of music criticism. When I suggested that I had never interviewed an artist whose ego was so large that he wasn't vulnerable to criticism, Schonberg replied that it is precisely because their egos are so large that they are vulnerable. He felt that a drama critic could "kill a show, but not a career. I can help a musician's career for a few years or hurt it for a couple of years, but not kill it. Artists make careers, not critics."[2] That is all very well, but there is a way of saying something that seems to escape some critics. A long time ago, I had a friend who was making his debut in a tenor role with a New York opera company. Before getting to the point and describing his beautiful voice, the critic felt impelled to allude to the tenor's "roly-poly" girth and "wedgie shoes." Anyone reading that was smitten with the cruelty, including my friend who subsequently left the company.

Radu Lupu once told me, "I have never questioned the right for a critic, any less anyone else, to express his opinion. It is just one opinion though, and what is the value of that? Ideally, there ought to be a conversation, a dialogue, even a symposium of opinions. The danger is that one opinion is read as the spoken word."

A final word on the subject of criticism. The recent Australian film *Shine* depicted the arduous career of pianist David Helfgott, including his complete breakdown and subsequent recovery. From the moment I heard about the "real" Helfgott's world tour I feared what the press might do to him; and, indeed, a regrettable feeding frenzy of reviews followed on his heels. With so many young artists performing unreviewed debut recitals, why would critics have to descend as sharks on an artist whose life deserves, rather, to be documented as a miraculous rebound?

We should listen to musicians like Helfgott in another way. What use is it to measure him against unafflicted performing artists? His playing is like the ingenuous stream of consciousness of his speech. I think I am an educated listener, yet I was curiously unoffended by the inaccuracy and eccentricity in his playing. I found it not only touching, but a thoroughly engaging phenomenon. The love he exuded, from the moment he bounded onto the stage to hugging folks in the front row afterward, was irresistible. It is how some of us wish we could feel if we weren't so bogged down emotionally by our so-called "normal" nervous tensions. That his playing is erratic and unconventional goes without saying; some things just ought not to be said. Would that we could have his grace when confronted with bad reviews: "It's all a game. They have to keep you playing your best. Play like a champion. Got to have guts." That's the wisdom borne of illness and pain, together with the gratitude borne of deprivation. There is certainly a place for kindness here. Moreover, every artist has something special to listen for. Helfgott's playing might not have delivered the profound messages we hope to hear at other concerts, but the struggle of his life is all there in the music. I was moved and awed by his survival and confidence to stand tall enough to perform again.

...

The green room—a strange name for a backstage chamber ranging from a closet-size cubicle to a lavish suite, from drab grey to clinical white, but almost never green—is a place where artists may have an ear cocked for response after the concert. It is a room that is transformed from an incubator of stress before the concert to paradise afterward. Recently I was reading a novel about a young pianist's career and became aware of a faintly recognizable, unpleasant little knot in the pit of my stomach. I was stunned to have to acknowledge my empathetic response to the mere fact that the fictional pianist was in the green room waiting to go on stage. (*He* was not nervous, but I was!) And, as extraordinary as this may sound, certain compositions, such as the *Egmont* Overture by Beethoven, cause me to feel jittery upon hearing them—even before I identify them by name—many years after I nervously abided their performance from the green room before going on stage to perform a concerto.

What people say to you in the green room or in any other place should not, ideally, take on as heavy an import as it does. I heard Hillary Clinton once quote some advice from her mother: You can either choose to be the main player in the arena of your own life, do the best you can for yourself and your loved ones and others, and be happy with that, or you can continually be concerned about other people's views of you. That advice, it seems to me, is as good after a single concert as it is on the grand scale of life. Some people might resent what you make of yourself, your accomplishments, and success, but then there are also the few good friends who are with you whether you are up or down.

But the truth is that the artist, usually in a state of excitement, relief, glee, misery, breathlessness, perspiration, semi-stupor, depression, decompression, elation, or any combination of the above, needs reassurance more than anything; after a performance is the most vulnerable time, particularly if it was not up to highest standards. You give everything to a performance, and it becomes your offspring. This is not the time for criticism unless the artist initiates the discussion. A great pianist once took my arm and ushered me off the receiving line and into his dressing room, closing the door behind us. I could not imagine why (and neither could my husband)! Once behind the door, he wailed, "It was awful." I had to set him straight and tell him not only how wonderful *I* thought the concert was, but also the raves I had overheard by other pianists in the hall. That experience proved to me how irrational and unrelated to reality our perceptions can be after we play. The best bet is to keep the green-room experience a social time, a time to come down to earth, to decompress.

You can tell a lot about the artist by the way he or she behaves in the green room. No matter how successful certain artists have become, they remain warm and gracious when greeting their audiences backstage. André Watts somehow can take the time to ask about the other person's news, focusing attention away from himself. Radu Lupu is modest, witty, casual, and easy to talk to. I can think of a long list of amiable postconcert exchanges I have had with many artists, but there are a few who snub their audiences and limit their after-concert contact to their own small coterie of friends. It can be mighty frustrating to wait for an hour or more while a performer stays cloistered behind a closed door in the dressing room with his or her entourage, without making even a cursory appearance.

Just as artists have their own green-room style, so do their guests. One could write a funny parody based on the postconcert exchanges between greeter and artist. One pianist I know always asks the performer, "Well! What did *you* think?" preferring not to commit herself. Another generally singles out one selection from the program saying, "I absolutely loved your Beethoven," leaving one to wonder whether the other pieces fell short. Someone else I know always comments, "That's a beautiful program. It's some of Schumann's best writing." (Yes, but how did I play it?) Some people are overwhelmingly generous and supportive, no matter what you've done, and others, totally grudging, cannot come up with a kind word, or any kinder word than "Nice." Some people simply do not know what to say, and others may be too shy, and scurry away with the misconception that the performer is too tired or distracted to make small talk. Small talk and noshing are the two great pay-offs after the concert.

A surpassing memory of Carnegie is the Russian Tea Room, where my parents made me a wonderful reception after the backstage post-recital party provided by some good friends. The Tea Room has since closed, but the fact remains that most of us are famished after performing. It doesn't have to be caviar and blini, but chances are that we haven't eaten for hours before the concert, and the main business at hand is to make up for that. I remember an amusing postconcert repast. Janós Starker was playing a cello concerto on Long Island and was coming back to our home for that important, well-earned late supper. We prepared him some delicate salads, got him his beloved imported Hungarian salami, a hunk of good cheese, and the Scotch he enjoys. In the green room after the concert, he casually let drop that the conductor and his entourage had included themselves in the invitation, and there was nothing any of us could do about it. To my alarm, the precious salami was suddenly and speedily shrinking in my mind's eye, and so I shared my panic with him, meekly explaining that I had planned for an intimate threesome and not a whole gang. "Do you have a good knife?" he asked. When we got to my kitchen, he rolled up his tux sleeves and proceeded to sliver the wurst so that you could read a newspaper through it! The slices magically and amply covered a big platter.

Many times I have provided the after-concert treats for myself and friends, because of my own great need for good food and good company after a performance.

15

Partner-Pianists

THE audience cheered and stamped as the great baritone returned to the stage, leading his reticent pianist by the hand, and not until both artists were equally center stage did he acknowledge the applause, jointly. The baritone was Dietrich Fischer-Dieskau, a name that has been linked to the highest level of lieder singing, and the pianist was Gerald Moore, although he could have been Jörg Demus, James Levine, or any other great lieder pianist. As Fischer-Dieskau and all great singers know, great performances of lieder presuppose a close partnership between the singer and the pianist. The word *accompanist* in such collaborations is neither adequate nor applicable. I once asked Fischer-Dieskau what the makings of a great lieder-pianist are.

> For me, the main qualities required for a partnership in lieder would be real musicianship and, of course, a very highly developed technical ability. Without trying to say anything against the professional accompanist, many of them, in former times, were pale technicians who tried to duck behind the soloist. The whole difference lies in the word "partnership" for which, perhaps, the best example would be Gerald Moore's artistry. The pianist should never be a mere shadow on stage.[1]

Gerald Moore's own wry and witty observations on the ups and downs of what most would consider an undervalued art are an important legacy, as are the recordings of his superb collaborative performances. The names of his several books reveal his droll style: *The Unashamed Accompanist* (London, 1943; revised 1947), *Am I Too Loud? Memoirs of an Accompanist* (London, 1962), and *Furthermoore* (London, 1983). He often expressed annoyance with the thankless, shallow task of accompanying operatic arias, as contrasted with the satisfying work of accompanying lieder. (I would make the same comparison between the joy of playing sonatas and the drudgery of accompanying virtuoso solo works for another instrumentalist.) As Moore suggested, in either lieder or sonatas, only the misguided pianist would assume a self-effacing persona and thus "commit professional suicide."

Indeed the piano part of art songs evokes the atmosphere and tells the stories, so that the pianist must understand the text explicitly. Some of the most demanding writing for our instrument appears in lieder: the poetry and meaning of the text at the core, and the musical symbolism and parallel expressive indications add to the challenge. But lieder also are among the most satisfying work. Schubert, and then Brahms, Schumann, Mahler, and Strauss epitomized the climactic meeting between words and music and made the pianist a true partner in expression, with more energetic force and drama than ever before.

Each partner also must understand the technical problems of the other. The pianist should have an idea about the difficulties of breathing and phrasing; the singer ought to know what determines the pianist's choice of an instrument, and be able to compromise issues of sound according to which instruments are available. "Territorial" prerogatives ought to be discussed gently (including, for example, the sometimes long introductions to lieder), and, of course, as each artist hopefully brings a concept to the work, an ability to converse congenially is essential.

The sweetest rewards come for the pianist who shares the stage with a partner of equal technical ability, artistry, and enthusiasm. It is not pleasant to have accepted an invitation and find oneself in concert with a wonderful technician who has no soul or with a perfectly sincere and expressive musician whose technical possibilities do not, alas, match his or her intentions. The best bet is to get to know a partner in informal sessions at home, get to know that artist's technical ability, style, and personality *before* one accepts a joint recital gig. For years I had been a closet lieder-pianist to my own inadequate voice, wanting more than anything to have a serious art-song collaboration; so, on several occasions I invited a soprano or a baritone to my home for an informal session which led to a couple of the most satisfying recitals I can remember. In the ideal situation, well-matched musicians will come closer to each other in all musical respects; then mutual respect and even real friendship can evolve from the musical partnership.

My late, great teacher, Leopold Mittman, had a flourishing solo career in Europe, having won distinguished competitions as a young artist. Then came the Holocaust, and he, along with many of Europe's cultured, intelligent, and persecuted artists and thinkers, came to this country, having to start from square one. The Atlantic Ocean is a great divide. Even these days, an artist can be well-known on one side and not the other. Mittman was "forced" into accompaniment to earn a living here, but soon he was among the collaborative pianists in greatest demand. Wherever I go, I am constantly looking out for his old recordings with Mischa Elman, Nathan Milstein, and many other renowned string players who invited him to concertize with them. Yet I always had the feeling that even though his collaborations led to friendships, he would have preferred to continue to give solo concerts and was never as thoroughly happy in duo engagements.

Some of my own happiest moments in music have been as an equal partner with another musician. Strangely, this would apply to almost any other instrument more than to a second piano. Although I enjoy informal sight reading with another pianist, I agree with someone's quip that a two-piano recital is one pianist too many. There are a few exceptions: I have performed Schubert's great Fantasy in F minor, Opus 103, Mozart's Sonata in D major for Two Pianos, K. 448, Rachmaninoff's fabulous Suite for Two Pianos, Opus 17, No. 2, *Souvenirs,* Opus 28, by Samuel Barber, and any number of other masterworks written for that genre, all with excellent partners. But when the concert is for two pianos (naturally not when it is for "piano four-hands"), there is the difficulty of matching the instruments and there is something else, not as easy to define: suffice it to say that when I played the Brahms Waltzes, Opus 39, in the two-pianist version, I yearned for those lilting, passionate, romantic, melancholy dances to be originating from *one* spontaneous heart (mine), instead of from a consensus of two. Possibly two pianistic personalities are more difficult to blend than are those of any other duo. I have heard exceptional two-piano concerts: Lupu and Perahia playing Mozart and Schubert stands out in my memory, but their collaboration resulted from a long, close friendship wherein they have always played for each other privately, sharing musical viewpoints.

When I interviewed Janós Starker about his prerequisites for a partner-pianist, he told me that when his usual partner is geographically inaccessible, he has to spend precious hours "unifying concepts and resolving myriad significant artistic details pertinent to an evening's worth of music. Such overnight affairs become less and less appealing and that is when permanent partnerships are formed."

We laughed about the fact that the audience often assigns the soloist priority because of all the promotional effects—posters and programs with bold print for the soloist, contrasting with fine print for the pianist—even though the collaboration is by musical equals; and we spoke about the artists who blithely park their seats or stands right smack in front of their pianists, entirely obliterating them from view by the audience. Then the pianist has to tread the fine line between expressing a desire to have some communication with the audience, without seeming to be an egomaniac. Recording microphones are usually placed in favor of the soloist, even in sonatas, and many an instrumentalist will bridle at the suggestion of an open-lidded piano even when it is explained that the sound may be muffled and muddy under a closed lid. (Cellists, who sit in the curve of the piano and are therefore right in line with the full sound from the instrument, will be most likely to mind an open piano.) But a fine pianist can produce as delicate a *pianissimo* with an open lid.

There are some misconceptions about pianists who choose to perform in ensemble rather than solo: the music is *not* any easier. Some of the thorniest passages for piano occur in Brahms chamber music of any permutation and combination. Yes, sharing the stage reduces tensions, and yes, the accepted use of the music in ensemble is another comfort. But the overridingly great pleasure is a sincere love of playing and sharing the varied and beautiful repertoire with an equal partner.

Starker spoke with great respect about the pianists with whom he has worked, and those who were legendary:

> What a joy it was when [Gerald] Moore sat at the piano and with a simple harmony and focus gave meanings to phrases until then neglected. What an uplifting experience it was when, in a repeated phrase, he brought variety of expression or threw the challenge of a rubato to the leading musical

> line, while maintaining disciplined boundaries. Real ensemble playing is not just playing together; it is living, breathing, and speaking notes and phrases with the same accents and beliefs.[2]

. . .

In a sense, it is a kind of marriage for those moments, and with the right partner, it can be made in heaven.

~ 16 ~

On Playing Chamber Music and Concertos

IF MUSIC is a universal language, chamber music is the most intimate and exclusive dialect. It is the music of a garden, not a jungle; it is civilized and democratic, not competitive and egocentric. It is the music in which great composers have created their most profound and spiritually uplifting messages, through which the interpreters may be similarly elevated; and although to most of the world, the genre may still seem obscure and highbrow, I am optimistic that appreciation for it is ever increasing among the general population. As Rubinstein once said, "The public isn't stupid."

Chamber music has been part of my life since I was a young girl. As I was always a good sight reader, adult string players in the community would ask my parents permission to come over, stick a trio or quartet in front of me, and presto, I was playing ensemble. I do not think I had a hoot of an idea about the depth of the music; I was proud to be keeping up with them, and I liked the blended sounds of the instruments. That is not chamber music as I now know it, but I think there are many adult amateurs who engage in a congenial activity fairly resembling those incomplete experiences, who are zealous, happy, stimulated, and rewarded by their hobby, and I say "Amen."

Lest that sound elitist, I will try to explain myself: it is simply that

I put chamber music on the highest plane of human experience. In the best of scenarios, when technique and artistry are evenly matched, chamber music becomes a social discourse within a kind of fellowship existing for the joint probing of great literature for its true meaning. A great part of the experience is the *unspoken* dialogue, a system of gesture that involves subtle movements of the body and eye contact between the members of the ensemble. The chamber player who is locked into his or her own page of music is totally missing the boat. To glance up from your page at another player whose musical phrase is exquisitely entwined with your own and to find that he, too, has glanced up simultaneously to acknowledge the moment is pure bliss. The intense listening, the ongoing consensus, the accommodations made, the musical balls volleyed back and forth, the deep, often audible inhalations between phrases, the laughter, the raised eyebrows, furrowed brows, nods, cues, flourishes, hunched, taut bodies, relaxed bodies, luxuriating in the music: indeed, there are sensual overtones—with all the heightened awareness, intense focus, minds and bodies attuned, communicating on the deepest level. Through the common love of the music, a real bonding takes place, at least for that session. This is music-making that brings one back to the enchantment it first had when we chose it for our own. When the profession makes us feel like quitting, cold turkey, and finding something, *anything* else to do instead, that's the moment to wrest ourselves from its centrifugal force and alight softly back to loving it, via a beautiful chamber piece.

Not all soloist-types who engage in chamber music know how to shelve their egos. I have heard ensembles composed of famous solo performers; the big names may attract audiences, but their ensembles don't always work well, because of an inability to subdue or subordinate a strong personality for the good of the whole. One might likely hear each part executed flawlessly but inappropriately virtuosic, and the integral concept is sacrificed for the gloss.

. . .

When I was in high school, an English teacher and her husband regularly threw chamber music parties; they were music-lovers sincerely intent on enriching the lives of the young musicians they knew. They had a vast library of chamber literature and invited random numbers of players to their home (often several pianists at one party, much to my chagrin) for these marathon sessions. We never knew beforehand what music would be brought out, or who would get to play in which ensemble. I remember my eagerness to be "the pianist," but I also remember learning to squelch my own ego and to enjoy listening to the others. It was in here that I first encountered the camaraderie and true spirit of sharing that is essential to chamber music.

Over the course of two months not long ago, I read through all the Beethoven trios with a violinist and cellist, both friends of mine. For works I had played before, it was paradise revisited, and we also had the wonder of discovering new ones. Even in the heat of the summer, our sessions never felt like work but rather sheer pleasure and play. One week we visited an old friend, Beethoven's "Archduke," the next week his "Kakadu," which I had never done before. There is nothing like a Beethoven trio to reaffirm the joy of being a pianist. The trick is finding partners as euphoric as you are about playing.

But as a pianist I am barred from playing the greatest music ever composed: the Beethoven string quartets. Nothing can top them; they are the most moving, beautiful works ever written. I may not play them, but I can listen—with the same reverence and dedication I would give over to them if I were playing. The essential and economic quality of Beethoven's impassioned utterances require serious study, and I am continuing to grasp and discover new meaning over time in this personal pilgrimage.

I had a powerful experience sitting in a stage seat at a Guarneri String Quartet concert at the Metropolitan Museum of Art's Grace

Rainey Rogers Auditorium. First of all, it was a strange experience to be on a stage *senza* anxiety, and be able to survey and contemplate an audience as individuals rather than a blurry sea of faces. I was touched to see how rapt this particularly attentive audience was—all ears and eyes focused on the quartet as they performed two Beethoven quartets (from Opuses 18 and 135 and the Grosse Fuge, Opus 133). I was particularly struck by a sense of privilege to be among eight hundred people who paid to be lifted out of the mundane and into the sublime. As a performer on stage, one does not generally have this luxury.

My second most poignant realization was the sheer enormity of the physical work involved in performance. This is, of course, something I have experienced firsthand many times. Rubinstein once said that if a pianist expressed the same physicality on a table that he expresses on a keyboard, it would be a shocking revelation. (But when one is deeply involved in performance, probably the *last* thing one ought to do is to take note of one's own kinetic output!) However, as I was sitting almost amidst these four artists, watching them play as a single organism under the blazing stage lights, the muscle, brainpower, and concentration were palpable. From my vantage point I experienced the huge expenditure of energy and, at the end, the utter exhaustion and the elation. It was almost voyeuristic to be so close, to witness the grimaces, the eye contacts, the heavy breathing, the whispered comments between movements, and all the little signals I know so well from the inner sanctum of a chamber piece. I alternately experienced the vicarious pleasure of being the performer and the relief that I was not.

. . .

The best motive for playing chamber music is the literature itself. As I write, I am thinking about an all-Brahms program that I prepared to commemorate the centenary of his death in 1897. Brahms wrote seventeen chamber ensembles, not including his sonatas, and each is a masterwork. The lucky pianist has five piano trios, three piano quartets, and one quintet to grapple with, but the rewards are unparalleled. Brahms was completely at ease when he wrote for piano and strings. These chamber works have both the difficulties and the charms of his two piano concertos; they also have the exquisite lyricism, the great sonorities and textures, the gentleness and the pathos, the lightness contrasting with dark moodiness. If the Beethoven piano trios make us rejoice as pianists, the Brahms chamberworks make us grateful to be musicians.

. . .

On several occasions I have been fortunate to experience the great joys of appearing as soloist with orchestra, which, at its best, can provide pleasures as deep as those of playing chamber music. In Brahms' Piano Concerto in D minor, the pianist's role is more symphonic than virtuosic; to be sure there are great technical demands and huge flourishes, but the piano part is so skillfully intertwined with the other instrumentation that the pleasure comes from being part of the beautiful whole. I will never forget the enormous thrill of sitting in front of the huge orchestra, hearing that first fortissimo thunderclap of the timpani's rolled bass D beginning the long, meandering tutti, feeling the force of that great music surging through me, letting it engage my whole being, so that my entrance after the protracted diminuendo seemed the most inevitable responsive action. Playing the D major Adagio movement, originally conceived by Brahms as a kind of Benedictus, was indeed, heavenly bliss: the sublime chorale episodes contrasting with the exquisite, almost recitative piano passages; and then finally letting loose in the last movement—restless, *buffa*, ecstatic. One had to struggle to keep one's euphoria in check.

I have also ravished in the delights of performing three Beethoven concertos (the First, Third, and Fourth), the Schumann A minor, the Mendelssohn No. 1 in G minor, and just two Mozarts: the A major,

K. 488, and the Double Concerto in E-flat major, K. 365. I have studied many more concertos than I will ever have the opportunity to perform; alas, it is a fact of life that orchestra series thrive upon the hiring of big-name soloists. But I am grateful to have had those chances because that is as close to flying as a pianist can get.

~ 17 ~

Some Privileged Coachings

WE ACCUMULATE a wealth of collateral from our early work with excellent teachers; then we strike out for independence and work for years developing our own voice and style from a composite of experiences. But from time to time a breath of fresh air from an altogether new source can reignite a spark and lead to surprising insights. Musician friends and I periodically exchange ideas, but the luxury of a coaching session with a distinguished pianist or pedagogue has been my rare privilege.

Among my fond and grateful memories is a session with Horacio Gutiérrez weeks before I was to perform the Schumann Piano Concerto in A minor. I had interviewed him for a cover story in *Clavier* and happened to mention my upcoming concert, whereupon Mr. Gutiérrez graciously asked, "Would you like to play it for me?"

"Would I!" He arranged for us to use the basement of Steinway and Sons on 57th Street, a veritable sea of black whales where many artists go to choose a piano before a performance. We threw off the tarpaulin from one of the vast armada of concert grands and got to work, leaving no tone unturned. My husband came along and wrote some poetry in a corner while technicians tinkered on other instruments. But for those few hours, in a generous spirit of true camaraderie, Gutiérrez gave me all his concentrated energy; I only wish I had taped the session, because over long years the splendid details do fade. I came away enriched by his intelligent and musical suggestions, and he came away with my best apple-nut torte, which was the only recompense I could get him to accept.

. . .

Jerry Lowenthal has offered his precious time and expertise to me several times. When his late wife, Ronit Amir, a wonderful pianist and teacher and radiant raconteuse, was still alive, I went to their upper west side apartment for a coaching and came away with a sense of their extraordinary musical life, some interesting new ideas, and a restored ego. Then, more recently, I asked him if he would listen to a program of Brahms, Beethoven, and Chopin, adding "but only on a *professional* basis."

"No," he answered, "only on a collegial basis." As chairman of the Piano Department at Juilliard, he had major teaching and administrative responsibilities and had stopped teaching privately. He told me he does not like to think of his personal time "in terms of dollars," but added that he still listened to friends. In addition to his schedule at the Juilliard School, he continues performing and recording, not to mention his frequent role as adjudicator for prestigious competitions. With all of this, Jerry asked me to come over on his day off. It was a great event for me. As a pianist I very much needed the dialogue, support, enthusiastic approval, and confirmation from an artist whom I highly respected.

Jerry shared his feelings about the pieces in question, which was a generous and touching gesture. One's conception of a musical work develops and evolves after years of hard work and creative thought. A conception is as personal as a fingerprint; one cannot and does not give it away. One can only choose to share it, as Jerry did, and I, in turn, had the pleasure of considering it as a precious gemstone in my hand, turning it over, examining it, grateful for whatever facets it might add to my conception. He knows exactly how to offer suggestions: he is open-minded and openhearted. I thought of how lucky his students are to have him, as I once again felt the joy of going for a lesson, hanging onto words, absorbing, registering, and assimilating ideas. On the way home in rush hour traffic, I recklessly held the wheel with my left hand and scribbled crooked, nearly indecipherable hieroglyphs of thoughts on the side of a shopping bag that was lying on the car seat. The euphoric rush came from letting in fresh air from another source. It is wonderful to work alone, to plumb and fathom one's depths, but there is the risk of staleness in recycled ideas.

. . .

Many years ago, on the afternoon before a concert on Long Island, André Watts yielded a precious piece of his warmup time in the hall to coach me on some Liszt pieces. I remember that I had difficulty focusing because a recurrent voice in my head kept saying, "Here you are with one of the world's greatest Liszt pianists coaching you on Liszt!" In fact, André is one of the pianists I most respect and love. Whether it be Liszt or Schubert, he wears his heart on his sleeve, and one is thus swept up into the heart of the music. He combines an uncanny visceral energy with an exquisite palette of coloristic effects. A technical command of the instrument allows him to do whatever in the world he wants to do, with supreme artistic control. He also has the fine taste not to exploit or indulge his assets. Yet he has remained one of the most unassuming and generous-hearted performing artists that I have ever known.

. . .

Following a project we did for *Clavier*, Claude Frank offered on several occasions to hear music I was preparing to perform. Frank and his wife, pianist Lilian Kallir, have an apartment on the upper west side where their incredibly gifted daughter, violinist Pamela Frank, grew up. A few floors above their apartment, Mr. Frank keeps a little *pied-à-terre* for his own practicing and teaching, and it is there that I was lucky to work on some pieces with him. He told me he loves doing the "abstract technical work necessary to keeping up the apparatus." He likened it to the "workmanlike" crafts of shoemaker or fisherman, adding that he enjoyed feeling like an "artisan." Although he finds learning new works the most fun, he spends the major portion of his time restudying old works. "The best-loved music is full of hidden beauties, and finding new things in familiar music can be most exciting."[1] Well, I had all my artisan-work accomplished before I entered his studio and welcomed his scholarly and intellectual insights, especially into the Beethoven sonata at hand—he is perhaps best known for his contributions in the literature of Beethoven, including his best-selling release of the thirty-two sonatas.

I remember asking Frank whether he thought that interpretation ought to be taught to younger students. With respect to teaching Shakespeare, it has been suggested that guiding an actor through a comprehensive analysis of one Shakespeare play might suffice for future guidelines and methodology. Can that principle be applied to teaching Beethoven? "This is where theory and practice part. A good teacher, in theory, does not superimpose ideas. We try to show the 'what' and help with the 'how'. . . . Some things are not personal, but rather musical points, such as phrasing."[2]

• • •

These privileged coachings offer two equally valuable gifts: the suggestions borne of these artists' vast experience on stage, and the reaffirming notion that in some crucial ways we are all reduced to common denominators, especially in the nerves department. Claude Frank, a very funny man, cracked me up when he quipped:

> The nailing down process makes the difference between knowing the music at home with no pressures and knowing it in concert under any adverse circumstance: with a fever, on an impossible piano, on a slanting stage, with flies on the

> keys, with insufficient orchestral rehearsal, with a nervous conductor, or, for that matter, a suddenly nervous pianist! There is no end to the possible pressures, and the need to spend time anticipating and coping with them increases, unfortunately, with age.[3]

How true.

. . .

Just as life is, or ought to be, an eclectic learning and growing experience, my life in music has been enriched with bits and pieces gathered everywhere, including live concerts. Seeing an artist like Jerry Lowenthal bound onto a stage and energetically lace into his opening notes before he is barely seated is a message not to forget the ebullient joy inherent in the performing mode; to hear André Watts plumb the instrument for colors beyond the imagined is to remember what a treasure trove the modern piano is; to encounter Radu Lupu's deep concentration and hear his transcendental recomposing of late Beethoven or Brahms regenerates one's own quests. Feeling the propulsive energy and wit of Alfred Brendel's Mozart and Schubert is invigorating. And remembering Rubinstein is an enduring lesson in the art of the piano.

18

Early Pianist Jobs

WHILE I was attending Queens College, I juggled classes, a new marriage, and the few jobs available to a young pianist. One job was accompanying ballet classes, during which I must have played every Chopin mazurka and waltz, every Schubert ländler, and all the incidental music to *Rosamunde*, *Swan Lake*, and *The Nutcracker*, not to mention anything else that I could improvise on that little upright piano. It was stop, start, stop, start again, for *pliés*, *rondes de jambe*, *arabesques*, and *petits battements*, and I found none of it musically satisfying. I remember having a Contemporary Civilization textbook on my lap and studying for exams while playing by rote. It was a job.

Many years later, I found myself doing an interview of a ballet pianist for the American Ballet Theatre. There I was in a ballet rehearsal hall on the basement level of the Metropolitan Opera House in New York; the room was further magnified by floor-to-ceiling mirrors on three walls. On the fourth wall was an enormous Dufy-like tapestry in bright orange, a brilliant backdrop for the emerald greens, pinks, and blacks of the leg-warmers and leotards of the members of the ABT corps de ballet, who were skittering across the floor or exercising at the *barre*. In their midst was Mikhail Barishnikov, then artistic director of ABT, and *danseur extraordinaire*, looking like a Cossack in cranberry leg-warmers and vest, bouncing his arches on the edge of a mat, then stretching into a split. Off in a corner, like a great black Russian bear, was the grand piano, and at the piano David Arden, who was then the official solo pianist for the American Ballet Theatre. *That* was a job!

Soon the room was cleared except for the two principal dancers for the evening's performance of Prokofiev's *Cinderella*. The conductor commanded of the pianist, "Give us four bars before the Waltz," and as though someone had dropped a nickel in a slot, the dark brooding bars of Prokofiev poured forth from the piano. Peering over the pianist's shoulder, I saw the formidable, three-staved manuscript of the piano transcription, and instantly appreciated the fact that this was no ordinary ballet-class accompaniment.

Indeed there are two types of ballet accompanists: those who "do classes" and those who don't. Those who do, have to be able to improvise and be quite creative, conjuring up a 3/4 or 4/4 tempo in an instant, using a *leggiero* touch or more oomph if the steps require it. Although there are special books for *tendus* and *grands battements*, the pianist must take spontaneous cues from the balletmistress and often make up something on the spot. Many take the material from the standard classical piano literature as I did or from the ballets themselves. And, in a sense, playing the rehearsal of the Prokofiev or the Shostakovich Piano Concerto No. 2, Opus 102, which was choreographed and performed that same season, is solo work, even though Arden was ultimately replaced by the orchestra (except in cases where the original scoring was for piano, as in the concerto).

If Arden's job and the garden variety accompaniment that I did had anything in common, it was the scant rewards and lack of feedback. "Take it again, David." (or "Take it again, Carol.") "We have to have a tempo change. We can't handle the turns at the same fast tempo." In other words, the technical problems and nuances of the dance are everything; the problems and frustrations of the pianist are nothing. Arden told me that a good class pianist is hard to find and highly valued, which made me feel a bit better about the drudgery of my experience.

. . .

Also in those early days, once a week in the evening, I accompanied the Queens College Choral Society under the direction of Professor John Castellini. I could never call that a job, although it was hard work. It was a privilege, a pleasure, and one of the richest facets of my college music education. Playing the piano scores of Handel's *Messiah*, of Bach's *St. Matthew* or *St. John Passion*, the Mozart, Brahms, and Verdi requiems, Schubert's Mass in G major, Mendelssohn's *Elijah*, Haydn's *Creation*—the list goes on and on—was not only pianistically challenging, but spiritually uplifting.

Professor Castellini had been a composition student of Respighi in Rome in 1928 and '29 and a student of Arnold Schoenberg in Berlin, and had the fiery Mediterranean temperament and high standards of a Toscanini; he brought me close to tears on several occasions, but I knew he had the highest expectations of me, as he did of everyone, and somehow my affection never waned, no matter how demanding he became. When Castellini was ninety years old several years ago, he sent me the manuscript to a piano piece he wrote and published in Rome that was ultimately orchestrated, called *Misty Dawn*. I hope to play it in concert some day. We were reminiscing, and he asked me, "Did I torture you?" He *has* certainly mellowed, but he has not lost his wonderful sense of humor. When he singled out a poor soprano and ordered, "You! Just mouth the words in that high passage," I almost giggled at the piano. Attempting to meld the chorus's consonants, he insisted upon comical syllabications such as "Ree-dee-meh-duh-stew-God" (Redeemed us to God). This is not to imply that the meanings of the words were ever lost on us. We had philosophical discussions about the text, and I, for one, filled gaping holes in my Bible education, elementary Latin, German, and the use of religious symbolism in music.

One season under the baton of Professor Sol Berkowitz, when Castellini was on sabbatical, we were even more adventurous with Stravinsky's *Symphony of Psalms*, for which Berkowitz, a wonderful composer and orchestrator, arranged an enormously challenging score for two pianos. I am still in touch with both professors and recently, after more than thirty years away, went back to my old stamping ground for a special celebration honoring Professor Castellini.

Places revisited often lose their sheen and the magnitude bestowed by memory. Indeed, the campus has been modernized beyond recognition. I learned that masterpieces revisited can also suffer. The sublime music of Handel would transcend almost any performance, and the messages and questions in the text—"Why do the nations so furiously rage together?"—are timeless. I sat waiting to be bombarded by greatness, as I was in those former years as a participant (when the orchestra replaced me, I sang in the alto section), but I felt a sense of loss. I regarded the backs of the now hoary heads of my three favorite professors, Castellini, Berkowitz, and Gabriel Fontrier, who were sitting several rows in front of me that night. Castellini could hardly resist the occasional involuntary conducting gesture. And I, who grew up with his conception of the work, his tempos, his passionate involvement, was left unmoved.

I am certain that those performers felt the same affection and pride in their concert. To be in it, to help recreate such a masterpiece, is unforgettable. The experience cannot be recaptured. It can only live in memory. Even if we were to do it again, it would be different because we are all changed. But even knowing that, we all whispered to each other wistfully, "It was different then."

. . .

For one mad moment in my innocent, more adventurous days, I thought I might get away from the piano and try being an announcer for a classical radio station. I went for a broadcasting interview which, in retrospect, had a kind of burlesque quality. Several days before the interview the auditioners were given ten sheets of possible radio announcements containing every conceivable tongue-twisting combination of human sounds ever before compiled; I was rendered nearly mute with the fear of not being able to utter a single intelligible syllable in my native tongue, not to mention everyone's else's native tongues. Prerecital tensions were child's play by comparison.

I enlisted exotic friends to help transliterate foreign names phonetically, and found a used tape recorder to listen to myself. A diction that I had always flattered myself had little or no trace of regional shades began to seem, in the replay, to reveal the very block I grew up on; and the frustrations of uttering three Russian names in series —"Galina Vishnevskaya, Nicolai Ghiaurov, and Gennady Rozhdestvensky" into a live mike began to take on dark implications, in spite of my lifelong involvement in music and two Russian grandparents. I called Josef Fidelman for a breakdown of the Russian syllables, but another form of breakdown threatened my equilibrium as he spoke: Vishnevskaya became "Vsh-nvsk-sk" and Rozhdestvensky transposed itself into "Rujz-gzez-vnsk," compressed blurbs consisting of a froth of consonants with no apparent vowels, practically unintelligible over the phone.

I entered the Spanish domain with the glottal-stopping conductor Artaulfo Argenta followed by Alicia de Larrocha, whose name continues to confound even some of her most devoted fans. A friend offered the authoritative "Aleethia delarrocha" and chided that Joaquin Turina is not pronounced like Joachim, friend of Brahms, but rather, "Hwakeen." Thanking heaven, at least, for my fluency in French, I almost, however, made the mistake of not practicing a phrase like

"*L'Après-midi d'un faune* by Claude Debussy performed by L'Orchestre de la Suisse Romande, Ernest Ansermet conducting." *Faune* is often mispronounced as "fawn" instead of "phone," not to mention how often Debussy is clawed and battered around.

A trip down the Rhine brought "Richard Wagner's *Ring of the Nibelungen, Götterdämmerung*, Fritz Wunderlich, Dietrich Fischer-Dieskau, Ursula Schroeder-Feinen, and Brigitte Fassbaender" all wrapped up by some diabolical sadist into one sentence. So I got an Austrian friend to help foil the conspiracy to trip me up.

These days I would have had an easier time with the Italian, but back then I had a false sense of security that years of *poco a poco diminuendos* would get me through "Tonight the Opera House will present *La gioconda* by Amilcare Ponchielli; Renata Scotto, Placido Domingo, Fiorenza Cossotto, and Renata Cappecchi will sing the leading roles and Francesco Molinari-Pradelli will conduct the orchestra of L'Accademia di Santa Cecilia" instead of demolishing me into a heap of cacophonous rubble.

Introducing gifted artists from Asia, for example, Kyung-Wha Chung or Kazuyoshi Akiyama on the air presented another brand of challenge, but the ultimate crisis came when such everyday phrases as "round trip to Fort Lauderdale with freedom fares to Florida" or "provides constant, intensive portfolio supervision" in commercial announcements began to addle my palate.

The night before the audition, horrendous fantasies invaded my sleep: "Aleethia Vsh-nv-sk will now play L'Après-midi de los Tres Picos, conducted by Yakamushi Bernstein." On the train the next day, commuters' heads swiveled to view the madwoman who was mumbling drivel to herself. Approaching the radio station, I experienced overwhelming nostalgia for the relative coziness of the stage; upon entering the building, I had a disconcerting hassle with a security guard who acted as if I were a Russian spy (just because I was muttering "Rozhdestvensky"?). Finally, seated in the radio station's anteroom, I listened to the piped-in, seasoned, middle-American, self-assured, voices of the announcers behind the glassed-in studios flashing ON THE AIR signs.

A cram course in radio followed: a congenial coaching session with an old-time announcer whose voice I had grown up with on that classical radio station and a fascinating recording stint in their studio, live mikes, and Rube Goldberg-type contraptions revolving and blinking all around me. The musical announcements went surprisingly well without any howlers (except for Lovro von Matacic which has "chich," not "chik" for its last syllable). But I was clearly not destined to have a brilliant career in broadcasting—not because of languages, musical background, or diction: apparently, I hadn't poured enough emotion into "investment stocks" or "artificial fluorescent plant lights" to convince the listener and placate the omnipotent sponsors who, after all, keep the recordings turning. Alas, the enthusiasm I projected when announcing Janós Starker's solo Bach suites was not matched in commercial breaks about bargain rates to Miami. I wonder why. But they do have me on tape, filed away probably under "Not For Use on the Air," unless they ever need someone on "Music Till Dawn."

~ 19 ~

The Art of Programming

TIMES have carried us a long way from the conventional program wherein the pianist begins with an appetizer, proceeds to the salad, then offers the main courses, and ends with dessert. There are a hundred creative ways to fashion a program, and a good part of the enjoyment of being a performing artist comes from conceiving of programs that will steer away from the banal and, rather, serve to elucidate and entertain.

A standard procedure used to be to present selections in chronological order. It still feels good to begin with Bach, Scarlatti, or Haydn, not necessarily for chronological reasons but rather for the strong rhythmic component and a sense of order that sets the recital off to a rousing start. Many performers are reticent to place a very modern work at the end of their recitals lest they lose a good part of their audience before that work. It's a sorry commentary, but I've seen it happen in New York City at orchestral concerts: an exodus to the parking lot by those whose listening range extends only to the early part of the twentieth century and Debussy; and here we are on the brink of the twenty-first century!

In a recent program at Carnegie Hall, Alfred Brendel entirely reversed the chronological order. His first half consisted of groups of pieces by Busoni and Liszt. On the second half, he played the great

Schumann Fantasy in C major, ending with a wonderful little Haydn sonata in G major. That Haydn struck me as the perfect thing after all that romanticism, almost like a sorbet to clean the palate. And as not too many pianists can communicate the wit and energy in Haydn as Brendel can, it was an upbeat ending.

Among the most original and provocative programs I have heard in recent years was one given by Andras Schiff at Carnegie Hall. He presented a fascinating juxtaposition of Bartók, Bach, Bartók, and Bach, progressing from early to later works of each composer. The concert became an ever-intensifying and visceral correspondence between the two composers, with Schiff in the middle as conjurer. So much did he bridge the gulf between the two composers that listeners marveled at Bach's daring chromaticisms and frequent atonalities, while Bartók's barbaric style began to sound less modern. Schiff went so far as to play Bach's Chromatic Fantasy and Fugue in D minor with barely time for a breath, as though it were the last movement of Bartók's Suite, Opus 14. The audience was shocked to realize it had been robbed of its opportunity to applaud, but the greater shock was the striking relationship between those pieces. Schiff made his point that Bartók revered Bach, and that there are many correlations between them. The third shock was that the audience was rapt and silent, a rarity especially considering that this was Bach and Bartók, and not Chopin and Schumann. The combination of great artistry and thoughtful programming is rare, and in this case the music was not only beautiful, but it challenged the audience to think and to concentrate.

Mitsuko Uchida is another artist who understands the art of programming. In two separate series of recitals in New York, she presented engrossing programs that made serious points while offering a bountiful musical experience. In one she provoked comparisons between Schubert and Schoenberg and more recently programmed Berg's Sonata, Opus 1, Schumann's *Davidsbündlertänze,* and Beethoven's final sonata, the C minor, Opus 111, in reverse chronological order. One came away marveling at the romanticism of Berg as Uchida's expressive reading hearkened back to Brahms; in contrast, the free-form disarray and constant mood shifts of the Schumann seemed more modern; and of the three masterworks, the Beethoven, of course, was the most forward-looking for its time, complex, and in Uchida's hands, an intensely personalized experience.

While I do not believe in spoonfeeding an audience, over years of presenting lecture-recitals, I have come to believe that there is great appreciation for whatever pertinent information is offered to complement the music. Sometimes I have chosen to write essays that appear as program notes, but I enjoy establishing a rapport with a group prior to seating myself at the keyboard; even if I only smiled and said "Hello!" that would be breaking down a kind of barrier. And as I have noted before, the research and planning of the commentary are as enormously rewarding as the practicing.

Considerations of key can be more important than many performers realize. An overdose of a single key or dissonances between the keys of consecutive pieces can be disturbing. Especially when there is a sequence of shorter works (a group of mazurkas or *Songs Without Words*, for example), attention to how one key leads into the next can establish a pleasant, almost inevitable continuum. I remember a period when the key of F-sharp was particularly beautiful and evocative to me (in fact, it still is). With a strange intensity, I seemed to crave the key as I did the color green one recent winter—an organic, nutritional requirement that led me to redecorate with predominant accents of green. In my fanatical F-sharp phase I caught myself planning a recital in which I had programmed not only Beethoven's great Sonata, Opus 78, in F-sharp major but also Chopin's Barcarolle, Opus 60, also in F-sharp, and a Romance in the same key, by Schumann. If you can believe this, the Prelude and Fugue in F-sharp minor from Book II of Bach's *Well-Tempered Clavier* was calling to me as well! That would have been *Overkill in F-sharp*, or some kind of an F-sharp Festival, and as much as I hated to part with any of it, I had to make several substitutions.

Yet understanding the power and suggestiveness of certain keys can be a major factor, even a determinant, in program-planning, if one agrees that keys have been used by many composers for their suggestive qualities. Beethoven's uses of C minor, for example, to connote tragedy, fate, moodiness, the bucolic and calming properties of F major, the majesty of C major, can be a veritable *raison d'être* for a program, although I have never tried that.

Planning a program around a certain theme makes it all a bit easier. On one occasion I did a concert based on fantasies, including Beethoven's Sonata, Opus 27, No. 1, "quasi una fantasia," the Fantasies, Opus 116, by Brahms, and Chopin's Fantaisie in F minor, Opus 49. I have already described my "Nature and Music" lecture-recitals—selecting compositions for the program was its most difficult aspect because of the enormous wealth of available material.

For years I played recitals of works by diverse composers, with a sense that the works were either related or contrasting in a significant way. But when I was invited to present an all-Schubert recital I realized that I most enjoy playing an entire program devoted to the music of a single composer. To be sure, I have heard all-one-composer marathons in which the listener's sitting apparatus turned to stone while the brain turned to mush—endurance tests to the saturation point. But as Alfred Brendel points out in his book, *Music Sounded Out*, one might liken a well-balanced concert from one great composer to a retrospective exhibition of a great painter.[1] Just as major museum retrospectives usually present us with more paintings than can be absorbed during a single visit, so the prospective recitalist might apply the same cautionary rule: to present only as much as can be digested. Those of us who are unlikely to present Schubert or Beethoven cycles and therefore can play only what can be delivered in one evening might limit the concert to early or late works, or arrange the program according to genre. I love to read as many biographies and essays as I can find, immerse myself in the life and times of the composer, and then select whatever information I can share without becoming tiresome.

When the Schubert invitation was offered, I went to bed with visions of *Moments musicaux* and *ländler* dancing in my head. The truth was that up to then I had been a closet Schubert pianist, yearning to play his music publicly, yet I had the notion that it was so fragile and intimate that it was better left on the vine, as a blossom that would wilt when picked (like *Heidenröslein*, the little heath rose in one of his lieder). That night I imagined that I might finally be ready to play Schubert the way I would like to hear it played. As any virtuoso display is alien to Schubert, a Schubert "performance" is, rather, an invitation for the listener to enter into the performer's private musical world. The pianist must approach the music with a pure heart, in a state of grace. As the names Impromptu or *Moment musical* suggest, there are qualities of spontaneity and songfulness for which we must try to imitate the human voice.

Schubert was among the most guileless composers. He offers a tune, for example, the theme of the second *Klavierstücke*, as though to ask, "Isn't that a nice tune? I give it to you." It comes to us from nowhere, out of thin air, weightless and transparent. Schubert once described a dream in which he felt "every time I tried to sing of sorrow, it turned to joy, and my joy turned to sorrow." The lied, *Lachen und Weinen* (Laughing and Weeping), epitomizes the bittersweet quality that is often expressed by sudden shifts between major and minor modes. There are many dualities in his music: modesty and ego, peasant and aristocrat, naiveté and sophistication, poignancy and charm. The moods are so ephemeral that they defy capture; one almost doesn't want to.

So I fashioned a program beginning with a group of waltzes and ländler, written by Schubert simply to give pleasure to his friends as they danced around him while he sat piano-bound at parties. Earthbound in body, his imagination soared, and he improvised more than 450 dances, ranging from the sublime to the bawdy, as listenable as they are danceable. Then I played two of the beautiful *Drei Klavierstücke,* which had been neglected among the many unpublished manuscripts found after his death and later edited by Brahms.

I would have loved to perform a sonata on this program, but I made the choice in favor of a group of lieder. Schubert's more than six hundred songs are among the most sublime musical expressions from any composer's pen. My fine soprano-partner and I chose a group ending with *The Shepherd and the Rock* with the addition of clarinet. Then I ended the program with a group of impromptus and *Moments musicaux*. It was one of the most deeply satisfying musical experiences of my life.

• • •

A year or so afterward, the same concert director invited me to do an all-Chopin recital. That also seemed to be a dream come true. I could play Chopin for days on end and never come up for air. It quickly became apparent that as the literature is an embarrassment of riches and I wanted to offer some commentary as well, I would have to eliminate many of my own and certainly some of my audience's favorites from the program. Again I embarked on a course of complete immersion and read everything from biographies as old as writer and critic James Huneker's (from 1900) to letters, current articles, and whatever I could get my hands on. Every day enlightening bits of information seemed to ignite and fuse with my work at the keyboard. One day a particularly remarkable fact emerged: I always knew that Carl Mikuli was an important Chopin student, but I never knew that he, in turn, was a teacher of the great Alexander Michailowski, with whom my wonderful teacher, Leopold Mittman, was a scholarship student at the Musical Institute in Warsaw, now known as the Fryderyk Chopin Music Academy. That missing link gave me a sense of lineage and extra purpose that further fired up my daily work.

I plowed through volumes of waltzes, nocturnes, etudes, scherzos, ballades, and sonatas, until a program emerged that I could love, that was widely representative of his beloved oeuvre without being unwieldy. As nobody reached so deeply into the soul of the piano nor stretched its possibilities as far as Chopin did, to perform Chopin for almost two straight hours is a veritable idyll. He changed the timbre and the nature of the piano forever, and we have to keep reminding ourselves how lucky we are to have the treasure of his legacy. I agree with Huneker, who said, "One can never play Chopin beautifully enough, but we can try."[2]

I had a wonderful time with that program. I started with three aristocratic, coquettish, animated, melancholic waltzes, because they generally present Chopin in his happiest moods. I could have played the whole book of nocturnes gladly but forced myself to choose among my favorites for the Nocturne in F-sharp major, Opus 15, No. 2, and I read Liszt's fanciful description of Chopin's genius with this poetic form. I played a group of etudes, each a Haiku poem, trying my best to combine technical skill with spiritual understanding (someone's pretty good definition of virtuosity); then, teetering dangerously close to my own dictum about keys, I played the great Barcarolle, Opus 60, in F-sharp major, because no program of Chopin would be complete for me without it. I think it is his finest work, the closest to being a tone poem, a kind of paean to the splendors of Venice.

On the second half of the program I played a group of pieces by those I thought of as friends of Chopin—"My Joys," the Chopin song arranged by Franz Liszt, a gem of a piece that exemplifies both the genius of these composers and the essence of their differences; and "Chiarina" and "Chopin" from the Schumann *Carnaval*. Five mazurkas followed, including the one he wrote for Mendelssohn's wife,

Cécille, Opus 59, No. 2, possibly his greatest. The mazurkas give the most intimate glimpse into his psyche, with innovative harmonies; some mazurkas are danceable, others are referred to as "dances for the soul," with that certain Polish susceptibility called *zäl*—a strange blend of sadness, nostalgia, and pain. I played the Impromptu (*in F-sharp*, but it was on the second half of the program) because I find it irresistible. Rules are sometimes made to be broken. It has the true spirit of impromptu: improvisatory, wandering, fanciful, restless, with some exquisitely wrought passages that are among the most satisfying and beautiful writing for a pianist's hand in the whole literature. I ended with the great Polonaise, Opus 53, in A-flat major, reminiscent of Schumann's statement, "Chopin's works are guns buried in flowers."

. . .

For the all-Brahms centenary concert that I mentioned earlier, I had the pleasure not only of presenting the works against the rich backdrop of time and change, but I also had the rare pleasure of playing with my son, cellist Dennis Parker.

Ever since I played Brahms' First Piano Concerto when I was nineteen, I have had a love affair with that composer. I grew up on Rubinstein recordings of Brahms, and I still have his sound in my ear, although I have been affected by Radu Lupu's Brahms in more recent years. Finally I can be happy with my own Brahms, but selecting a group of *Klavierstücke* for a major part of the program was a wrenching experience: as my little daughter once lamented many years ago while contemplating a bed full of stuffed animals, "I can't decide which to love." I forced myself into a group of seven, drawn from Opus 116 through Opus 119; following that, the Sonata, Opus 120, No. 2, in E-flat major (transcribed by my son for cello from the viola), and then the Trio for Piano, Cello, and Clarinet, Opus 114, in A minor. (The program also included Schumann's Adagio and Allegro, Opus 70, for cello and piano.)

Brahms wrote seven duo sonatas: three for violin and piano, two for cello and piano, and two for clarinet or viola with piano. I think that the Second Sonata, in E-flat, from Opus 120, the last chamber work he wrote, is the most poignantly beautiful. His indication Andante amabile exactly describes the music: it is amiable and ingratiating from the very first phrase, and with the last predominantly slow movement, Brahms bade farewell to chamber music. The Trio was among the first compositions Brahms wrote after deciding to terminate his creative work. Eusebius Mandyczewski, a close friend of Brahms (and a music historian and museum librarian), wrote about this trio in a letter to the composer, "It is as though the instruments are in love with each other." A good friend, Gene Keyes, was the excellent clarinetist. I felt quite lucky to be playing those masterworks with two such superb musicians.

. . .

As I write, I am at work on an all-Mozart program, feeling both thrilled and privileged. If I could project future concerts-with-commentary devoted to the works of a single composer, my choices would be Bach, Beethoven, Ravel, and Schumann. Schumann might be the hardest to program, because as Andras Schiff once said to me: I have the feeling I would like to study and play every note he ever wrote.

. . .

A postscript regarding encores: they can ruin the whole thing. If a musician has carefully crafted a program that has successfully made its mark and has set the audience to thinking, a frivolous little piece can throw it all off. If the program ends with a strong or profound statement, why would anyone want to sit down and play again? In the old-fashioned menu-type programs that are composed of one from column A, then one from column B, all is well if appetizing delicacies continue to come forth. Sometimes it is possible to please a frenzied audience, pleading for more, with a short work that is within the same mood, time frame, and genre, and still end up ahead. But so many performing artists hurry over to the piano just as the applause is slackening lest they miss out on the opportunity of doing an encore, as though it would be the measure of anything significant.

I must add that I have heard renowned pianists offer their most relaxed and affecting works as encores, after a long, unaffecting concert. On the other hand, I have experienced an overly generous bestowal of gifts by performers who seem unable to stop themselves, when even their most devoted fans are quite ready to go home.

There's no rule of thumb. The determining factors ought to be the nature of the program, the stamina of the artist, the receptiveness of the listeners, and the hour of the night, but inevitably it will be the impulse of the moment that will propel the pianist to the bench yet again.

~ 20 ~

The Essential Ego

THE importance of ego for a successful performing career should not be underestimated: the belief that you have something worth sharing that justifies not only a lifetime of sacrifice and hard work on your part, but the price of the tickets your audiences pay to hear you, to put it bluntly. Any student who has ever asked me what I think about "should he or shouldn't he" has, in fact, given himself the answer. The belief and conviction leading to commitment to a career ought to be made independent of anyone else's opinion, and made *early*.

The irony is that the awful specter of self-doubt haunts even the most well-grounded ego, and this doubt, too, must be resolved within oneself. Granted, to have a supportive teacher, good friends, and expert ears, all reconfirming one's own convictions, is wonderful, but the strengths have to be interior. One can find nourishment in a million places: as Robert Louis Stevenson wrote so charmingly, "The world is so full of a number of things, I'm sure we should all be as happy as kings."

Ego is often confused with conceit. Ego is a pleasant trait. We are all attracted by people who have a certain confidence and ease with themselves, and there is nothing wrong with the benign vanity that comes from good hard work and the pleasure of achievement.

The same is true for assertiveness. Assertiveness, to me, means the energy and action it takes to support one's ego. It is not aggressiveness, which is experienced as an unpleasant character trait. To assert means to state or declare positively, and as Hillel once asked, "If we are not for ourselves, who will be? And if not now, when?" It is the energy to call the press or design a flyer on your own behalf if you want to be assured of an audience, and to insist that you require a fine instrument if you feel you deserve it. It is the courage to charge a fee that you feel is fair, regardless of who is doing what for nothing. It is the energy to resubmit and resubmit a book manuscript until you get a publisher, and it is certainly the energy to resubmit to one audition or competition after another, as so many young artists do, until a door opens. The music business is a tough game; someone once called it a "blood sport."

There is no dearth of real talent in this world. A census of all the first-rate pianists running around whose names we have never heard of would shock us. These artists eke out their livings making supreme sacrifices to be heard. Many play for embarrassing "honoraria" that come to a dime per hour of preparation, and yet the value in being heard is too precious to pass up. The artists twinkle and flicker like the myriad lights dotting a big city's skyline at night. Occasionally by good fortune, good politics, good timing, or maybe miraculously by sheer merit, a glimmer becomes a flash, and if there is real substance and talent, a career will survive and develop momentum. But this will never happen without ego.

It is amazing how one's belief in oneself begets respect; unfortunately, it may also beget more than a raised eyebrow from a grudging colleague who may not understand the value of ego, who may mistake it for egotism, and who may not have learned to act on his or her own behalf.

The *sound* of ego is something I talk a lot about with students who may not have experienced enough to have developed sufficiently in real ego. But one can learn to sound convincing and, in doing so, convince a listener and then eventually oneself. By loosening up and broadening out in gesture, by getting down deep into the key bed, we can make things happen in a free and powerful way.

It is real ego that allows the pianist to trust her instincts and to play spontaneously with a sense of adventure. This is not to suggest capricious indulgences, eccentricities, or distortions, but rather the expression of freedom with integrity—within the boundaries of validity. Ego is the enabler for taking risks and allowing the music to mingle with your own life experiences in order to come out speaking in a way that is fresh and astonishing even to oneself. It is the basis for the irresistible spirit behind Rubinstein's playing that made old favorites sound fresh under his hands. Alfred Brendel defined "piano-playing of genius" as:

> Playing which is at once correct and bold. Its correctness tells us: that is how it has to be. Its boldness presents us with a surprising and overwhelming realization: what we had thought impossible becomes true. Correctness can be attained by the expert. But boldness presupposes the gift of projection, which draws the audience into the orbit of one's personality.[1]

. . .

The most difficult moment in which to revel in ego is backstage before going "on." I try to force myself to recall how many times I have played the piece well, and even utter the words, "I can do it! I have done it! I will do it!" Then, no matter how I dread walking that last mile, I try to effect a look of happiness. I read a scientific study claiming that folks who smile and laugh more convince their brain that they are, indeed, happy, and then the brain releases chemicals supporting that mood. A direct line links facial muscles to brain, reason enough, I think, to try to look happier than one might feel. Radu

Lupu once lamented, "Why do they want me to smile? I don't feel like smiling." He does, indeed, have one of the more serious visages on stage (and one of the best senses of humor offstage), and certainly no one ought to have a problem with that. I am saying what works for me. If I can project confidence and lightness and joy, I can often remind myself of my own *real* joy in playing the piano, and approach the instrument with a more sincerely positive frame of mind.

A good part of the ego of a pianist is the realization of what we have trained our hands to do. Rubinstein once pooh-poohed it when I asked him to show me his hands. "It's all up here," he insisted, pointing to his head. Well, I think it's in the head, heart, and hands, and I have sometimes studied my hands which are far from the delicate, feminine ideal, but good strong hands that, thank God, have rarely caused me any grief with tendonitis or arthritis. They are certainly in better shape than any other part of me, and I am grateful for their flexibility and strength, whether it be for gardening, carpentry, or the piano. (My harmless predilection for rings—obviously when I am not at the piano—may relate to the notion of embellishing a hand that is hard-working and productive!)

As live concerts are both auditory and visual experiences, a more superficial pleasure is the projection of one's personality through self-adornment, for example, in the choice of a gown. I have been to concerts where the pianist wore a glittery gown that spawned lightning bolts and sparks with every tiny movement, transforming her into a mini–fireworks display. This unfortunate decision drew the audience's entire focus to the visual and away from the music, as the gown says "Look at me, look at me!" and not "Listen to me." Other artists might err on the side of apathy or reverse chic; a certain famous male cellist recently wore several casual overblouses in a row, color-coded to each piece in his program at Carnegie Hall, and sure enough, the reviewer made a point of mentioning the affectation. Comfort ought certainly to be a prime factor, but I think there is something to be said for trying to create a charismatic image, as though the concert were an important event for the performer as well as the audience.

I enjoy these last-minute considerations because they are so mundane when compared to the serious business of playing—finding something to wear that will be comfortable, pretty, and flattering, and even having my hair done by Deborah, my charming young hairdresser, whose capable hands are as skilled for her craft as mine are for music and who touches me by getting into the spirit of it all, taking special care that I look my best. Looking and feeling good doesn't hurt a bit.

Then you're out there and it's you and the piano. I "caught" a habit from André Watts, who comes out and strokes the instrument as though to say "It's you and me, baby!" That seems to help, too. But finally all else falls away, and you are left with your convictions about the music, your concentration, your technique and musicianship, all backed by the ego that allows you to play as though you are saying, "Here, I give you this music. Isn't it beautiful?"

~ IN THE STUDIO ~

My business was song, song, song,
I chirped, cheeped, trilled and twittered.

ROBERT BROWNING

~ 21 ~

Why Teach?

IF I won the lottery, I would still want to teach, and that, I think, is the bottom line. Would I want to continue to teach all my students? Probably yes, although it looks like my deep-seated desire to be a "lady of leisure" will never be realized in this lifetime. I am teaching as much now as I could ever do without relinquishing all the rest: two packed days per week. The trick is in keeping the balance so that I continue to give my best to it without feelings of overwork that could lead to resentment. As Secretary of State Madeleine Albright quipped, "Work hard and have a good time."

Once, in an interview, I was asked a version of the question: Would I choose to teach if I didn't have to for economic reasons? When I answered in the enthusiastic affirmative, the interviewer seemed surprised. She said that she had interviewed many people in the arts who were reticent to "give it all away." "It," I suppose, is their craft or know-how, and I think she implied they jealously guarded their expertise from perceived competition. I find this attitude incomprehensible, as I have the impulse *to teach everything I know even as I am learning*, at every lesson I give.

Throughout the thirty plus years I have taught piano, I have continually remarked to myself how much I learn at every lesson. Had I kept a journal all along, or reread my students' notebooks, I'd have twenty books by now. The frustration of writing this section on teaching lies in the ever-changing dynamic of the profession. The moment I think an essay is complete along comes a student who will play something in such a way as to trigger new ideas, discussions, and results, and I will want to add them to these records of discovery. My students have gotten used to my scribbling at lessons, and have been amused at finding themselves in print in an essay or a column, even if they exemplified tricky problems; they knew it was in the interests of problem-solving, and that the context was affectionate. I also write copiously in their notebooks, in the hopes that they will process the ideas that emerged at each lesson. Some of my best suggestions and intuitions have been laid out in those bedraggled little spiral books; I could never be accused of having a pat methodology; each student receives a custom-tailored education based on individual goals, potential, and style. At times when I have wondered if a particular student is reading my words of wisdom, I have been known to sneak a little box in amidst the instructions, with the question, "Are you reading this? Check box if yes." Many an unwitting student has been caught with an empty box the next week, and a few wise-guys have written in "No!"

Each lesson is an event and ought to be approached in a positive and enthusiastic frame of mind to the best of our abilities. Goodness knows I have at times received a disturbing and even tragic piece of news a moment before the arrival of a student, and have had to postpone my own emotional response until the end of a long afternoon. If I were about to go on stage, the show would have to go on, no matter what, and I feel a similar commitment to carry on when lessons are scheduled. Sometimes the student may walk in with excess baggage as well. An angry teenager may come in with a chip on his shoulder, slamming the door, and I may walk him back around to the entrance, asking if he could possibly leave the anger outside the door. I believe that we bring all the elements of our lives to our music-making, whether we are students or concert artists; my point is to try to clear the decks before working.

Talking it out often helps, provided the session doesn't reduce itself to psychiatry; all my students are aware that I would rather be told it was a difficult week and expect to have to work extra hard, than to be deluded and disappointed. A good teacher knows the possibilities of her students better than they do themselves, and therefore even if they don't allude to the extramusical problems in their lives, the situation quickly becomes evident. Then I might stop a student and say, "Multiple choice: A. I really had a productive week and practiced hard every day, B. This wasn't an extraordinary week, but I did a fair amount of work, or C. I hardly went to the piano at all because I was too swamped with everything else." Invariably this unleashes a barrage of confessions, and finally we are free to proceed unfettered by sham and pretense.

The challenges come one per minute. I love it when a student says, "I can't" and I prove within a couple of minutes that he *can*, indeed. Vladimir Ashkenazy spoke to me about "finding the possibility"—that you can almost will your hand and find the approach (even with a small hand) to accomplish whatever you need to do. Certainly watching one human hand do it authenticates that it is doable; therefore, I demonstrate liberally at the keyboard. Trying to describe the process of shaping a phrase to a student by saying "fall," or "drop your hand, rotate the wrist, and then lift" is so entirely insufficient and inferior to *doing* it, then having the student try to do it, and perhaps even helping to shape the student's hand until the movement is understood.

I also find myself using a vast array of verbs to describe appropriate movements, including thrust, hover, sidle, grab, overlap, and cling. I am always telling my students to "ping" certain accented notes in an upper voice. The other day, after I told an adult student to "bong those lower basses," he quipped mischievously, "Oh, I get it. You want me to ping the treble and bong the basses!" It sounded like a couple of ancient Chinese dynasties, but he knew exactly what I meant, and he did it, too.

I am always careful about choosing *le mot juste* (even if I have to invent a word) because it can communicate a world of difference. For example, I loathe and avoid the use of the word *Loud* as a translation of *forte*. Almost any other word would be better: strong, deep, full, large, or rich, to name a few. *Loud* conveys the very caustic, percussive, and brassy quality we try to avoid in the quality of our *fortes*. I will never forget the time I was in a shoe store in Italy, trying to ask the saleswoman for a wider shoe. "*Ah! piu larga!,*" she exclaimed. At that moment, and unbelievably for the first time in my life, I realized the true meaning of *Largo*. Not any of my excellent teachers had ever implied anything more than *Slow* as an explanation. But how inadequate! *Wide* and *broad* and *expansive* are philosophically so much more than just slow.

. . .

Although I have been told I am an "original," in certain musical ways I can trace my teaching style to my teachers'; from Josef Fidelman comes my insistence on fingering and from Leopold Mittman comes my predilection for demonstration. I can still fairly "taste" his inimitably beautiful sound.

I know one thing for certain: I seem to do my best playing when I demonstrate for my students. I want them to love the piece at the moment I am giving it to them. Once they see the sound is in there, they know it's in there for them to get out as well. Something about the sensation of holding them in the palms of my hands and wishing to make the most striking impression brings out the best in me. It probably hearkens back to how I hung on every tone Mittman ever played for me. I learned partly by osmosis and by watching his hands move over the keys. I am still awestruck when a student's sound and approach evolve as we sit at two pianos and dissect a piece, phrase by phrase. After my proffered example, the student tries the same passage, and it is exciting to hear the music emerge entirely from the student's own hands and self. Oftentimes when I introduce a masterwork to a student, a strange phenomenon occurs: playing it gives me an irresistible urge to restudy the work, myself. The act of enlightening, whetting appetites, and watching eyes light up with revelatory insights renders me strangely possessive of the composition. I ask myself why I haven't touched it for so many years, and it is like revisiting an old friend.

I hasten to add that because there is never one single way to play a passage, I certainly do not want to produce clones. There is plenty of room for the tug-of-war between the inalienable "wisdom" of the teacher and the budding ego of the young artist. If I demonstrate, I offer several options and open up a dialogue that allows for a free exchange of ideas. I try to teach my students to make their own musical decisions; we discuss questions such as why we would not play the same phrase twice exactly the same way: that just by virtue of its having already existed, that phrase has changed, philosophically.

I ask them to try to define how they feel about the music in question. If they feel sad, or reverent, or dreamy, I try to remind them to keep their own responses in their consciousness. How easy it is for any of us to sit down and play mechanically, without reverence, for example, to accomplish feats of technique and lose the essence of its meaning. They may well be playing excellently and flawlessly, but not necessarily meaningfully and beautifully. So I might suggest writing in a word of reminder: "distant," "tranquil," or "jubilant."

I am a firm believer in the power of visual aids, and I make frequent references to the visual arts. Aside from the obvious comparisons between the music and a painting from the same period, it is valuable for matters of *process*. For example, when I ask a student to count a piece like "The Little Shepherd" from Debussy's *Children's Corner Suite*, with every rest and beat accounted for, she might question why an impressionistic piece must be so exact. I explain that before she can take the expressive liberties she might like, she must understand the work literally; a good analogy might be that painters must know how to render their subjects realistically before they can effectively alter or distort reality according to their style, or before they have earned the right to distort! (Witness early Picasso as compared to late Picasso.) At a recent lesson, a student expressed difficulty grasping the juxtaposition of the classical form of the sonatina with the dissonances of Ravel in his *Sonatine*. I tried to explain about neoclassical style, and homage to another age, expressed in twentieth-century language. When I pulled out an art book and showed the student the seventeenth-century painting by Velasquez, *The Maids of Honor,* alongside Picasso's reinterpretation and studies of that painting in which the same composition and forms were passed through the semiabstract lens of his imagination, the student got the point more clearly.

Another useful connection between painting and playing that serves me well when I teach addresses the difference between craft or skill and Art. When a student plays proficiently but has failed to move me because nothing of her own emotion has gone into it, I call it "typing." Although I might praise her technical accuracy, she knows that my use of that *T* word is no compliment. I might liken it to someone who has the ability to capture an excellent likeness of something or someone on paper or canvas, who is highly skilled and even talented, but is that Art? Although it may sound presumptuous for me to offer my own definition, I merely suggest that true art must pass through the prism of the pianist's or painter's own imagination, and contain interpretive elements.

Then, obviously, the task at hand is to teach the craft: the many components of technique that would allow my students to play a passage joyfully or majestically, using all the tools at our disposal. I happen to have a rather hands-on approach that has sometimes amused or disconcerted a student who is getting to know me. (I must also keep reminding myself of cultural mores, and the fact that certain ethnic groups do not come into physical contact with others as readily or casually.) I have been known to pick up a student's hand and place it where or how it ought to be, and to shape or manipulate it. I "play" on their arms when I think they might benefit from feeling the actual depth of touch required for a beautiful tone; I vividly recall a moment, many years ago, when Mittman took my arm and depressed his fingers into it, suggesting that I, henceforth, think of the keyboard as human flesh, and "knead" and sustain my touch. I don't think I ever played the same from that moment on.

My strongest argument for a teacher also to be a pianist—so many piano teachers I know can hardly play—is to be a trailblazer. "How did you know that?" my student once marveled when I offered a little trick, a special fingering, that immediately enabled him to play a difficult passage that had hitherto confounded him. "I experienced it with my own hands. I found the way for myself, so now I can offer it to you!" I answered.

"It is as though you are my guide," he responded. Treading the same paths as others before us and as our students after us connects the generations and defines teaching as a mission.

I have begun to talk seriously with my students about breathing correctly. No one ever mentioned the word *breathing* to me, except figuratively, as in between phrases; I'm talking about breathing, literally. Of course wind players and voice students are taught about breathing, and you can even hear string players' deep intakes of air before they draw a broad bow across the strings, but when I was growing up in music, attention to breathing was not a concept that pianists talked about. It makes all the sense in the world for us pianists to breathe too: appropriately, restoratively, supportively to the music (as they say, the alternative isn't too terrific!). János Starker jolted me into consciousness about the importance of breathing after

I had played some Bach for him in my home, and the guidance has enhanced my playing enormously.

. . .

Finally comes the largest lesson of all, and one for which not every student is ready: to learn how to *live* in the music, to translate the dots into human thoughts and feelings.

. . .

Not every great musician will make a great teacher; Sir Clifford Curzon was quoted as saying "If I ever fell on hard times, I would rather trim a hedge than teach lines and spaces."[1] Better that he knew it and did not inflict himself upon some poor student. I have attended a few so-called master classes presented by visiting artists who are in the area to perform a solo concerto with an orchestra and are lassoed into doing an extra gig with a group of gifted young pianists. In more than one case it became painfully clear that as talented as they might be as pianists, they have no business working with the fragile psyches of young musicians.

We all remember teachers who have made an important contribution to our lives. My husband recalled one particular teacher from elementary school who "instilled confidence," made him feel that he was "intelligent and creative," told him he was "making important contributions," and just made him feel generally good about himself. I remember how I was armed by praise from Mr. Mittman for hours and even days afterward. Certain compliments still ring in my ears: "Your little fingers are as strong and fast as bullets" may be the foundation for my gratitude for my fingers as a mature pianist. Giving praise is so important. When a student plays a piece particularly musically, I might ask him to play it for me again, simply for my own pleasure. I take my chair across the room to simulate the feeling of a real audience and he plays it even more beautifully. Then he asks me if there are any more pieces "like that one" that he could study. We both feel rewarded.

I would rather see my students take a class with a great teacher of wallpaper-hanging than a poor teacher of piano. A fine teacher will transcend the subject and enrich the student no matter what the basic material. Similarly, we ought not to limit ourselves to the subject of piano *per se*, but bring in anything and everything that may be relevant in this world, for example, an anthology of letters in which a composer has written information relevant to that composition. The room in which I teach is complex, interesting, and filled with resources: paintings, pottery, and great books. It has an aesthetic atmosphere that I personally respond to, and is therefore an extension of myself.

I would venture that we owe it to our students to set an example of living creatively; to be an individual, an unforgettable character in the best sense of the word; to give them something special to come away with and keep forever, something musical, and to the best of our abilities, beyond music.

~ 22 ~

Playing Classes, Recitals, and Auditions

FOR years I have held periodic group playing classes for my students which fill me with excitement about teaching in general and affection for each student in particular. The sessions follow a now-familiar pattern: at the outset we talk about expectations (trying to fulfill one's potential and convey the meaning and essence of the work) and attitude (trying to remember to love the music and to concentrate, rather than thinking negative thoughts such as "what if this or that happens"). I stress the informal nature of the class, and the fact that I may ask students to begin again if they are not playing up to par. They might even choose to do so themselves.

We are seated in a large circle, and before the playing starts, we enumerate, on paper, the elements of music and performance, with each student, in turn, suggesting an item: accuracy, tone, phrasing, rhythm, tempo, dynamics, interpretation, touch, articulation, pedaling, poise, and so on. This list is meant as a listening guide because the classes are as much a course in listening critically and intelligently as they are in playing. I remind them that there is something to love in each person's offering, and to listen for the positive things as well as whatever might need improvement.

I owe this unforgettable point to Krystian Zimerman, who in our interview was comparing various recorded interpretations of a

Chopin piece: although each rendition was quite different from his own conception of it, he "could find something to love in each."[1] He even added that he used to be more critical of concerts that left him unsatisfied, but now he hears the positive elements rather than the negative. I explore that notion with my students and encourage them to find the charm, the intention, the uniqueness, the loveliness in each other's efforts, and then we can go on to offer some constructive advice as well. I watch with pleasure as they jot down their impressions with serious intent. It is delightful to hear them praise and encourage each other and gently offer their well-considered advice. Most often they are right on the mark and I hardly have to utter a suggestion, but if I think a student deserves more praise or more help, I offer my own observations.

Usually the group is quite eclectic: adults who have made the piano their avocation, teenagers, one or two younger ones participating for the first time, and several students trying out works before competing in a young person's competition, audition, or master class. I never urge any student to play who doesn't truly want to, but I insist that they attend. Often someone who comes determined not to participate actively cannot, in the end, resist the impulse to get up and share her own efforts, much to her own surprise (but not mine). An infectious spirit of sharing envelops the room, and seeing that no one perishes or succumbs under pressure and indeed that all look like they are enjoying themselves is the best inducement to have a go at it, too.

Instead of fearing and rejecting our humanness which may manifest itself in memory slips or inaccuracies, and instead of expecting ourselves to be as infallible as computers, I remind my students that we ought only to strive to do the best we can. I remember one workshop when an exceptionally gifted young girl held all the rest of us in the palm of her hand with a performance of Chopin's Nocturne in C-sharp minor, Opus posthumous. She played so beautifully that my hair stood on end, and although she had a momentary memory slip, it did not break the spell. Even she knew she had expressed something special. What pleased me the most was that she did not feel the slip had invalidated her performance or negated its beauty. I am not condoning inaccuracy; naturally the idea is to play well without slips. For this we need to develop the ability to concentrate, a special skill that is difficult to teach and enviable in those who possess it.

If all audiences sat as respectfully as this class does, no artist would ever complain. When a student plays beautifully, eyes dart around the room exchanging silent glances of appreciation. If a student struggles and founders, an empathetic expression of quiet despair appears on the others' faces; they discreetly look down into their laps, rooting for a speedy recovery. The more verbal participants cannot wait to share their responses, and I sometimes have to quiz the more reticent ones for theirs. If someone plays a piece that another has studied, a wink of acknowledgment passes between the listener and me as though to say, "We have traveled that path, too."

Isn't that what it is all about? The time-honored masterpieces and even small gems like the *Solfeggietto* are little journeys we make with our students, first taking them by the hand, then little by little attempting to establish enough experience, taste, and know-how for them to venture forth independently.

After some refreshments my students leave, and I gather their scratch sheets left behind. A lump rises in my throat at one young student's page: "Tone, Tempo, Dymanics, Peddling, Poys, Rythm, Balince." She may not have the spelling right, but her comments, "I thought your second movement was beuitfull, but try when you make a mistake to keep going, and maybe you could slow down on the last few notes" were my sentiments exactly.

. . .

As certain as I am about the great value of the playing classes, I am filled with skepticism on the subject of student recitals. My announcement of an end-of-season recital triggers emotions that range from expectation to sheer dread. On some occasions when I could have sworn that my students were exceptionally well-prepared and reliable, the recital has left me disappointed, feeling as though I ought to throw the towel in; other times when I have faced the experience with trepidation, somehow the students came through it, making me feel like a miracle worker.

I have had separate recitals for advanced students who played longer works and for intermediate students playing one or two shorter pieces. Sometimes I coach them on the work's history, background, and composer so that they can speak to the group before playing. But most of the time I like to combine both groups so that the younger students can be inspired by the older ones. I also like to scramble the levels instead of progressing upward, placing an advanced student at the opening slot to get the event off to a rousing start.

I know piano teachers who rent prestigious halls, including Weill Recital Hall at Carnegie, for student recitals; I find this practice to be utterly pretentious, and devaluing for the serious recitalist who scrimps and saves his last penny to rent that hall only to step on stage following some ambitious piano teacher's little crop of pupils. Granted, few teachers have a home or studio that comfortably accommodates all the students and their parents. If my local library would make their community room available for private use, I'd be delighted to use that space, but it is limited to public events. So my husband and I shift furniture around to open up more space in the living room, pack in as many folding chairs as possible, and pray for a cool day. Somehow we get everybody in, and there is something cozy and unthreatening about the atmosphere. One big drawback, however, is the proximity of the audience to the pianos, and the difficulties of concentrating with folks practically sitting in your lap as you play. After years of borrowing chairs from a friendly local funeral parlor, I finally invested in some of my own. Now my guests can enjoy the music without the incongruity of the funeral home's name on the back of each chair, and I needn't trek into their storage shed, midst all the spare coffins, to pick up and deliver the chairs.

For years I had the distorted notion that the piano teacher ought also to be the dessert chef. Before each recital I cranked out sheets of cookies until it finally dawned on me that baking cookies has nothing whatever to do with my rating as a piano teacher, nor with the success of the recital. Now I accept any and all offers from others to help me with refreshments.

To cut through the air of nervous tension and establish an informal atmosphere, I usually say a few words about our goals. I might talk about audience behavior, the fragile nature of concentration, and the love of music that inspires us to share this experience with others. I discourage my students from thinking dark thoughts about what might go wrong, and caution anyone from exclaiming, "Oh I studied that!" As the recital begins, I close my eyes, cross every finger, and hope that each student will play close to his or her potential and finish with a feeling of satisfaction and pride, along with a taste for the joy of playing for others.

I look around during the recital, and what do I see? Fretted brows, wringing hands, bodies huddled into mothers, and general anguish, with very few exceptions, no matter how much I have lectured on positive thinking, relaxation, and loving the music. By the end of the program I begin, once again, to question the value of the experience. The level of the performance, though generally high enough, is rarely the group's highest level of achievement. Those most hampered by nerves, if given the choice, would opt not to play again. One of my most talented students played the Chopin Waltz in A-flat major, Opus 42, the so-called "2/4 Waltz," less than perfectly at a recital and quipped to me, "That's it for me and Chopin. I'm never playing another Chopin piece again!" A girl who is my Bach maven, who bowled me over with her excellent playing at lessons, lost her center at a recital and ran away with herself. Afterward, she, too, blamed the composer, but later admitted that after the first small glitch, she threw it all to the winds. With every little crisis my own heart flips over in empathy for the panic each student feels. When things zing along I, of course, feel warmed and proud of their efforts, but I can't help wondering what happens to all my insistence on taking a moment to focus in on the music before starting to play. And what happens to my reiteration of the fact that we are not computers, that humanness implies irregularities, and that perfection is a mythical concept?

Although at lessons the students play their pieces with understanding and expressiveness, at a recital they may approach the piano as if they were walking their last mile and proceed to play like a stick, marching zombie-like back to their seats. No smile, no nod to acknowledge audience applause, despite my coaching on this protocol. Too many display a just-get-me-back-to-my-seat-alive mentality. A student even asked me whether I might consider having frequent recitals, as her former teacher had done, so she could get used to performing. I have neither the time nor energy for that, nor am I convinced it would help, since I know too many concert artists who give more than a hundred concerts per year and still become deathly nervous each and every time they approach the stage.

Why am I disquieted about my students' harsh responses to their stress and disappointment? Have I not witnessed firsthand the backstage severe self-criticism from artists like Lupu and Watts, after concerts that would make a listener swoon with pleasure? Self-doubt and stress are, and always will be, part of the parcel. I heard the Caribbean painter Frederick Brown suggest that perhaps the reason for all the self-doubt is the lack of a certain measure of how good one's art is. "A doctor knows how good he is if the patient lives; a lawyer, if he wins the case." But who is the arbiter of standards for art, and what defines its value? Brown concluded in this television interview,

"I must just be a positive being, and leave my traces behind me, as many and as beautiful as I can."

Only a tiny percentage of piano students, indeed of musicians in general, respond positively to an audience and play even better than they do at lessons. For those few, I would gladly give over my studio and home, set up chairs, bake cookies, and afford them the opportunity of having a legitimate solo recital; and for the few who planned to continue their piano studies in college and graduate levels, I have done this. Most piano students do not study the instrument with thoughts of a career, but simply to have a music education, to enhance their artistic sensibilities, widen their horizons, and learn a wonderful skill. If they are not natural performers, I question the need to undermine their feelings of self-worth, foster competitiveness, add to the already high load of tension in their lives, and chance turning them off about something they would otherwise enjoy.

These concerns recently forced me to rethink the conventional recital format. I had been convinced that it satisfied the families more than the students—it primarily served for parents to bask in the pleasure of their offspring's accomplishments and to justify their investment in his or her musical education. (I reject the theory and the rationalization that it motivates the student, unless we are talking about the born performer, and I continue to encourage students to focus on the accomplishments of understanding and playing great music as a sufficient motivation.)

But at the last playing class, in order to pursue further options, I passed around cards on which I asked my students to answer several questions regarding the relative value of the classes and the recitals. Almost every one chose the informal learning experience of the class and admitted to fear and stress concerning the recitals. Half of them thought their parents would miss the opportunity to hear them in recital, and the other half felt that their families would understand and be glad that they decreased the tension in their lives.

But here was the big surprise: most of my students, including the ones admitting to the stress of playing for an audience, expressed reluctance to dispense with the event! One card read "Recitals not only give us a chance to show what we have learned, but they challenge us to play in spite of our nerves, and then we feel a sense of accomplishment and pride. I think the recitals are worth the struggle." Another: "A little pressure can be a good thing; we need goals and deadlines." And "I kind of dread the recitals, but I still enjoy performing in a relaxed atmosphere." "If we stopped the recitals, I would feel short-term relief; however despite the stress, it's usually worth the extra work." "It would make me very sad, although I dread them." When I got over my surprise, it occurred to me that my students suffered from the same syndrome as their teacher: the Love-Hate Paradox of Performing (see Chapter 11).

An astute and gifted student made a superb suggestion, one on which I will model my future events: "Why not let our parents attend a playing class?" We can keep the informality and enriched learning supplements to the playing, and they can be privy to the process. We are all bound to have a better time.

. . .

Recitals are not the only events that beget tensions for students. I accepted a twenty-three-year-old who wanted me to help her prepare for an upcoming audition for admission to a master's program in piano. She had two large hurdles to overcome: her piano repertoire was sparse (after majoring in music education and splitting her instrumental requirements between piano and strings), and she was grabbing odd hours to practice on an old piano in the elementary school where she teaches because there was no piano in her apartment. I located an available old upright, overcoming the second obstacle, but her relatively weak piano background presented the bigger challenge. Her strengths were musicality, intelligence, and the fiercest determination I have ever encountered in a student, along with an enormous capacity for hard work and a driving desire for perfection.

Yet the task before her seemed so daunting after a long workout at one lesson that she began to cry. She came to the right place because I, too, am a determined person; when her will wore off, mine took over. It occurred to me to ask her whether she had seen the movie *A League of Their Own* in which Tom Hanks coaches a women's baseball team and the pitcher begins to cry under pressure. She nodded that she had seen the film. I asked if she remembered when Hanks chided the poor young woman, "Baseball players don't cry," and I changed it to "Piano players don't cry!" She giggled through her tears and we started again. I told her we would knock down each hurdle like bowling pins, one after the other, until she could play the required pieces for her upcoming audition. If this had been any other student it might have been sheer folly, but I felt that with her will and the right approach, she might have a chance. As it turned out, this student was not accepted to the Master's program. I didn't hear the audition, but I feel confident she acquitted herself well enough; certainly the preparation process had elevated the level of her playing.

I fully agree with Vladimir Ashkenazy's belief that often when technique leaves off, the sheer force of will can take over, leading the hand to accomplish things that never seemed possible, or that by rights should not be possible.

In places where "I can and I will" still fails, there is yet another set of options to tap, called "tricks of the trade." I'll never forget when my teacher, Leopold Mittman, showed me a trick for a passage that my hand could barely reach in Brahms' First Piano Concerto. He winked mischievously and whispered, "I challenge any member of that jury to understand how your little hand did that!" (They didn't, and I succeeded by winning the Queens College Orchestral Society Award for best performer on campus.) Some students balk at the mere suggestion of easing a situation in any way; they think of it as cheating. I do not. Mittman claimed, and I concur, that if an educated musician's ear cannot detect the minute change, then it is legitimate. I would never suggest changing the score or an alternate way to grapple with a spot unless it can make or break a situation.

I remember with amusement a conversation with pianist Peter Frankl, whose playing has the greatest integrity. I was about to give a joint cello and piano recital at Yale University with my son, and I was fretting about the "millions of notes" between the Mendelssohn and Chopin sonatas on the program, and the brisk clip at which my son was taking it. Frankl offered with humor and sympathy, "Oh, but I am *sure* that Mendelssohn didn't mean for us to play *every* note!" (I am sure I played all the notes, just as I am sure he does too, but I was comforted by his acknowledgment that if one or two dropped on the floor under the piano, not a soul would have known.) Some of the world's greatest pianists have admitted tricks to me. These are not dirty tricks: composers like César Franck, an organist who wrote bass lines as though the pianist could render them on pedals, or Rachmaninoff, who wrote for his own hand which resembled a garden rake, invite an occasional ruse.

Tricks of the trade may not involve omitting anything; they can simply mean refingering or redistributing a passage between two hands instead of one, or using the hands in any number of ways. What a wondrous, adaptable tool the human hand is! We learn something about the "mechanism" and its infinite possibilities every time we go to the piano. If we play flat-fingered and slither and sidle along like a crab on the sand, certain effects are possible; if we attack from above in short vertical strokes, we create other sounds. André Watts once showed me how he aimed obliquely into a note at a certain angle in order to get it. The fingers used for a trill depend on the notes in the figure. I love to see a student look at me in disbelief when I suggest trilling with 2 and 4, for example, if the music calls for it; and then seeing him try it successfully; or to demonstrate the delightful relief of shifting fingers midstream in a trill that is several bars long; or to teach the secrets of overlapping for a true legato.

These devices are known and used by experienced pianists and pros. As teachers we should pass them down to students along with everything else we know. I love to see the relief and gratitude when a student suddenly plays a passage after I refinger it. One of my teachers, Josef Fidelman, was a whiz at refingering. He was also a tyrant about insisting that his students copy "his" inimitable fingerings into their own music. At the time, I often rebelled at the laborious chore, but it certainly reduced many a tricky passage to child's play, and I learned the art of fingering firsthand. Troubleshooting, whether in preparation for special challenges or simply during the course of a lesson, is among the most enjoyable facets of teaching for me.

• • •

While working with another student under a lot of pressure to learn Beethoven's First Piano Concerto for a competition deadline, I realized that the time frame had forced her to focus on the technical aspects, allowing no emotional energy for experiencing the great joy and beauty in the music. She got herself squarely on top of the technical considerations, with every phrase beyond fault. But then my task was to help her to understand and transform a well-played staccato passage into a witty, buoyant musical statement, or a succession of repeated notes in both hands into a playful dialogue. I had to call her back from the anxieties of accomplishing a physical feat and remind her about something that is not so easy to put into words: that music is an abstract representation of ideas and feelings, and that not only must she try to express the composer's intentions along with her own responses, but the listener, in this case the jury, has to end up feeling them as well.

It was one of those lessons during which our exchanges were so astutely in tune that I would have loved to record the session for future reference. By reminding Yuka that a great musical masterwork is as much a work of literature as a great book, and that one ought to come away with the same enriched sense of journey and experience, she was brought back to the crux of the mission: to get to the core of the work, to don the cloak of the composer and convey with every part of her inner self—along with her fingers and hands and arms and body—the force of the great Beethoven. This approach also took a considerable burden away. Turning toward loving and being in the music is much more engaging and enjoyable work than being preoccupied with the evenness of a scale passage. And chances are, if one plays a scale with the sense that it is part of a soaring phrase, or a diminishing phrase, or connecting a dialogue, or accompanying a singing line, or with any sense of its role and function, that scale will be much more sensitively executed.

The preparation for that audition, particularly that last lesson, was a major turning point for Yuka. In a succession of pieces she was studying after that—some Rachmaninoff preludes and the Chopin Fourth Ballade—I noticed an unbelievable change: a heightened awareness of the underlying meaning of the music, along with an unstoppered flow of emotion from within her. It was a high moment in her piano education, and therefore a high point in my teaching career.

~ 23 ~

Students I've Known and What They've Taught Me

I HAVE both beautiful and bizarre tales to tell, and still it's only the half of it because I failed to jot it all down over the years. Half my students are adults, and they are committed to learning and fun to teach. Relatively few of my students have made careers in music, but there are important lessons to be learned from each.

After a long career teaching music in the school system, Arthur retired and came to study piano with me. He had had many years of technical grounding on the instrument, in fact there was almost nothing he couldn't pull off with ease, including Liszt paraphrases, Moskowski etudes, and Godowsky and Leschetizky plums. He played with enviable technical aplomb and a reasonable and well-based cockiness, but I had to wonder about the taste and goals of his teachers who kept him on a diet of technical exercises and rich desserts, without providing the steak and potatoes of great literature. His idea of a successful rendition of a work was one which proceeded without any technical glitches, and he made excessive apologies for the occasional wrong note.

Arthur's innocent, incomplete approach to music was more challenging to me than a young person's. I found myself discovering new modes of expression, and fresh new analogies just to help him through new processes. One day when he asked me to name the most beautiful piece of music I had ever played, I realized how little guidance he had been given in understanding the essence of great music. His question grew out of his enormous emotional response to the first Brahms composition he had ever worked on, and it generated a discussion of what distinguishes the greatness of Brahms from, say, the greatness of Bach. I didn't have to point out the shortcomings of his many years of intense study that produced so few insights. "I was a stuntman," he lamented, "and my teachers were only interested in showing off my prowess on the instrument."

The most effective way I know of to teach nuance and meaning is simply to play, and parody the "typing" approach followed by a musical reading of the same passage. In the best of situations, the student responds with a sigh of acknowledgment and the willingness to try again; invariably there are dramatic changes, and with enough demonstrations and trials, words become superfluous as a student imbibes the essence of the music. Discussions of form, structure, art, and so on, are a wonderful supplement, but if a student cannot hear the difference, we are in trouble. The concept of breathing—that the music has an ebb and flow that mimics our own, and that we must breathe between phrases, take time to pause, and move on—is futile if a student is afraid of being a millisecond late for the next beat. I introduced Arthur to the stylistic idiosyncrasies of each period, including *rubato*, which he resisted mightily, and the interpretations of such indications as *energico, agitato, molto espressivo*, that often imply tempo and dynamic changes, especially in Brahms. Gradually he discovered that each phrase was a new thought and, as with spoken language, there ought to be pauses to reflect, reconsider, refuel. And little by little, he let go of his inhibitions about wavering from the straight and narrow.

Consider the magnitude of the challenge: it was as if an adult had suddenly emerged from a primitive forest into a highly developed civilization. He knew all the words without understanding the language, which is to say he was fully mature technically but not artistically. The union of body and mind that are the components of a complete artist had not occurred, leaving a well-trained vehicle able to execute virtually any composition, with precious little to express. The most surprising concept for him was that music, as much as any more concrete form of artistic expression, reflects feelings about the human condition; and he learned how infinitely richer an experience it is to delve and discern what the composer sought to say.

The best way to learn each composer's mode or style of expression is to hear as much of his work as possible. (I am always amazed to discover how little exposure to orchestral and operatic music even some of my most talented students have had.) Arthur has become a voracious attender of piano concerts, and watching artists breathe and move expressively, getting to know and love the repertoire as it ought to sound, has made an enormous contribution to his artistic development.

He can spend a major part of each day with his new Bechstein. He says he's "having a love affair with Becky." It takes time for an adult to abandon former strictures and transform himself from a rigid, exacting pianist to a musician who allows a free flow of feeling; and I am happy to report enormous changes in his playing. He leaves the lesson breathless from the hard work and discovery, and is generous with expressions of gratitude and enthusiasm. The process has been elucidating and enjoyable for me as well. I am always thrilled with the challenge of trying to verbalize and explain that which I have loved and known, and of watching a responsive pianist emerge and express the wonder of a newcomer.

. . .

I met Charlotte at an exercise class, and we got acquainted running around the gym. She too recently retired from a career in music education and eventually realized that she wanted to resume her piano studies. The most delightful aspect of working with her has been watching her astonishment at her own dormant potentialities. In no time she has left her careful sonatina-playing behind and is digging into Brahms and Schumann pieces, a Beethoven concerto, and a Bach Partita, and playing them exceedingly well. With each new piece, she looks at me with a dubious frown, expressing doubt that she will ever play it, but soon afterward she finds herself able and excited, so that now the major part of her day is spent in making up for lost time at her piano. Her expressions of love for my guidance feel like garlands.

. . .

Margeaux was the assistant to the carpenter on a renovation job on our home. She wielded big tools, carried lumber, and exhibited the expertise generally associated with men. In fact she was so excellent that a month later we hired her to repair and paint our front porch, and to do some demolition work. I kept remarking at her quiet efficiency, brawn, and our good luck to have found such an excellent handywoman whose talents were as exotic as the spelling of her name. I was completely unprepared for what followed: when the jobs were done, she came to the door and asked if she could talk to me about something.

"I would like to study piano with you," she said. "I studied when I was younger, and as I listened to you teach while I was working, I realized that I never had a teacher like you. It's something I really want." My first reaction was skepticism, but something about her earnestness led me to explain the scant availability of my time, as well as my policies. I invited her to prepare something to play for me at a later time.

When she came, she apologized for the bad habits she had accumulated over the years during which she had been autodidactic, and expressed doubt that I would accept her as a student. She had no idea how good she was, and she bowled me over. She is one of those multifaceted people whose hands can accomplish anything she sets her mind to. At thirty-something, this young woman has an aura of capability about her. She does, indeed, have bad fingering habits and a slightly casual approach to details, to which she readily admits. Yet I am amazed that her fingers are as strong as the rest of her; even though she sometimes comes to a lesson straight from a physically demanding job, her smaller muscles respond vigorously, and she is in complete control. Margeaux is a superb sight reader and can fly through every sonatina ever written. When I played one back to her at our first lesson, she immediately picked up on all the nuances and became excited about the process of refining her own playing. I would say she has a definite gift; talent sometimes comes in unexpected packages.

. . .

Some of my colleagues have refused to teach adult students at an early level, and there are good reasons why. It is difficult to find material that neither embarrasses them nor undermines their lifetime fantasies of playing the piano. Adults who studied as children are often unwilling to do the technical work necessary to catch up to their former levels. Adults usually have more anxiety before lessons than younger students; some come to the lesson with the notion of showing the teacher what they can do, and they are the hardest to teach. Then there are those who, figuring that a piano-lesson fee is much lower than a psychoanalyst's, openly refer to the lesson as therapy. The teacher, reduced (elevated?) to counselor, has to be an artful dodger to stay focused on the music and avoid becoming ensnared in their private lives. It always starts with an explanation of why they could not practice as much as they had planned, because of this or that tension; then comes the unburdening. It is tricky to straddle the fine line between lending a sympathetic ear when you do care about your students, but then easing them back to the business at hand.

Even the most conscientious adults come up against the unavoidable realities of everyday life, from having a sick child at home from school, to an unexpected business trip. But I have had some unbelievably lame excuses from adult students from "I wrecked my body doing the Jane Fonda workout" to "so what if I am an hour late, you can always practice or clean the house." Needless to say those students looked for another teacher the following week.

My least favorite adult students are the dilettantes with the attitude, "If it's Wednesday, it must be my piano lesson, because tennis is Tuesday, and toenails are Thursday." Such dabblers make me feel like a kept woman, essentially paying me to listen to them practice. One showed her true colors when I informed her that I would have to discontinue with our lessons. "You ought to be happy that we are maintaining a connection with each other, and I with music!" she insisted. How's that for egotism? Some adult students try to bargain for a bimonthly lesson. I dislike the lack of continuity and commitment and have rarely taught on that basis. On the other hand, I have had many advanced students who only come for a monthly or occasional coaching session before a concert, and we simply schedule those at random.

For the adult students who have already developed strong preferences, often rigid, finding a selection that will both please and educate can be difficult. A dentist whom I used to teach wanted the moon immediately. She was an excellent sight reader, bright, musical, but impatient. After a series of suggestions and rejections, I played some pieces from Schumann's *Kinderscenen* and she seemed interested. I assigned her two short pieces from the collection, and a day or two later, I received what can only be described as an hysterical, accusatory call, "How dare you give me something I studied when I was eleven years old?!" She had retrieved her old music, marked and dated, and felt betrayed; worse, she felt that she not only had made no progress but had regressed.

Suddenly I was on trial to defend myself as well as the greatness of those little masterpieces, to explain that the timelessness transcends age, that Rubinstein, Horowitz, and Horszowski performed them publicly late in life, that as an adult she could bring much more to those pieces than a child merely playing the notes. Another adult student bit the dust.

Then there was the psychiatrist who flung herself down on the couch and said, "Oh, I don't feel like playing today; I haven't practiced anyway. Play for me, Carol."

"Oh, no," I said in my quasi-serious voice. "Let's go. There's plenty to work on, especially if you didn't practice." She insisted that she would rather listen than have a lesson, so I said to myself, "Why not? I would rather play any day than teach this dame, and she knows what she wants to pay for." Then a moment of guilt set in, when I questioned myself (while I was playing!), whether I should have insisted on teaching her, but then I realized that my fee for playing was much higher than my fee for teaching, and that she was getting the bargain! This same woman came early one day and did sit-ups on the rug in my studio for the last ten minutes of the previous lesson. But most of the time she was late, so I simply gave her a "psychiatrist's hour." Needless to say, I soon helped her to find another poor soul who would try to teach her.

. . .

The crop of students I have these days is a superior bunch. I am not bound, as I once was, to accept students for reasons of economics. But I certainly remember past students, including the old gentleman who fantasized about being a pianist after having played the violin for many years. He had enormous trouble learning the bass clef and coordinating his two hands, and he was continually frustrated. Apparently so was his spouse. This kindly fellow brought me a cartoon his wife had given to him; in it a man, not unlike my pupil, is seated at the piano, obviously intent on getting it right. Two matrons are on the couch in the same room, and one—his wife—says deadpan to the other: "After our daughter stopped her lessons, Burt took it up. So

I'm having him killed." (I put the cartoon up in my office. It kills me.)

In the past I have had many kind, well-meaning, and generous adult students who were passionately eager to learn how to play the piano. (I would love to be a ballet dancer, but certain things were never meant to be.) After years of hard work in situations where I began to feel unethical to continue taking payment when there was little progress, or I began to find myself glancing at the clock or wincing at chronic clinkers, I finally wondered how I could have put myself into such binds. In one case, when I tried to let go delicately, the student clung to me, saying, "You're the only one I want to study with. It's not only the music, I look forward to talking to you." She expressed appreciation and sympathy for my struggles with her, and, indeed, I had grown fond of her. We hugged, I felt like a heel, but I had firmly resolved to limit my teaching in ways that were nourishing to both the student and me. I found her a teacher with whom I think she has made progress: sometimes a lot is gained in changing teachers.

. . .

One of my adult students is a young woman whom I taught for six years when she was a very musical young girl. As gifted as she was, she was irresponsible in certain ways: never on time, returning my music in bad shape when she remembered to return it at all, or forgetting to bring the monthly payment. Then one day she phoned me fifteen minutes before her lesson. "Mrs. Montparker, I want to take two months off from lessons because I need the time for school, and then when I catch up to my classes, I'll come back. O.K.?"

"No. Not O.K." I explained about the commitment, that I could not keep that time for her, and that she would have to make the decision to continue or to quit. "Well," she retorted, "I guess I'll quit." No apology, no thank you, no nothing. Six years invested in a gifted young person, out the door. But once she passed through the difficult period of adolescence and was well into being an adult, she had the courage to phone me expressing a yearning to continue, and we resumed her lessons. Now, ironically, *she* is successfully teaching early piano, and her lessons with me consist not only of piano but also piano pedagogy *and* advice on coping with thorny business problems—not my forte. And we are good friends.

. . .

I am generally very successful dealing with teenagers, no matter how tricky their adolescence may be. A rare few, like Jessica and Andrea, are intellectually curious and voracious learners. Others are shockingly lazy and want to be spoon-fed and taken through the practicing process that they ought to have done at home, step by step at the lesson. Admittedly teenagers can be both great fun and exasperating, even at the same time. Megan, who is about to go off to college, has been my student for many years. From the first few notes she ever played for me, I was glad to be her teacher. Intensely musical, she grasps concepts and produces appropriate sounds before I have finished making my suggestions. One day when she was about fourteen, she placed her hands on the keyboard revealing nails polished in black lacquer. (This predates the current nail craze that has overtaken the country and that occasionally shows up on the keys of my piano.) My first impulse was to recoil in horror, but instead I offered, "Hmm, interesting." She giggled, and proceeded to have as excellent a lesson as ever. As the lesson went on, I got used to it, indeed it became a fascinating visual experience: shiny black piano, ten dazzling black nails flying over black and white keys—an Art Deco event. Pondering this phenomenon, I realized it comes with the territory: the most talented people are also the most creative and avant-garde, and originality emerges in diverse ways. Over the following months and years, Megan expressed her creativity both musically and with a form of self-graffiti: a succession of nail colors, then hair colors, including orange, fuschia, and jet black, changing weekly; then came multiple ear piercings and some facial "jewelry," only to return, full circle, during her last year with me, to her own lovely hair color and fewer adornments. She is off to a fine college, having kept on top of her academic life throughout her years of finding her center. My acceptance of her gestures of self-expression went a long way, I think, to strengthen our relationship.

Some students are distinguished to me as much by their sweet good natures as by their musicality. Kaitlin embodies these qualities, and I will miss Jaime, who has left for college—especially for the joy she always exhibited upon making the acquaintance of each new work she was to study.

Several other teenagers have come to me from teachers who warned, "You'll see, she won't last more than a couple of weeks with you; she has bad habits," or "You'll see, she has a very difficult personality, very obstinate," but in each case it worked out. I expended a lot of energy with one such inherited girl because she devoured large chunks of material each week, and I had to try to focus her excitement on details. But I loved Tricia's enthusiasm and sparkling eyes which reminded me of my own teenage spirit. With cajoling and perseverance I succeeded in modifying her work habits, and her mother told me she was practicing longer than ever before and listening to classical records rather than the rock she used to prefer.

. . .

Lisa, despite any words of caution offered me, is a teenager who is eager to please, with the special bonus of being musical. She and I do this little dance around several options whenever we are about to study something new because she has a solid ego and a definite set of likes and dislikes, and I have the firm conviction that one is much more successful studying and performing music one loves. That is as true for experienced concert pianists as it is for students. We are blessed with a vast literature and we needn't ever perform or study a work unless it appeals to us. Therefore I am always thrilled if a student expresses a desire for a particular work, provided it is within the realm of possibility and will serve to educate and develop the student appropriately.

One day as I was about to suggest a new piece to replace the Poulenc pieces she had just completed, Lisa waved her hand to forestall the search, crying, "Wait! I heard something I would love to study."

"How does it go?" I asked. She started to hum, out of tune, an entirely indiscernible nonmelody, and I was completely at sea. I wanted more than anything to identify what was lurking in her mind's ear, so I asked, "Where did you hear it?"

"In the bookstore." She tried singing it again, struggling to reconstruct the melody to which she had responded so positively, poked her finger around the keyboard, fishing desperately for the right notes. I plumbed the depths of my musical sensibilities hoping that the mystery fragment would resonate with anything I had ever heard and stored. This time a tiny trigger mechanism deep inside my brain, a primal twinge, responded to a couple of notes, and I said, "Shhh, let me think." Suddenly something occurred to me.

"Is this it?" I sat down and started playing the Schubert Impromptu in F minor, Opus 142, (how *would* she sing it?), and before I got three bars into the piece, Lisa cried out in delight, "Yes! That's it!" She looked at me with the greatest respect, adoration, and gratitude, and I secretly congratulated myself. Now we were guaranteed the love factor, and ultimate success.

I never want to sit at my piano without loving it, and I never want to teach without love in my own heart for the student and the music. In a perfect scenario, my students, too, will share in that happy state.

• • •

Eric is one of the most exceptional young people I have ever worked with and among the few, I would venture, who has what it takes for a career. He, too, is off to college soon, to study pre-med, but I have felt great pressure, albeit pleasurable, to impart as much as I can to him during these years he is entrusted to me. When his father first called me, he was eleven, had studied for three years, and was obviously very talented. I asked to speak to the child on the phone so I could question him about his current repertoire. He cited some pieces, including the opus numbers, then added "and a sinfonia by Bach."

I asked, "Can you sing it for me?" Without hesitation he sang the opening Andante from the Bach Partita No. 2 in C minor, in the right key, and without another moment's hesitation, I invited him to come and study with me. He has defined the word *protégé* because he trusts me, follows through on every suggestion I make with commitment and hard work (despite his heavy scholastic responsibilities) and at seventeen is playing like an artist.

• • •

In contrast, the mother of another young fellow I used to teach wanted me "to prepare her son for Juilliard." The boy was quite musical, but the parents were the most ambitious I had ever dealt with. I got monthly calls asking "How is he doing?" and they sat in on lessons, sighing audibly with each wrong note their unhappy son chanced to strike. I could only imagine the pressures at home. I asked them what their goals were for him—did they expect him to be the next André Watts? I told them that realistically their son, while talented, should not plan a career in music, and that he would not be at all happy in the competitive atmosphere of a music conservatory. The mother reluctantly replied, "Well, if you don't think he will be a concert pianist, I suppose we would be satisfied if he could at least—er—well—be as good—as say—you are." Let's just say I was stunned into silence. Although I was tempted to tell them of youth competitions I had won at an early age and to explain my career choices, I decided to let this comment go. I told them to get me the current Juilliard catalog and said I would be happy to start preparing him right then and there for the audition. I believe in justice for all: students *and* teachers.

~ 24 ~

Teaching the Nitty-Gritties, Marking the Music, the Human Factor

I BELONG to the marking school, and it begins with my own music, into which I put any conceivable visual aid that helps, from humorous warnings, to red circles, to well-chosen words for moods and images, and of course fingerings. I am certain that my habit was formed in my teachers' studios because both Mittman and Fidelman were heavy markers. Mittman would often grab for whatever art material was at hand, no matter if it was a blunted crayon or chalk, and it never occurred to him that he didn't have every right to do it. I also wrote in his remarks if he didn't, if I found them useful or amusing. The classic case was the time I dragged out a romantic climax in a Schumann piece ad boredom, and he admonished gently, "You know, Carol, when one gets passionate, one cannot take so long!" After I stopped laughing I jotted down the remark, and his droll point is still well taken when I play that page. Fidelman's insistence on marking every correct finger and his delineation of phrases heightened my consciousness on those points evermore.

Not all my students are pleased to have their music marked, nor do I do it indiscriminately without ascertaining their response. With each new piece, according to the level of advancement, I write in whatever fingering I deem essential, not only because my teachers did that for me, but because of the atrociously careless habits I have encountered, especially from inherited students. No one complains about fingering marks; it is the correction marks that cause the most grief. I asked one of my more mature students whether he minded my corrections on his music, and his sarcastic response was, "No, I love graffiti." With another student I had three weeks' worth of marks around a single note: first a lightly penciled circle, then a darker (angrier?) penciled circle, and the third week's red mark. When the note was still wrong the fourth week, I brought out my next weapon, a yellow highlighter.

"No! Not another color!" cried my student in anguish, shielding the page from further defacement. "I swear I won't play it wrong again." He never did. One student's music had too much marking even for me, and together we flipped back through his notebook to see how many weeks he had worked on the piece: too many. In an unpremeditated frenzy I whisked the music off the stand, put it out of sight, and said, "That's it. *Fini*." It was a shock and relief for us both. I once heard of a student who took white-out and obliterated some troublesome notes from his music!

A piano teacher I know shared her tale of an unfortunate episode in which her student played a wrong note for the umpteenth time; she took a red pencil and gouged the page with increasingly large circles around the note until it resembled a bull's-eye at an archery range. "What will his mother think when she sees that page," she wailed afterward. Even piano teachers are entitled to lose it once in a while, and isn't there a way to determine the age of trees (and errors) by the number of concentric circles? A friend, who emphatically declined to be identified, said, "If they play it wrong a second time, I mark in pencil; if it's wrong a fourth time, I mark in red; after that I mark the student."

One woman who had studied piano since childhood admitted that her mother once warned her against having an accident while returning from her lesson; if her music should fall haplessly open to a particularly worked-over page, what an embarrassment that would be! Whenever a student expresses dismay at the well-worked look of a page, I take out a copy of anything I have ever worked on intensively and show it to him or her. I tell them how I regard those pages with pride: each notation represents a thought I do not wish to lose, a direction, a clue. The page is not only the composer's but my own unique view and experience of it; my markings don't embarrass me at all.

But I have stumbled upon an excellent alternative to marking the music. On rare occasions when I simply cannot stand to hear an error one more time, I have said with a straight face: "O.K. If you play that wrong again, I will leave the room and make myself a cup of tea." I have never had to follow up on that action, because the mere shock of the notion that I might do that has acted as a miraculous cure!

• • •

Genius teachers who can surmount any problem notwithstanding, is there a normal teacher who would not agree that a student who cannot count is the most challenging of all? Maybe "challenging" doesn't quite express it. Frustrating? Confounding? Infuriating? Exasperating? Hopeless? I'm referring to those who cannot perceive the steady tick of a metronome and budget triplets and quadruplets, or even duples, to coincide with the quarter-note tick. A metronome notch away from those are the ones who can stay with the tick but cannot be weaned from it. The moment they are on their own, each bar assumes a life of its own. Then there are the students who start a piece at breakneck speed while we sit back and wait for the inevitable slowdown at the first tricky bar. I am constantly trying to get students to acknowledge that evenness is a virtue, and that playing a piece at a slower tempo until all of it is safely learned needn't mean sacrificing the beauty, that the greatness of masterpieces is apparent at any tempo. The importance of using a tempo that will allow the piece to be played accurately can be underscored with the warning that each time a note is misplayed, *it is being practiced inaccurately* and is becoming more deeply engraved into the muscle memory. (At the same time, slowing down for a difficult bar is also being practiced.)

Having no sense of pulse is a tragic flaw that will prevent students from succeeding who are quite musical in every other way. In the early phases we talk basic arithmetic: fractions, pies cut into halves, quarters, eighths, and so on. We bang our hands on our laps: the right hand beats the quarters "Pie Pie Pie Pie" while the left hand beats the duples, triplets, quadruplets. We say "Apple apple apple apple, Blueberry blueberry blueberry blueberry, Huckleberry huckleberry huckleberry huckleberry." I search for analogies—"the pulse is like the heartbeat; the timing is like the skeleton keeping the flesh of the music in shape"—to indicate its critical importance.

I find myself nodding, tapping, grunting, and breathing loudly to suggest beats, rests, and entrances, hoping that the rhythm will be absorbed at least by osmosis if not through understanding. One rhythmically challenged woman admitted that she desperately tries to hear my gasps and sputterings and to feel my nudges at home to suggest the beat. Her music looks peppermint-striped with the strobes of beats suggested first lightly in pencil, then emphatically in red if needed. (Sometimes in an Adagio, she has required the eighths and sixteenths indicated as well.) Without them she confronts the printed page with fear and trembling. This is an intelligent woman who writes well and is sensitive to art and music, but is rendered Neanderthal without visual devices to indicate pulse. With cruel irony, there is nothing she wants to study more than a good Grave movement from a Beethoven sonata or a Largo from a Bach concerto. Her eyes glaze over when she confronts the thirty-second or sixty-fourth notes, the stripes I have drawn fuse into blackness, and I hurry in with red pencil and smelling salts. In such ways do we try to bring music into the lives of those who yearn to play it.

Someone once said that the measure of a good teacher is not what you do with the talented students but what you can do with the non-talented ones. While this may hold some truth, it doesn't speak to the joys and frustrations, which are, in turn, closely allied to a teacher's effectiveness. And although the notion that certain inherent musical abilities cannot be taught may sound like a cop-out, I believe it is true. A sense of timing is one, and sight reading is a close second. To be sure, exercises and drills can help improve the level to some extent, but my feeling is that sight reading is related to the facility for reading in general, possibly intelligence (reading disabilities notwithstanding), and above all, visualization. The person who perceives the music in terms of its "topography," which is to say the peaks and valleys of the melodic lines as opposed to separate dots, lines, and spaces, who can readily discern the minute differentiations between intervals, and other details, will have an enormous advantage. Other important factors for sight reading are a good ear, the ability to anticipate harmonic progressions and melodic directions, eye-hand coordination, and that essential ego. (Timidity and hesitation are the enemies of sight reading.) Somehow the skills all come together in certain individuals; and although fluency in sight reading is not a critical component of fine pianism, it is a useful and enjoyable aptitude.

• • •

Teaching a student to play with a beautiful tone or to dig in, using energy from the whole body, is another challenge. I remember Fidelman's highly original concept that certain phrases are "fingered," some are "handed," and some are "armed." It is fun to show a student the many ways we pianists use our hands. Articulating fingerwork as in lively Bach pieces is the easiest to understand. But clusters of notes under a rotating wrist, such as the sixteenths in *Aufschwung* by Schumann, can be described as "handed" or "handled" in groups. Chords passages, for example in the Brahms Rhapsodie in E-flat major from Opus 118, or in the opening page of Mussorgsky's *Pictures*, are played from the arm. Grabbing those chords like so many bunches of grapes and holding the clusters lovingly in the palms of your hands, so to speak, until each has its full sonorous due, letting them shimmer, becoming aware of their vibrations, approaches the sensual. I try to awaken the students' awareness to the pads of their fingers where good tone is produced, to experience the tingling sensation that may, with time and experience, be perceived even through the circuitous route from string, via wood, felt, and ivory, to flesh.

. . .

When a student asked me what we figure out in advance and mark into our music, and what we leave to the moment of performance, he asked a million-dollar question. I believe in laying out a plan of dynamic contrasts, tempos, pedaling, and so on, and generally mapping out the color and shape of a piece, but I also believe in the moment: taking risks, making discoveries, allowing for sudden impulses as they happen. Students may require help with the creative aspects (in contrast with the re-creative elements.) Imagination often requires a fuse to ignite it. We all have to guard against sitting down to play in a less-than-inspired mood and letting our machinery run us. A well-chosen word written into the music may be sufficient impetus to remind us to play creatively. If a plaintive phrase is repeated three times in a row, and a student plays it exactly the same each time, a discussion of its philosophical meaning, the reiterative quality, intensification or diminution, and even a verbal phrase that might fit the music or suit the mood, might be in order.

There are so many ways to prod a student's imagination. While I worked with a student on a Debussy piece that was inspired by nature, I pointed out that the music needed a shift in dynamics, without suggesting any choices of my own. But I did say, "The tonal color shifts there just as surely as the dusk softens the light, or a cloud covers the sun." The student then produced an amazing array of tonal contrast within those few bars.

Improvisation is a corollary of imagination; the two gifts are closely allied, but few have a flare for the former. Cadenzas are good conduit for teaching improvisation. The Italian word *cadenza* was meant to imply a flourish, an invention, and "the execution of spontaneous and elaborately decorative passages," according to *The Oxford Companion to Music*. It ought also to reflect the personality of the artist. There ought to be a measure of astonishment, and an unrestrained indulgence of enthusiasm and whim.

I encourage my students to take an original approach to cadenza interpretation, starting with a discussion of the term *a piacere* (as you wish, or to your liking). I have even suggested that my talented students try to write or at least embellish their own cadenzas; few are ever willing to extemporize using thematic material from the concerto. Precious few can, especially in front of someone else. Improvisation, again, calls for a strong ego, lack of self-consciousness, technical assurance, relaxation, concentration, and above all else, imagination, the rarest element of all.

It is interesting to note that the word *capriccio* was at one time interchangeable with the word *cadenza*. At a recent exhibit of the paintings of Tiepolo at the Metropolitan Museum, I read a marvelous definition of the word *capriccio* by Antoine Furetïare, taken from the *Dictionnaire Universel*: "poetry or pieces of music wherein the force of imagination has better success than observation of the rules of art."

On a small scale, Gershwin's Prelude No. 2 invites a little fancy with the return of the main theme after the middle section, as I once heard Leonard Bernstein do. I urge (and sometimes have to force) my students to invent little riffs around the tune with the right hand, jazzing it up with syncopations, embellishments, whatever they wish, while keeping a strict 2/4 tempo with the left hand. It is incredible how reticently and shyly they start out—has our puritanical society wrought such repression?—and how jauntily and happily they eventually proceed to play the theme once I manage to help them overcome their inhibitions. Little Bach pieces, for example sarabandes from the suites and partitas, are another wonderful vehicle for improvisation. I believe we all have much more imagination than we know, waiting to be unleashed.

In an age where computers are insidiously permeating every conceivable facet of society, most strikingly music, we can justify our objections by playing as expressively and unmachinelike as possible. Electronic keyboards reproduce the timbres of harpsichords, pianos, organs, and other instruments; electronic musicians can play a Liszt etude at practice tempo, then speed up the tempo of the recording to surpass human possibilities without altering the pitch; and now electronic instruction packaged with the new instrument is advertised on television as surpassing "the old knuckle-rapping variety of human piano teachers"! All this miraculous equipment lacks one important ingredient: humanness. They can simulate it with tonal gradations and fluctuations, but the result is calculated, *Ersatz,* and frightening. As this ugly trend pervades our world, we should place a premium on individual expression, before it is too late and we all not only sound alike, but like computers.

25

Leopold Mittman: A Memoir

LÖLI has been dead for more than twenty years, and I rarely sit at the piano without a sense of him; I suppose one might say he is my muse—listening to me or playing for me with the special pleasure he seemed to have. An almost imperceptible tap on my shoulder indicated he wanted to demonstrate, and I yielded the seat gladly. His hands were usually cut or bruised from carpentry chores, and after he offered a string of excuses about the injury or a lack of time to practice, his face took on a serene and almost vacant expression; the eyes, unfocused, the jaw dropped open in an attitude of classic rapture, knees locked closely together, sitting rather high with the boost of a volume of music, and on the very edge of the seat, he began to weave his spell with tone as beautiful as I have ever heard. He was a little vain of his tone and yet so humble and modest of his person that he often asked me not to watch him while he played.

He once gave me a wonderful photo of himself as a young artist, a dramatic black and white study of an intense, handsome man; in his haggard aged face there were still the beautiful eyes, but the fiery intensity was long since replaced by resignation. The photo reminded me of the book he gave me, *Jean-Cristophe* by Romain Rolland, wherein an old professor excuses the flabby shape of his old Blüthner piano (as Löli often did) by depressing two still exquisitely resonant notes and saying gently, "You see, it still has beautiful eyes." In fact, the tone, though thin, remained singularly sweet and irresistible.

I called him Mr. Mittman until he invited me to use Löli, a diminutive of Lölek, the equivalent of Leopold. I clearly remember the excitement with which I approached each lesson during those twenty-odd years from age eleven: a mix of happy expectancy with a degree of nervous tension. My mother had fortuitously found exactly the right teacher for me, and our family moved to Forest Hills so I could walk the few blocks to his lovely Tudor-style home, bordered with his wife's beautiful flower gardens. At the big oak door, there was always a bear hug, and by the twinkle in his eyes I knew he had looked forward to the lesson as well. Then came the trek up two flights of stairs to Löli's world: his third floor garret studio with its beamed ceiling, reminiscent of Vuillard's painting *Room Under the Eaves* reproduced in one of the many art books he gave me, signed "In everlasting friendship." It was a rarefied and cozy atmosphere filled with his most beloved possessions: fine paintings, old photos from his earlier years in Europe, books, beautiful rugs, tubes of oil paint, a large easel with his own latest painting drying, all surrounding his Blüthner, the prize for winning the much-coveted Blüthner Competition in his youth. He was born in Kiev in 1905, then the Ukraine, studied first in Warsaw, then in Berlin. Later he lived in Paris until he had to flee from Nazi-infested Europe. Somehow he managed to transport a small portion of his personal belongings, including some paintings and his beloved piano.

The change in Löli's stride upon the stairs over the years was plain evidence of his spiritual and physical metamorphosis. I remember how the younger man scampered up the two flights, thinking nothing of flitting down and up again if he had forgotten a score on the Steinway in his living room. But more vivid is the image of his slow trudge, his increasingly slouching body and rounded shoulders approaching a hunch. At the top of the landing, there was often another hug and the bestowing of some token. My home contains many of these bibelots of friendship which are constant reminders of how he gently but purposefully went about the business of my art education through paintings, books, and sheet music from his youth. I have a few of his own paintings, presented to me still wet, including one he admitted to painting behind the back of an excruciatingly dull student. His blues rivaled Cézanne's and his still-lifes and landscapes were all distinguished by a keen sense of color and composition. He also gave me two still-lifes by a Polish painter named Sveter, with a wink and the assurance "These are *good!*," as if the appraised value would be of any interest to me.

We sometimes swapped pictures. I felt presumptuous in these trade situations, no matter how kindly he assured me that he really wanted my watercolor. I was afraid he considered my work superficial and decorative, especially as he had a dubious view of watercolors in general. Once when I was defending aquarelles as a genre of lasting value, I stupidly offered as evidence the fact that I had recently sold a good number of them at an art exhibit. "Well," he retorted in an elitist voice, "if everyone likes it, that's the best proof of all that it is not great!" He wanted me to paint a "substantial" canvas in oils. He even gave me a set of paints, as well as a wonderful box of pastels, and I remember showing him my first oil painting, and his fine praise, "I would like to have painted it myself."

I can still conjure up some of his paintings along with others by Maurice Utrillo and Max Weber that covered the walls of his home. One year on my birthday he handed me one of the most loving gifts I have ever received from anyone: a little book which he had made and bound together himself, consisting of color photos which he had taken of my favorites from all his paintings, each mounted on its own page and put together not so much with ego as with the joy of sharing. Among those paintings was one with a special tale. In return for teaching Max Weber's daughter, Löli was paid with Weber's work.

He also taught Löli a lot about painting. One day right in the middle of a lesson, probably right in the middle of a phrase (such were his irrepressible and spontaneous impulses), he dragged out a large painting and proudly propped it up for me to see, explaining with a mischievous wink that he had "weaseled it back" from a friend years after having given it as a gift. I got up from the bench to admire it at length, and after a long silent spell of appreciation (as he watched me anxiously for my response), I pointed to a particularly delicate and adroitly painted little tree in the landscape and said, "How well placed and delicate that tree is." At which Löli fairly attacked me with a strange mix of mock livid rage and tenderness.

"You little witch! Max Weber put that tree in after I finished the painting!" Behind his sham of anger was merriment and delight at the perverse manner in which the discernment he himself had taught, had backfired. This name-calling was another part of the lesson to which I was accustomed. "Idiot!" he might shout if I played something mechanically or absent-mindedly, "Little gypsy" if I got too schmaltzy, "Rascal" if I found a clever way of handling a tricky passage. But most criticisms, no matter how severe, were tempered with a wistful pat on my head and a reflection, "You know, I remember doing the exact thing." Löli, in fact, made me feel like a musical reincarnation of himself. Sometimes I found him looking at me quizzically as though to ask himself or me, "How did you come to play that just that way?" He also enjoyed my achievements as his own, including the competition when I played Brahms' Piano Concerto No. 1 in D minor, having learned it in a fit of inspiration in record time. In work sessions he frequently showed me tricks to cover spots where my small hands or my endurance threatened to fall short of the mighty demands of the score.

There were the disappointments, too, and on one occasion I felt I had been ill-advised by him to enter a certain contest at that particular stage of my development. Mittman was a teacher guided solely by instincts. His guidance was not in the least methodological—no rules or formulas, each problem tackled as it came along. His intuitions were sharp. If a student was weak in double-thirds, for example, he pulled out just the piece to focus on the problem. However, he also held some questionable viewpoints: if, in his estimation, the double-thirds presented insurmountable problems, he shrugged and indicated that one could go successfully through life never having to play double-thirds at all. His rationale was that no one did everything well anyway, so get to know your territorial boundaries, focus on your own talent, and be grateful for it. In fact, I know many pianists who do not choose programs intelligently for themselves and are unrealistic in their expectations. But it wasn't until later on that I realized I wanted to face squarely and work out certain technical hang-ups which I might have done earlier with him. It was Josef Fidelman who ultimately helped me fill in whatever loopholes were left in my piano education.

I would undoubtedly have learned even more about the piano from Löli had we not had so many other things to talk about. We never squandered time on idle chatter. The discussions were charged with new ideas, although most of the musical portion unfolded with demonstration rather than in words. He had a wonderful sense of humor, and my sheet music is annotated with his screamingly funny *bon mots* uttered over the years. The lesson, which sometimes had to be squeezed into a tight schedule, was crammed with urgent conversation about music, art, poetry, and nature, as well as reminiscences, so that especially in the later years our session became more a course in humanities than what most people think of as a piano lesson. Because of this and despite his longstanding refusal to take any money from me, Löli became paranoid about the musical value of the lesson to me and constantly had to be reassured that I wanted to come and that it was worth it. Worth it! At that time in my life, who would underestimate the value of learning about Goethe or Romain

Rolland, gazing at paintings of Vuillard and Bonnard, hearing his firsthand accounts of the gruesome yet fascinating dynamics of the Nazi rise to power, including his own involvement in the exciting ferment of the creative arts? He related the tale of his early years as a child prodigy, apologetically showing me the yellowing clippings from a Warsaw newspaper, reporting that only Chopin himself could have played his concertos as Mittman had done that night. I heard tales of his student days, first with Michailowski in Warsaw, then on scholarship at the Hochschule fur Musik in Berlin, and his concerts all over Europe. I learned about the increasing suppression and his flight, his struggle to remake a career in America, and anecdotes from his illustrious collaborations with Nathan Milstein, Mischa Elman, Gregor Piatigorsky, and countless other famous musicians to whom he became a partner. Who would ever deny that what I got from Löli was more precious and rare than some more Chopin etudes?

In retrospect I have to acknowledge that in making me his protégée in the most complete sense of the word, Leopold Mittman made a more profound impression on my life than any other person.

Sometimes if time permitted, Löli and his wife Sala would invite me to stay for a little lunch. There was always a delicious aroma from her kitchen, and she more than gratified his gourmandise. The peasant in him emerged unabashedly as he dunked his rolls, picked and nibbled at the cheeses, devoured the crumbling pastries, stirred a bit of jelly into his coffee. He once climbed a ladder in their garden to pick some cherries from their tree so I could go home with a big basketful. I seemed to go home with a gift every week for years—art books, music, prints, paintings, or something edible from Sala's kitchen.

. . .

My lessons gradually became less frequent simply because the demands of my family life made the long drive from Huntington difficult. Besides, there was a period during which my musical needs were languishing. He seemed to understand the juggling act of raising two kids and trying to practice, and implied that he would be available and delighted whenever I could come. I visited with my children on several occasions, and his delight in hearing their progress over the years on cello and flute was matched by their sense that they were playing for an especially distinguished person. His approval and blessing meant the world to all of us. Once it struck both Löli and me that Dennis had reached the age that I was when my mother first brought me to study with him. In a strangely prophetic moment, Löli expressed a desire for my son to play for his friend, the cellist Aldo Parisot. (Many years later Dennis took his master's degree with Parisot at Yale University.)

At a few of my last lessons, we listened to Löli's tapes of the Debussy Preludes, which he was in the process of recording. He was a supreme colorist, and each vignette was like an exquisite painting. He promised to send me a recording, but as things turned out it never materialized. Over the years I knew him, he had already acquired a kind of apathetic, almost cynical attitude about fame. Here was a great artist whose career had been at its peak when it was nipped in the bud, never to regain its full momentum in the United States.

. . .

How it happened that this beautiful friendship was marred in the end, I hardly know. But suddenly I was confronted with a bizarre ultimatum: to study every week—or not at all. I know, just as surely as anything, that these were neither his own words nor his inclinations. Löli, out of distaste for the more mundane side of teaching, preferred to have the administrative end handled for him. Perhaps it was with the best motives and in his "best interests" that this decision was made for him. But there it was. Both he and I knew that I was not only unable to come regularly, but I no longer required regular lessons, and neither of us could do a thing about it. We had a couple of painful conversations, fraught with strain. He was too old to cope with stress, so he had taken the path of least resistance. We had less and less communication, but once he suddenly appeared in Huntington, having driven all the way himself. We had a rather quiet tour of the nearby Heckscher art museum, with minimal verbal exchange.

When I made the decision to give a New York debut recital a year or so later, there was no question that I could never go back and study with Löli again. I was fortunate that Josef Fidelman agreed to help me prepare the program. I never felt disloyal about changing teachers. I would always think of Löli as my dear friend and greatest artistic influence. He himself had often said that he probably had given me all he had to offer as a teacher. There was everything to be gained from a fresh approach, especially as the two teachers were the direct antithesis of each other. Josef was able to zero in on the more neglected elements in my technical training, and in a meticulous, scholarly, and generous way, he helped me to achieve my goal.

At the same time I was entirely aware of the irony and pain of a teacher who has worked with a student for twenty-three years only to see the greatest accomplishment achieved with another teacher. Löli had urged me for years to consider presenting a New York recital, but it would have been premature. No one knew that better than he, but he was restless to see me do the things he would have wanted to do himself, or to relive certain events in his past.

I tried to share some of my excitement with the Mittmans. I sent them announcements of my prerecitals in the New York area and the flyer heralding the Carnegie Recital Hall concert, on which was proudly cited my long years of study with Leopold Mittman. I sent them tickets with an affectionate note in the hope that they would respond. With cock-eyed optimism, I peered through a crack in the curtains that eventful night, praying and half-expecting to see his beloved old face somewhere out there, but he never so much as sent a note. A cryptic remark resurfaced from our last conversation (when

I had cried from the utter disbelief that our friendship had, indeed, ended): Löli had said with great weariness, "My dear, we are all creatures of circumstance."

A few months after my debut in 1976, Josef Fidelman, who knew how close I had been to Löli for so many years and how much I loved him, called me and said, "Carol, I have bad news for you. Leopold Mittman is dead." He had read it in the *Musicians' Union Journal,* and he knew I would like to know. Like a flash flood, all those years of love plus two years of regret came pouring out. With the tremendous sense of loss was the inconsolable feeling of irresolution and irony. I don't know how many hours later it was that I thought to call one of his students whom I knew slightly. I was then very much pacified to learn something that I should have known, perhaps did know deep in my heart: that Löli was there at Carnegie—in spirit. Apparently he was showing my flyer as well as my *New York Times* review to his pupils with pride, according to this student's account.

. . .

And so I have chosen to chalk off the last two years of the relationship as some kind of mistake; and whenever I want to crystallize my years with Leopold Mittman, I open a beautiful book he gave me, this one leatherbound, on Impressionism, and I read the fond, handwritten inscription:

> *In the beginning a brilliant, gifted young girl—and now a lovely woman, a fine, mature artist, and a very dear friend of mine. To Carol. L. M.*

~ 26 ~

On Being Respected and Loved as a Teacher

FOR every teacher who has loved and missed a student, and for every student whose beloved teacher from years past remains an ever-present muse, a return visit with the tender assurance, "I never left you; don't you know you are always with me?" will cause tears to flow. In a *New York Times* article, Stephen Sondheim wrote about his teacher, Oscar Hammerstein, "When I hear the word 'teacher' I get teary. For me, the word 'teacher' is similar to what God and saints represent to religious people."

Not many of us routinely receive that kind of affection or respect even when we spend inordinate energy and love. Most students vaporize and disappear after leaving our studios, with only a fraction staying in touch. It is certainly the exceptional student, at any level, who is verbally expressive and grateful. When my husband recently retired from a long career in education, he was given a large and heart-warming retirement party. Teachers and administrators who work in large institutions get summers off, pensions, and gala send-offs, none of which is enjoyed by those of us who teach privately. Our rewards must be in the less tangible elements of the act itself, and only rarely in the future fruits of our labors.

Some of my most satisfying moments are the continuing contacts with a few exceptional former students who have gone on to carve paths for themselves, not necessarily in music. Sometimes at a final lesson I jokingly enact a ritualistic raising-of-the-right-hand and extracting of a promise to keep in touch. Even so, whether from laziness, shyness, or the basic exigencies of life, many a talented student has vanished into thin air, and no explanation can take that hurt away.

. . .

As part of an ongoing project to simplify my life and overhaul my work space, I have reread hundreds of old letters, saving some and discarding others. I found one batch from a student who went to Harvard after coercing me to teach him Bach Preludes and Fugues from *The Well-Tempered Clavier,* almost to the exclusion of all else during his high school years. I managed to sneak in some Beethoven and Brahms, and his voracious appetite along with a keen intellect were unforgettable. His letters from college were a touching and intense chronicle of high and low times with occasional avowals that I had been "one of the best friends he had ever had." He went on to Harvard Medical School, and after a while the letters ended abruptly. My curiosity was piqued and I had an impulse to reestablish a connection; after a series of frustrating calls, Harvard offered to contact him for me in California. One day my phone rang and it was Robert. We spoke for over an hour; he remembered and recognized what I had given with all my heart. In spite of his success in medicine, he told me that his creative fulfillment in life still comes from music. When he visited this past summer with a lovely wife and daughter, I should not have been surprised that this beautiful eight-year-old played a Bach Invention for me, extremely well.

. . .

I taught another young man after he majored in music at college and could not decide between careers in medicine and music. He fence-straddled for many years, continuing to study seriously in both fields, all the while asking my advice as to whether he could "make it" in music. He had considerable gifts, but I never touch that question with a ten-foot pole. I firmly believe that a strong personal commitment and conviction, independent of anyone else's opinion, is an essential sign, and so many other factors come into play that I should not deal in predictions. (I also do not believe it is necessarily the happiest profession, even in the best of circumstances.) We continued to have an excellent working relationship and friendship until one day when he called to ask whether I would "put in a good word for him" with a famous performing artist who was coming to town, whom I knew personally. He wanted to play for this concert pianist, and he became fixated with the notion that I would, and should, arrange it.

It is true that over the many years I have conducted interviews for *Clavier* and other publications, I have come to know many famous artists. But as I tried to explain to this young man, I have never exploited those associations for my own, or anyone else's benefit. My student became positively furious, accusing me of a lack of loyalty and concern, and that was that: I never heard from him again.

. . .

During the eighteen years since I taught the Stevenson brothers, their parents have become our close friends; yet I have had only rare chances to talk to the sons at length. Each brother has redirected his artistic talent. Glenn has earned a graduate degree in psychology but has also produced a rock CD that, even to my subjective ears, exhibits traces of the gifts I recognized and encouraged years earlier. Dave got a degree in fine arts and is a talented, struggling sculptor whose monumentally scaled works dance to the music that will always be in him.

. . .

The return of Howard to my life during recent years has been the deepest pleasure. I have mentioned his late father, Wally Schreiber, my piano doctor. When Wally died, his gifted and already accomplished son began to study with me. We were only occasionally in touch during his college and law school years, but there was always an abiding affection between us. He often showed up at my concerts and said he kept up-to-date by reading my "Carillon" columns. Now, thank goodness, although he and his partner, Robert, both writers, live in Los Angeles and New York, he is like a member of the family. Whenever he is in town, we set aside time to work together, most recently on *Jeux d'eau* by Ravel and Beethoven's Piano Concerto No. 4 in G major. He is a wonderful pianist and true artist, a soulmate.

During a visit we had the luxury of time to listen to some old tapes of my performances, and I discovered that the now-historic tape of my Brahms First Piano Concerto performance, recorded when I was nineteen, had all but decayed, gone forever, at least on the cassette recording. Then we listened to my Schumann Piano Concerto performance that still pleases me. I had only shared that tape with a handful of close friends, but Howard's enthusiastic and sensitive response gratified and moved me. A few days later he called to tell me he was going to have several of my past performances preserved on compact discs: the Schumann concerto, the Schumann *Symphonic Etudes* along with the rest of my Carnegie Recital Hall debut, and the Brahms concerto (rescued from the original reels), lest they, too, deteriorate. No institutional benefits can be measured against the magnanimity of that loving gesture.

. . .

Those of us who have been lucky to study with patriarchal or matriarchal figures, vestiges of the old world who were refugees from oppressive European regimes, entered a realm in every way dissimilar and unrelated to home life, school, and the rest of society. I have written of my years with Mittman, and I also would pay homage to the late, great pedagogue Josef Fidelman, a Russian émigré in the 1920s who brought with him not only his Old World ways but also his wonderful heritage as a student of Heinrich Neuhaus.

. . .

No one can underestimate the importance of the earliest lessons. After teaching me the rudiments at home until I was five, my mother took me to Miss Esther R. Bernstein (whom we glimpsed briefly in Chapter 8). Miss Bernstein, a serious and attractive woman who had studied at the New York College of Music, lived near us in Brooklyn. I recall that her fee was $5, and I became a happy member of her thriving studio for about three years. I remember my first ensemble experiences on her two fine grand pianos, and the first thrills of blending my part with another's to produce a greater whole. I remember her neat white silk blouses, her warm weekly welcomes, her dogs Whimpy and Terry, and the moment she spoke to my mother about my continuing my studies with her teacher, Harold Henry. This was a supremely generous gesture and further proof of her selfless and serious concern for my education. Only when I was an adult and read his name in Harold Schonberg's book, *The Great Pianists,* did I realize that he was so highly regarded. As a child, all I could think of was my carsick subway ride to Manhattan, Mr. Henry's scary glass eye, and his big watchdogs. I missed Miss Bernstein, so after one year, I returned to her studio for another year. Her recitals were my first "public" performances, including the bizarre little ritual of facing me away from the piano and demonstrating to the audience how I could identify notes and chords by ear. She was so loving that she even bought me a special recital dress one year. Esther Bernstein's enthusiastic voice is as vigorous and warm as ever; I am sure it is her love of music and her students that has kept her young well into her nineties. One can only hope to be held in as much affection as I feel for her, but I doubt I will wait that long to retire.

~ 27 ~

One Door Closes and Another Opens

WHATEVER my talents and aptitudes may be, the business side of teaching is definitely not one of them, but my many years in the profession have taught me to survive all sorts of situations and even to challenge myself to see whether I am improving in that department. The answer is still "not very much"—I know what I ought to do, but I don't always do it. An amazing thing about teaching piano in one's own studio is the mercurial, unpredictable nature of the business.

Just recently a relatively new student, a highly musical adolescent girl with a rare intellectual curiosity, thrilled me when I asked her what piece she wanted to begin with at her lesson. "Oh I don't care; I love all the music I'm working on!" That kind of thing is music to a teacher's ears, and for several months, she bounded in, fully prepared and dripping with enthusiasm. Yet I almost lost that student when she suddenly began to feel that I was "too serious a teacher," and her mother told me she was "scared" to tell me she had trouble with her Bach. To re-engage this student's enthusiasm came as another one of many challenges. Yes, I take my teaching seriously, but I have been confident that my students view me as good-natured and harmless; I even consider myself too lenient. Occasionally, I have been known to cackle with mock ferociousness to a student waiting for a lesson, "Next victim!" But I trust that my playful antics are not misconstrued, and that my students do not find me scary.

Nevertheless, this type of occurrence prompts deep self-questioning. I have never raised my voice nor used sarcasm, and the few times I have sensed that my gentle chiding has brought a supersensitive student to the brink of lip-quivering and tears, I have backed off. For some children, the mere question "Did you practice this?" is devastating. No doubt my students sense my serious intent, my expectations that they fulfill their own potential, and my disappointment when they don't. Perhaps for them "serious" equals "scary."

One very musical student, Bénédicte, has a delicate ego, and it took me quite a while to establish a thoroughly unthreatening presence to her instead of what she (especially as my youngest student) probably perceived as my serious persona. At twelve, *she* is serious about every one of her many pursuits. She puts the highest expectations on herself and can hardly cope with her own disappointment if her results fall short of our goals. She is a lovely-looking child with impeccable manners and elegant ways, respectful, responsive, and punctilious about her preparation.

For our first two years together, I was struck by the solemness of her demeanor. I wanted more than anything to lighten things up and I practically stood on my head to get her to laugh. One day I went to see her perform in the starring role of Clara in *The Nutcracker* ballet. I was astonished by her ego and confidence, the great joy that was written all over her face, and the security of her every gesture. She seemed like two different girls. At our next lesson, after telling her how much I loved her performance, we had a long talk about the development of ego in her piano-playing and about expressing the same kind of joy that I saw in her dancing, provided she felt it. She assured me that she loved her lessons and the piano, and felt no stress at all associated with coming; I told her that was good news, but I hadn't been able to discern that from her behavior. We hugged, and it was a moment that clearly broke the spell of formality that had imbued our meetings until then. Ever since, her inherent sweetness and the pleasure she takes in music have been a constant delight to me.

When an adult student uttered the oft-repeated lament, "Things never go as well for you as they do at home," I asked her, "Is it because I scare you?" If she had answered "yes," I would have gone straight away to a plastic surgeon; instead she replied, "No, but one wants so much to please you." So perhaps that's it. That a student would want to please a teacher is a pleasant notion, one that I remember with fondness from my own youth; and certainly I respond generously when things go well. Whatever else I might be accused of, I am never unresponsive or grudging. Still, I want my students to succeed for their own good, not mine.

I find it particularly odd to hear, from even the rare student, that I would scare anybody, because as a matter of fact I have often gotten into silly moods and have hoped that my students don't think me too frivolous. A case in point was the day one of my two grand pianos was restrung. Those of us whose pianos have undergone that surgery know that the new strings must settle for a while before any attempt is made to tune them. With three strings per key, the instrument is as far from well-tempered as it can be: absolute gobbledy-gook. In walked Seth, my first student of the afternoon, and quite a talented young fellow. I said, "O.K., Seth, play your sonatina for me." He sat at the ill-humored keyboard, played a bar, and stopped, horrified. Usually quite secure, he did something that seemed incredible to me: he examined his hands as though some gremlin had taken hold of them. (It never occurred to him that the trouble lay in the instrument.) I said, deadpan, "That's all right, Seth, you got a bad start. Try again." Seth played the same opening bar, again began to examine his hands, spied me across the room, holding my sides, and said, "Hey wait a minute!" I shared my banana-peel sense of humor with him, teaching him about the strings, and he wasn't sure he liked my joke until I promised that he would get to play it on the student after him. He had his usual good lesson on my other piano, emitting a secret chortle in anticipation of the fun he would have at the end.

Justice was indeed done when the next student was treated to my weird humor and had the same response: instant self-doubt, examination of hands, an optimistic second start, sudden realization, slight discomfiture, and finally glee at the promise of the payoff to come.

I do have a lot of fun with my students, and I am confident they enjoy my occasional forays off the deep end. For example, one of my editions of the Chopin Nocturnes is *Editio Musica Budapest* which would have been quite expensive had it not included two nocturnes printed over one another in a kind of double exposure. I have been known to show these indecipherable pages to unwitting students saying in deadpan, "This is your next piece." For the moment of abject horror reflected on their faces, I satisfy my harmlessly mischievous whim, and then we have a good chuckle.

When an adult student attempted to play a Chopin mazurka timidly with no strong rhythmic impulse and no spirit, I cajolingly asked her how in the world she thought anyone could dance to that? I showed her a flyer from a recent tour of a Polish ballet troupe showing the dancers in brilliant costume, and I even danced her a mazurka (this was another of my wilder days). After that I said, "Come on, now. Convince me!" This time it just wasn't the same person playing. Whatever one might think of my methods, I assure you that it is possible to coax or bully the most reticent student into sounding as if she really knows what she is doing, and even loves doing it. We both had a pretty good time that day.

. . .

Nowadays I have a crop of students all of whom I thoroughly enjoy, but it wasn't so long ago that because of economic considerations, I found myself with a mixed bag, including students who were studying because their parents wanted them to, and for other less-than-glorious reasons. In those days, I might easily have lost my love of teaching had I not committed certain sins of the trade that are better expunged in a doctrine of confession: I birdwatched. After making a correction for the tenth time, I consciously decided to let the error go, shrug my shoulders, think "Hopeless," and mentally say, "Hello woodpecker. Thank you for coming to the feeder just now." I have taught only the first movement of certain sonatas; I have even left off at the end of the Exposition when things were truly bleak, and I knew that the persons who would ever hear it would not feel the lack of resolution from having left off in the dominant key. Once or twice I whitened out the couple of notes that stood in the way of ever finishing a piece. But before I commit myself to piano-teachers' prison, in my defense is the fact that they all played to the best of their ability, and they had a good time for as long as they lasted.

. . .

The mother of another gifted student called one day: "I'm sorry to tell you this, but Judy has so many school activities until she graduates from ninth grade that she won't be able to take piano lessons." Flabbergasted, I asked "You mean anymore?"

"She doesn't have the time."

"If it's a question of rescheduling—"

"No, she feels she is doing too many things."

It is usually the most gifted and versatile student who seems to be able to juggle many activities, but there it was. We exchanged polite goodbyes, and I hung up particularly upset: partly sadness, partly anger. This was a girl I taught gratis during the months her mother was out of work (even though the family drove three beautiful cars), a girl I took to concerts by young female artists, hoping that these role models might motivate her to achieve her considerable potential.

This student was invariably cheerful and well-prepared for lessons. She seemed to enjoy them, but apparently I failed to notice the conflict within her. I was hurt that all my extra effort, time, and care on her behalf were wasted. I was angry at the ingratitude and callousness of a teenager who lacks the courage or breeding to call her teacher herself to explain, no less say goodbye. I wanted to write a letter teaching her some basic manners and telling her of my disappointment; then remembering all the tardiness, last-minute cancelations, late pickups by her parents, and presumptions on my time, I realized that I had failed to see certain signs of irresponsibility and that my lecture would fall on deaf ears.

I tried to convince myself it doesn't pay to become too emotionally involved with a student. Phrases like "easy come, easy go" and "no expectations, no disappointments" flashed through my consciousness, but these are not my way. I cannot teach without trying to connect with each student as a human being, find what is unique, and help to cultivate it with all my energies. Naturally that makes me vulnerable. My husband tells me that teaching is not a profession for those who need frequent endorsement, and no doubt he is right.

. . .

By far, the most unpleasant issue of all is the question of payment. Now that I am teaching seriously committed students, I no longer run into problems of this nature, but it used to be a nightmare. Apparently it is an age-old nightmare, as in 1782, Mozart wrote to his father:

> I have three pupils now, which brings me in eighteen ducats a month; for I no longer charge for twelve lessons, but monthly. I learnt to my cost that my pupils often dropped out for weeks at a time; so now whether they learn or not, each of them must pay me six ducats. I shall get several more on these terms, but I really only need one more, because four pupils are quite enough. With four I should have twenty-four ducats, or 102 gulden, 24 kreutzer. With this

> sum a man and a wife can manage in Vienna if they live quietly and in the retired way which we desire, but of course, if I were to fall ill, we should not make a farthing. [1]

To avoid collecting payment every week and to discourage canceled lessons, I have requested that students pay for each month's lessons at the beginning of the month. For those who used to forget that the new month had arrived, I ought to have been able to ask as they sidled out the door, "Would you like to pay for the month today?" It is a simple enough question, but I could barely bring myself to do it. I used to have to deal with last-minute cancelations, make-up lessons, "June mothers" who inform the teacher that their child will be taking the last lesson on the seventh of June because of early departure for summer camp, and affluent families who expect time off for their many vacations, or who leave their offspring for free and prolonged babysitting services after the lesson ends. I solved that last dilemma with a pat explanation: I would like my next student to have the same undivided attention and privacy their child enjoyed and would appreciate their picking him up punctually.

Finally, there is the whole question of establishing one's fee. My husband shamed me into raising mine by quoting the astronomical hourly fees that high school tutors of math and languages charge, more than twice what most piano teachers charge. (The fee I paid to my computer-guru per hour also exceeded my own.) I used to think that the fee ought to be a consensus among the professionals in the community, according to what the traffic will bear, but I know of one or two good teachers in my own community who for reasons of their own continually and considerably undercharge for their services. Does that mean the others should too? We all have to make independent assessments based on what we think our time is worth and then let the public make their decisions too.

Parents and teachers consider many factors in choosing a teacher, and for a few the fee may be the most important. Teachers who undercharge may, indeed, end up with quite a full schedule, and that may feel like some form of success. I have never refused to teach a student who could not afford my fee. I have taught a few of them for less and have also given full scholarships. Some particularly generous parents have offered to pay for playing classes and recitals I present at various intervals throughout the year but for which I have never charged. Others offer to pay for extra time when I keep a student long past the normal duration of the lesson. Paradoxically, those are the ones I would gladly teach for nothing; I have to explain that it was my prerogative and pleasure and that I do not expect any remuneration for it.

In the end I really believe in honesty and openness, in being able to say to those who might put you in compromising positions, "Listen, I wish I could tell you I teach for the sheer love of it. I do love to teach, but the hard fact of life is that, alas, I also teach for economic reasons." Surely no one who heard that would ever try to exploit you again. Or would they?

~ IN THE FIELD ~

We are the music-makers
We are the dreamers of dreams.

ARTHUR WILLIAM EDGAR O'SHAUGHNESSY

28

In the Field

I DO NOT know how I became a country girl. I have felt energized by the big city from my early childhood when I braved the New York subway system from Brooklyn to Manhattan to take my piano lessons, with my mother as chaperone; and later from Forest Hills during certain teenage years by myself, I felt my step buoyed up by the lively tempo. I felt as though my head were on a swivel, lest I miss a single exciting sight; my eyes drank up the variegated colors and shapes; my ears recorded the jazzy cacophonies and beats of the city streets. Never for a moment did I worry about what evil might lurk behind some dark alleyway. The city has always been the great source for the things I loved, particularly art and music. A day at the Metropolitan Museum of Art, exploring one gallery after another, or an event at Carnegie Hall sustained me for weeks afterward. Those are still my two favorite haunts, and I still love New York City.

I was in a friend's upper west side apartment overlooking Central Park recently. There was a piano at the window, and from the balcony I could have reached out and touched the hawks that were soaring over the park. I thought, "I could work here and be nourished." At dusk, the lanterns and the twinkling lights of the beautiful buildings came on, and nothing could have been more romantic. But the truth is, our home and its wooded environment, with the red-tailed hawk that perches on a tree in our own backyard, nourishes me more. The city has become the welcomed occasional field trip.

We go in for concerts, lectures, ballets, and dinner parties; and it is in the city that I have conducted most of my interviews of performing artists who were passing through town. I always experience great expectation and excitement whenever I drive from Huntington to Manhattan, and I have never ceased to wonder at the way the multicolored city rises magically out of the grey bedrock: the UN in celadon jade, the Empire State in rose quartz, all the fool's gold and copper towers oxidizing to turquoise, the opalescent facades, and my favorite—the Chrysler building as a marcasite and sterling brooch, adorning the skyline. Over the years, each new skyscraper has added another architectonic dynamic, and sometimes even the smallest fire-escape with a pot of geraniums takes on the special aura of the city.

Gradually, however, I am shedding my cloak of cosmopolite and becoming a townie, basking in the pride of Huntington's rich cultural life, which includes the same circuit of concerts that hit the big city three days later, great restaurants, and the lovely balance between good hard work and a stroll on the shore.

. . .

During my twenty-some years of interviewing artists, I have never experienced the kind of anxiety associated with performance. As I am a compulsively on-time person, I often find myself sitting in hotel or apartment-house lobbies, killing a half-hour before the agreed time of the appointment. It gives me time to reflect—and not necessarily on the interview to follow. More musicians per square foot live on the upper west side of Manhattan than perhaps anywhere else in the world. While checking my apparatus—tape recorder, batteries, notes—I enjoy watching the city folks stream in and out of elevators. I am always punctilious about my preparation and have become increasingly comfortable in any situation. Probably this ease is related to the development of my confidence both as a pianist and as one who can discuss music, even though I know that most musicians distrust and abhor describing their art in words.

As the painter Edward Hopper said, "If I could say it in words, I wouldn't have to paint." And Felix Mendelssohn:

> People often complain that music is too ambiguous—that what they should think when they hear it is so unclear, whereas everyone understands words. With me it is exactly the reverse: the thoughts which are expressed to me by music that I love are not too indefinite to be put into words but, on the contrary, too definite.[1]

Yet we persist, and a skillfully posed and provocative question will prod and engage the subject in spite of himself. The ego implied in being an artist involves some vanity, and once the ice is broken, I find that most artists, initial protestations notwithstanding, take pleasure in describing their work process.

. . .

I remember how easy it was to get my first interview. I literally bumped into André Watts at a PDQ Bach program given by Peter Schickele at Carnegie Hall about twenty years ago. There he was, one of my heroes, several feet from me in the lobby, and I seemed to have stepped outside myself, with no preparation or plan, to approach him. I simply greeted him, told him how much I had enjoyed his concerts over the years, mentioned that I was a pianist, and asked him whether there was a chance he might agree to being interviewed. At that time I had written only a couple of freelance pieces and had never conducted a single interview.

With his characteristically easygoing and affable smile, he immediately said, "Sure! I'll give you my phone number, and we can set something up." Not his manager's number, his home phone. A week or so later, we met in an upscale ice-cream parlor on Central Park

South, which turned out to be too crowded, so we walked over to a hotel and set ourselves up in the lounge. In the space of that half-block walk, we were already engaged in a lively conversation about the two Brahms concertos; he was to perform No. 2 that week, and I had performed No. 1. Watts is probably the most open, unaffected, and engaging personality in the business, and for that reason the conversation that ensued was rapid-fire, rambling, enthusiastic, and thoroughly enjoyable. I came away feeling that a friendship had been established, and ever since, through several formal interviews and informal meals and meetings, he has been a friend.

But I was in for a shock when I got home from that first interview. In listening to the tape, I was embarrassed and mortified at the extent to which I had participated in the conversation. Watts had stated up front that he did not want me to fire one-liners at him but preferred a discussion, and it seemed I needed no encouragement! There is as much of my voice on the tape as his, and my only consolation was that no one else would ever hear my uncensored, ebullient participation. So I went about the business of extracting all the rich material of his remarks and the substance of the interview, and thankfully what emerged was an exciting article that was forthwith accepted by *The New York Times*.

My next interview was with Vladimir Ashkenazy for *The Piano Quarterly*. I imposed all sorts of restrictions and resolutions to limit myself to concisely posed questions, and then to back off and let the subject speak. Ashkenazy is very different from Watts. He has an extremely serious visage, searches for *le mot juste* for as long as it may take, putting up his hand to disallow any suggestions; and, of course, English is not his native tongue. The resulting tape was just about as boring and dry as the first was supercharged and dynamic. I think that I crafted an interesting enough article, but I realized something central to the process, which would guide me from then on in all my interviews: that my own enthusiasm and involvement in music were a vital catalyst and infectious stimulant to the conversation. Henceforth I would not prevent myself from participating or even expressing animated thoughts as they occurred; nor would I go on in the unbridled way I started out.

I learned to let the conversation shape the writing, and I have found that the resulting piece has the natural flow of the original discourse. I prepare a long list of questions after reading all existing press materials, and if I have studied sufficiently, I can weave in whatever ideas I have brought with me. I never go in with a preconceived order of topics, and often the conversation takes an unexpected turn that might be more fascinating than anything I could have prepared or imagined beforehand.

. . .

Not all interviews are as easy to come by, and not all artists are as engaging, accessible, and generous as Watts. For example, I would have loved to interview Martha Argerich, whose talent I greatly admire. In spite of her reputation for granting no interviews, I entertained the frivolous notion that if we ever made even the slightest eye contact or casual verbal exchange (as I had been able to do with certain other more-than-reticent artists), she might agree to it. But neither a letter via her personal representative nor several attempts to greet and congratulate her after concerts led anywhere. One comes to the realization that some pianists *really mean* NO interviews and either greatly fear or disdain the press and public. I am not at all unsympathetic to their choices; in fact, I think it must take a superior resolve and strength to stick to their decision. Goodness knows it's a difficult life; I am a harmless and sympathetic journalist (and pianist), so I appreciate the fact that for whatever reasons, a self-protecting mechanism is an essential element for those in public life.

One artist who has routinely refused personal interviews is Maurizio Pollini. I made several attempts to meet him, both in New York and in Milan where he lives, but to no avail. When I received an invitation to be part of a small caucus of journalists gathered to meet the artist at Carnegie Hall, I jumped at the chance. The meeting was interesting but less than ideal for preparing an article. Mr. Pollini read some prepared notes on the subject of the Beethoven sonata series that he was presenting concurrently in New York at Carnegie, followed by other major cities. Then he allowed about a half-hour for questions from the assemblage. I managed to ask several but the mixture of unrelated questions, his struggle with the language, and the ban against tape recorders all presented stumbling blocks for creating a cohesive piece of journalism. It wasn't until after the question-and-answer period that I had an opportunity to speak to him informally, at which point he was thoroughly gregarious and relaxed.

• • •

Radu Lupu is a musician for whom I have the highest degree of respect. He most definitely is among those pianists who are not only reticent, but wary of the poverty of words to describe something as transcendental as music and who therefore patently resist making finite remarks which may be misquoted or misunderstood. By 1981 when I wanted so much to interview him, the Romanian pianist had managed to resist publicity and keep his name and his superb artistry unfamiliar on this side of the Atlantic despite annual tours here and major international prizes. With characteristic shyness and resolute avoidance of media and promotion, Lupu would come and slip away quietly, content to leave whatever trace his audiences carried off from direct contact with his music. "Radu who?" was the reply I usually received when I mentioned my desire to meet him, a phenomenon that was difficult to correlate with my experience of his top-grade artistry. (Even now, the general public is surprisingly unfamiliar with his name.)

Determined as I was, I wrote him a letter stating that I was a serious pianist who had some journalistic experience and that I understood and respected his decision to refuse all interviews but if he would agree to allow me to interview him, I promised to stick with musical issues, to stay away from the mundane, and to show him the resulting article for his approval and emendations before sending it on to be published. I put the letter in an envelope, went to hear him at Carnegie Hall, and stood in line to greet him afterward in the green room. When it was my turn, I congratulated him for his wonderful concert and asked him if I might give him a letter that he could read later on, if he would. He answered cordially, "Certainly," and put the letter into his tux pocket. I went home with visions of it going to the cleaners the next day, unread.

The next morning the phone rang, and a deep voice with a decidedly Romanian accent said simply, "O.K.!" And that is how I met Radu Lupu, who later explained to me, "I am not a world conqueror, and I do not have to sell records on the moon. If I had to conduct my career according to what managers advise me is the best idea to stimulate publicity and increase audiences, I would go crazy. I would rather have 300 come to hear the music, than 3000 who come to hear some sort of a stage personality and have to be seduced by publicity to come."[2] These high ideals, along with a certain impatience with the increasing distractions of disrespectful and unruly audiences, have helped to create rumors that Lupu is a complex and difficult personality. In fact he is a disarmingly amenable, warm, and funny man, brutally honest about his own technical problems, and generous. In spite of his continuing resistance to the media, he has allowed me to reinterview him several times, "because I trust you," a distinction about which I am particularly proud.

Alfred Brendel, a pianist whom I very much respect, is open and accessible backstage after concerts. Few artists enjoy the rapt, loyal, almost cultlike devotion that is typical of Brendel's audiences. He is an intellectual in the finest sense, insisting that "Most people want to believe in myths; they want to believe. I want to know." He gets right to the essence of the work in a no-nonsense approach characterized by great clarity, wit, and a tremendously vital and propulsive rhythmic drive that infectiously catches the listener up into the momentum of the work. His probing and active mind expands way beyond the piano into literature, art, and writing, and he has described his routine as a kind of commute between his library and his music room.

At the time of my interview,[3] Brendel had what seemed to be a virtual militia of personal representatives shielding him from the public. It was like moving heaven and earth to gain permission to do an interview; and I might add that I never had to deal with a more difficult personality than his former manager. I am quite certain that Mr. Brendel was never aware of the tactics taken by that office on his behalf, and I would venture that he would not have been happy to know it. Once engaged in the interview, he was witty, candid, and very interesting, and exhibited an impish, playful side, in relief to the scholarly discussions. During the conversation, the red foam-rubber ball that slides over the microphone dropped onto the floor. In one spontaneous, almost bizarrely funny gesture, Brendel swooped it up and placed it on his nose, explaining, "I have a strange attraction to clowns." A rather incongruous image, this music-philosopher wearing a clown nose, but he has kept the child in himself alive, and the good humor is often audible in his performances.

I have been fortunate to confine my interviews to artists whom I respect and admire and about whom I am genuinely curious. For a brief stint I was hired by a PR company to write awestruck-sounding profiles of performing artists for their files. That didn't last more than a few days. Press kits by the dozens are sent to my address because of my associations with a music magazine; most end up in the trash, not because the subjects are in any way unworthy (I believe that every artist has something unique to say and every right to be heard) but simply because I have had to make compromises in order to pursue each facet of my work. I have had to limit and forego many exciting opportunities.

The best thing about the interviews I have been fortunate to do are the friendships that have evolved. Also of great personal value to me are the shared insights I can apply directly to my own playing or teaching; with a curiously converse stroke, these two occupations have helped me become a somewhat credible journalist.

~ 29 ~

That Infernal Little Machine

IN AN age when scientists can walk in space and create clones, it is difficult to understand why they cannot invent runproof stockings and more substantial tape recorders. (Perhaps they can but choose not to for commercial reasons.) In the past twenty years I have bought at least ten new machines for one reason or another, each conspiring to subvert an interview. I have had interviewing experiences ranging between panic and disaster which have transformed me into a paranoid maniac, constantly checking my apparatus with bulging, crossed eyes to insure that everything is still functioning. The awesome responsibility one feels to an artist who has set aside a good piece of time, whether willingly or reticently, is magnified considerably by the threat of losing the precious words that can never be adequately paraphrased. I always feel a great weight of accountability when I do an interview; invariably the person has parted the Red Sea of his or her schedule to accommodate me; most are leery of the press, but their managements urge them to go ahead for promotional reasons. I truly want to represent their ideas as clearly and accurately as I can, and the tape recorder is an essential tool.

Whether it be an ill-functioning machine or other electronic catastrophes, I doubt there is anything I haven't yet experienced. I won't recount all the little disasters, but a few may be good for a chuckle or two. Interviews conducted in the artist's studio or home are unquestionably the most enjoyable because of the added perspective suggested by the workspace and environment. Most often, though, the interview is conducted in a hotel room or restaurant, with no local color at all.

Only once did I agree to do a telephone interview, and that was with Krystian Zimerman, the pianist to whom Arthur Rubinstein willed the gold button he always wore in his lapel at performances throughout his long career. Because of last-minute travel changes, Zimerman had to leave town one day early, making a phone interview the only possibility. I ran out to purchase the device used to tape phone conversations and tried it out with a friend before trusting my interview to the electronic age. In rereading that interview, I am amazed at the natural flow of the conversation; it is also amusing to read Zimerman's remarks about his discontent with the recording process and his dependence on the audience almost as a drug to elicit a kind of dialogue between himself and his listeners. Little did he ever know the problems I had with my recording process during his interview that day.[1]

When we finished our conversation, I hung up the telephone, disengaging the little earphone device, rewound the tape in order to listen to an interview that I considered to have been extremely successful even though it had not been conducted in person. Zimerman's sincerity and warmth were transmitted telephonically, and I wanted to start transcribing the tape at once in order to write the article. Instead, what I heard was a high pitched, mile-a-minute Minnie Mouse voice, much too fast to decipher a single word. I quickly discovered that this was the sad result across the entire tape; and when you depend on a tape to record an event and you see that it is turning around with the red recording light on, you don't take backup notes. There is virtually no way to reconstruct a richly animated discussion and so I prepared to throw myself into Long Island Sound and thank the Lord for the good years leading up to that moment. Before I went down the street to the water, however, it occurred to me to call a friend who is a sound engineer for CBS-TV, Larry Schneider. Larry calmly explained that it sounded as though the recording speed had gone out of whack, and that he thought he might be able to salvage a good part of the tape on his sophisticated equipment, which he kindly did and which is why I have survived to tell the tale.

• • •

During one of three interviews I did with Vladimir Ashkenazy, he had his baby boy on his lap in the New York hotel room. For the first few minutes of the tape, I have the pianist's voice saying to his son, "Say 'Papa,' Sasha, say 'Pa-pa,'" and for the next ten minutes, I basically have scratching noises rendered by his cute little toddler clutching the mike. I had tried, ever so delicately, to disengage the tiny fingers, entwined quite resolutely in a kind of prehensile grip, but the father kept firmly assuring me, "I am sure he will not damage your machine." Whatever conversation took place in those long moments until the maid came in to take the child away, the world will never know.

• • •

When I interviewed the painter Robert Dash in his eastern Long Island farmhouse, I was charmed by the old colonial structures that he had managed to bring together into a kind of compound of living and working space. His wonderful gardens and mellow eighteenth-century frame houses blended into one of the most picturesque and enviable settings I had ever experienced, except for one tragic flaw. During the course of the interview I chanced to peer into the display window that reveals the revolving tape, only to see it all at a standstill. I put up my hand to stop the conversation, as lively a one as I have ever had, and to inform the unhappy artist that I had heretofore captured none of our talk on tape. He was exasperated and barely civil, and I was flustered and beside myself with mortification. What saved the situation for me was the discovery that Dash, himself, had plugged my recorder into a dead socket in his old barn wall, and the unfortunate situation was neither my fault nor my much-maligned little machine's. My husband was also present at that interview, and all the way home we tried to reconstruct the portions of conversation that had been gobbled up. Fortunately, Dash had also tried to reiterate some of his comments, and as he is such a natural and colorful raconteur, I had enough material for several articles.

. . .

In order to avoid ever being plugged into another dead socket, we went out and bought a superdeluxe machine that came with its own rechargeable battery and a guarantee of lifelong energy. All night long, before my interview with the late, great Shura Cherkassky, my new recorder's battery was being charged according to its instructions. I drove the thirty-odd miles into Manhattan and arrived with plenty of time to spare before what was promised to be a luncheon meeting with the artist at the posh Pierre Hotel. Imagine my chagrin when, in the hotel lobby, I pushed the power button on the machine to record "Testing, one, two, three,—," and nothing happened. Panic, opus 347A. I had blithely and confidently left the electrical connections at home, and I had to find another apparatus, pronto. I called Cherkassky's management agency to ask whether they could run me over a tape recorder from their office, but they had none. I asked the concierge of the hotel whether they had a tape-recorder, and they did. It, too, was out of order, which did not come as a surprise to me. I ran around the corner to a drugstore to buy disposable batteries, in case the problem was the superdeluxe rechargeable battery and not the machine itself. Mercifully, once I popped them in, the recorder worked perfectly. With what little remaining energy I had in me, I phoned up Mr. Cherkassky from the lobby to let him know I had arrived and to ask him if I could come up to his room. That conversation and the ensuing encounter were truly the pay-off, and the stuff that never gets into the article-proper.

"Hello, Mr. Cherkassky. This is Carol Montparker. May I come up?"

"Who???"

"Carol Montparker from *Clavier* magazine. We have an appointment for an interview.[2] Are you available now?"

"Impossible. I have a flight to catch. I cannot do any interview."

"Mr. Cherkassky, I made the appointment over a month ago and have reconfirmed it with your management several times. They assured me that you had agreed to do this interview."

"But I have a limousine coming soon to take me to the airport!" he moaned.

"Mr. Cherkassky, I just drove for over an hour to have this opportunity. Even if you have only a short piece of time, I would greatly appreciate it."

"Well, can you come up now?"

"Yes, of course. I'll be right up."

I entered a room that had the remnants of a most elegant brunch spread out on a table in the living room. Visions of my elegant luncheon floated out the window, as he asked whether I would rather do the interview sitting on his unmade bed in the adjoining room that also contained an upright piano, or at the brunch table. I selected the table, and we set right to the business of the interview. We must have been talking for at least a half-hour when a bus-boy came in to clear the table of the used dishes, along with some perfectly beautiful untouched croissants and jams that I most probably had subliminally eyed during the course of our conversation. I think I emitted a sigh or uttered a gasp as the waiter pulled the delicious treats away, and with great charm, Mr. Cherkassky, in his gnome-like

Russian inflected voice, asked me, "Oh, are you hungry, dahlink?" Then with surprising paternal indulgence, he began to prepare me a roll with preserves on it, and to feed me his leftovers, which I was only too glad to accept with relish in my famished state.

Cherkassky was the oldest remaining exponent of a genre of playing referred to as nineteenth-century Russian romanticism. Aside from his brilliant virtuosity, his playing had great lyricism and breadth, and he eschewed any labels, explaining that he played "the way he wanted to." What resulted was an eccentric and spontaneous style that had considerable charm and appeared to be almost effortless. The rhapsodic, fantastic quality of his playing, his delight in producing wonderful sonorities and devilish feats, and the way he flitted around like a sprite were all refreshingly different from any other artist I had ever encountered, either on stage or off. In many ways he was an entertainer, amusing and good-natured. When I reminded him of the plane he had to catch he said, "No, no, no. You make me feel so comfortable. Ask me another ten questions!" I didn't ask him any more, but I'll remember him more for his generosity than for any preliminary difficulties in getting started. He sent me a copy of Morton Gould's *Boogie-Woogie Etude* which he had played as an encore and which I had mentioned I had been unsuccessful in locating.

. . .

Another glitch worth mentioning, one that stood between me and a most significant interview, was not electronic but viral. I had met Arthur Rubinstein on several occasions, but when he finally agreed to do a formal interview, it had to be canceled because the great artist contracted shingles, a serious and unpleasant illness that affects the central nervous system and which ended up destroying a good part of his vision. On many occasions I had conducted interviews feeling quite ill myself rather than risking rescheduling and then possibly losing the opportunity altogether.

. . .

On one occasion many years ago, I drove up to Connecticut to interview Victor Borge, the hilariously funny comedian who is also, incidentally, a very fine pianist. He greeted me at the door of his mansion situated on the shores of Long Island Sound, wearing a tuxedo jacket over dungarees, and I thought to myself, "Well, I am about to have a very good time."

As it developed, about fifteen minutes into the interview, the phone rang just as I was posing a two-part question: "Do you ever play for your own amusement at home, and if so, what kind of music do you enjoy?" Mr. Borge, obviously flustered as his secretary had just entered the room to ask him about the phone call, suddenly became upset, first shouting at his secretary that he had interrupted an interview, then turning on me with, "And you! learn how to do an interview, young lady. Ask one question and let me answer, not many questions all at once!"

My heart was racing—I think my reaction was part anger, part affront. A pitiable little voice inside me responded, "I'm sorry. You must be very tired, Mr. Borge. You had a show on Broadway late last night, and perhaps you would prefer to do this some other time. I could always go home and practice."

With that, his voice took on a new, kinder tone, and he asked, "Are you a pianist? Play something for me."

I sat down at his Bösendorfer and played the Praeludium from the Bach Partita No. 1 in B-flat, after which he said, "Well why didn't you say so? You're an artist."

The interview proceeded with respect on both sides, and after we said goodbye, I drove away from his house. But as soon as I could, I parked my car and rewound the tape until it came to the big blowup scene; at that point I pulled a Rosemary Wood antic: I erased his shouting because I never wanted to hear it again. Now what I have on tape is the sound of a phone ringing, a gap of silence, and then my timid voice asking him whether he wanted to end the interview, followed by the Bach.

Of course to this day I regret having lost that footage for all its local color. I could handle it well now, but I was younger then, and that sense of failure was too upsetting. With every incident over these many years, I became more inured and experienced, and now I enjoy the challenges and welcome any intriguing, unexpected turns my interviews may take.

~ 30 ~

The Most Jazzy Encounters

FOR many years I have listened to jazz with great pleasure, ruing the fact that the twain (classical and jazz) would never meet on my piano. As a square, classically trained musician, I would only look from the outside in, wishing I could "do it." In reality few musicians have bridged the gap and are able to play successfully in both modes. Friedrich Gulda and Keith Jarrett come immediately to mind, but they would be the first to aver that the separations between the two genres are nebulous and that the struggles and problems each type of pianist faces are the same: the approach to phrasing, concentration, response to criticism, gestures, unconscious mannerisms, back and neck problems, tendonitis, annoyance regarding unruly audiences, grappling with strange pianos, and the quest for artistic freedom. But to a pianist like me, it is the seemingly loose and flexible way the jazz pianist's fingers respond to the brain's split-second, spontaneous, improvisatory whims that represents the greatest distinction between the two styles.

I once heard a remarkable concerto performance with a cadenza that set me to wondering what has happened to the art of improvisation in classical music. Mozart and Beethoven, who were both wonderful improvisers, might have been partially responsible for the decline of the art lost to most players today: in lieu of trusting soloists to improvise original cadenzas to their great concertos, they provided written ones, and who could have conceived of better cadenzas than they?

Nigel Kennedy's recording of the Beethoven Violin Concerto includes a cadenza that begins conventionally enough, then takes off to never-never land with a free flight of his fancy. The often dissonant result may have little to do with Beethoven but everything to do with Kennedy's impulses of the moment in response to Beethoven. I surprised myself by loving it and reveling in his freedom and originality. Such phenomena are all too rare.

It seems to me that Kennedy is a true modern artist who can play the traditional literature as beautifully and faithfully as anybody, but he has managed to bridge the past and present with grace. The Beethoven concerto performance marked his voluntary retirement from performing conventional concerts, and his unusual cadenza was his parting gesture.

I know several classical musicians, including my daughter, Kim Parker, who came to a moment in their lives when the standard repertoire ceased to challenge their intellect, flex their freedom, and offer sufficient stimulus to their curiosity. They play jazz or new music now, and goodness knows, our contemporary composers need them.

To my surprise, the jazz musicians whom I have interviewed expressed similar desires and frustrations about "the other side," wishing that they were able to execute and interpret the great classical literature. However, it always seems to me that jazz must be even more demanding than the re-creative art of the classical musician. The jazz artist's mind must be thinking and planning every moment to keep the music within the structure; the hand must be well-trained in the idiom to be able to draw from a kind of wardrobe of jazz patterns, scales, and arpeggios that suit the music; possibly most important, the pianist must be sufficiently free, emotionally, to trust and follow through on impulses.

. . .

George Shearing, one of the great jazz pianists, keeps one foot in the classical world by freely adapting elements from all periods of music into his jazz technique. Shearing may treat "Taking a Chance on Love" as the Brahms Intermezzo in E, Opus 116, No. 6; "Should I?" à la Poulenc; or "No Two People Have Ever Been So In Love" in the manner of a Bach fugue, all with impressive success. He listens extensively to classical music and gets concerto engagements with symphony orchestras. The fact that he is blind has not seemed to hamper him one bit. He can read Braille music but says that doing so is a much more laborious task than learning a new work by ear from a tape. His ear is so sharp that he can reproduce a ten-note chord on the spot and has learned complex contrapuntal works of Bach in that manner. The ease with which he glides around his apartment on the upper east side of Manhattan, slides his finger along a formidable wall of recordings and stops strategically at the very one he seeks is so impressive that I asked him whether he has been blind all his life. His answer characterizes his quick wit: "Not yet!"[1]

When I asked him whether a classically trained pianist like me could learn to play jazz, his answer may have oversimplified the matter: "It depends whether you read the eighth-notes in a piece of jazz as 'doo'n dee' as though you could hear a horn playing with all the articulation, instead of a bunch of square-sounding 'tah-tah-tahs.' It also depends on how readily you can pick up another conception; whether you have the ability to transfer or transport an idea from some other source, and then adapt it in your own way."

George Shearing enjoyed himself the most after the interview-proper. We sat down at his two pianos and I accompanied his playing of all three movements of Bach's Clavier Concerto in D minor, which he had committed to memory impeccably. Subsequently, he invited me back for similar stints of Mozart on two-pianos.

. . .

My husband and I visited the incomparable and highly original jazz musician Dave Brubeck at his Connecticut estate. Brubeck is philosophical, articulate, direct, and hospitable. Since his heyday when he produced "Take Five" in 5/4 time and "Blue Rondo à la Turk" in 9/8, his career in jazz has gone outside the standard jazz idiom, toward twentieth-century so-called classical music. His teacher Darius Milhaud encouraged him to travel and collect influences wherever he could, and he has, indeed, incorporated everything from African to Brazilian, challenging the traditions that exist in jazz as they do in the classical world. He regrets the long time that jazz artists have waited to be fully recognized as American composers, and he considers Duke Ellington, George Gershwin, Leonard Bernstein, Aaron Copland, and Charles Ives, all composers who use the jazz idiom, to be the best this country has come up with. In our interview he described his early music education at Mills College in California:

> Milhaud was a stickler on Bach and Mendelssohn, and we had to study fugues and follow all the rules. When we started to write, though, Milhaud gave us complete freedom. Schoenberg was as different from Milhaud as he could be. He imposed complete discipline on his students and their compositions. Schoenberg and I barely got along, and I worked with him very little. . . . He wanted a reason for every note, whereas Milhaud felt there should never be a system for composition, that it should not be done with a slide rule, but should come from the deepest part of your mind. . . . We have our Tatums and our Shearings who can do almost everything, but there's no way to teach a composer except to open his mind to many areas and disciplines.[2]

Brubeck particularly loves the quote from Stravinsky's *The Poetics of Music*: "Composition is selective improvisation."

. . .

My interview with Dick Hyman was one of the liveliest and most enjoyable meetings I have ever had. At the time, Hyman lived on 42nd Street in Manhattan, an address altogether fitting for someone whose lifestyle, pace, and work so perfectly fit the show-business capital of the world. His studio, with its two grand pianos, console organ, albums, tapes, photos, and posters from his illustrious career, is as vast as his territory in music. Since the fifties, he has counted among his many successes club dates, jazz festivals, concert appearances, radio, television, and movies, and the scores for most of Woody Allen's movies. He considers his "commercial work" as enjoyable as everything else, but jazz has been the closest to his heart. "It happens as you do it, and it's all up to you. Jazz lives at the moment, with no pre-planning and no regrets if it doesn't work. Being a jazz artist is like being an acrobat. There are risks in music, mostly to your pride, and the tensions of composing on the spot."[3]

I think that with the issue of risks he put his finger on the difference between jazz pianists and classical pianists, except that here our views diverged. To me a classical pianist's risks seem comparatively negligible; except for spontaneous bursts of inspiration, a rubato here, a flashier-than-usual octave passage there, the notes are memorized or planned, and the margin of individuality is rather contained within the confines of validity. On stage Hyman sits down and with assurance laces into a stride bass or a jazzy right-hand riff with complex configurations that would rival some Chopin etudes in difficulty. Hyman discharges these with no apparent tension. He says, "I don't get nervous at all if I can improvise to some degree. It is only when I have to play someone else's music note-for-note that I get tense."

At that point in the interview he asked me to play something, and I rattled off two Chopin etudes which happened to be under my fingers. Hyman insisted he'd give anything to be able to play "other people's music" in that way, but to hear his high-energy jazz performances is to want to make a bargain with the devil and trade off all one's years of training in order to be able to improvise in that manner. Dick Hyman studied piano with his uncle, Anton Rovinsky, who had studied with Artur Schnabel in the early 1920s, but there was never any doubt as to the direction his playing would take. He admits to an indebtedness to the classical literature, particularly Chopin, and a quirky big book called *Thesaurus of Scales and Melodic Patterns* by the late Nicolas Slonimsky, which consists of every conceivable permutation and combination of notes arranged into patterns. From these sources Hyman draws lush chromaticisms and complex designs, and guided by his whims, he incorporates them, along with his sophisticated harmonies, into his jazz solos—as much a feat of mental as physical gymnastics.

Hyman's lecture-concerts at the 92nd Street Y in New York are thoroughly delightful, energizing, and amazing. Presenting marvelous examples of each style, he makes his point that in art as in life, all categorization is fuzzy at the edges. "Beethoven didn't know he was composing stride in the last movement of the Concerto No. 1 in C, in the A minor section!" His advice about faking is equally funny:

> Faking really means improvising, particularly to cover up an unpredictable performance situation. An aptitude for faking tends to develop quickly when, for example, you are playing at a seashore concert and your music blows away, or when a singer's faulty entrance throws off the entire accompanying orchestra, resulting in what is known in the trade as a train

> wreck. At such times confusion reigns and the conductor will very likely wave everyone else out except the poor pianist, who has to figure out alone where the singer has wandered and fake his way into a suitable connection.

Hyman insists that this sort of nonjazz improvisation has been going on for a long time, and that pianists in particular have been expected to produce appropriate music for all manner of situations. His opinion is that "Bach, Beethoven, Mozart, Mendelssohn, and other cats like that who could improvise four-part fugues, could probably blow any of our modern day jazz musicians right off the bandstand." To add a bit of controversy to his own thesis, Hyman composed some little variations—from stride to fugato—to "Ah! vous dirai-je Maman," the group of Mozart variations (on the tune we know as "Twinkle, Twinkle, Little Star").

Hyman's view of pianos is no different from that of anyone I know in the classical field. He declares mystically that the instrument tells you what it wants. "You have to have a little meeting beforehand to get the instrument to cooperate with you, and if necessary, tell it who is the boss."

Any classical pianist who thinks he expends more energy in an orthodox recital program than a jazz musician does should watch Hyman's perpetual motion. He stays on top of the action, whenever he plays.

31

Coping with the Extraordinary

ALTHOUGH I have never suffered from the strain of nerves in anticipation of an interview, I have been thoroughly winded afterward. Whether I faced unexpected challenges in meetings with famous artists, logistical problems, language barriers, or simply cutting through layers of hype to get to the core, I have landed on my feet to tell the tales that may never get into print.

A "legendary" figure does not often appear in our midst, nor does the term necessarily apply when it is used, but in 1982 Magda Tagliaferro, the ninety-one-year-old Brazilian-born French pianist, whose colleagues included Gabriel Fauré, Vincent d'Indy, Alfred Cortot, Jacques Thibaud, and Pablo Casals, breezed into town, and I was most anxious to meet her. "Legendary" can also imply myth, but a few moments in her lively presence—whether in sparkling conversation or in concert—attest to the complete authenticity of this legend. No one had warned me that she hardly spoke any English, and thankfully my French is better than adequate, but it takes a moment or two to enter the mode of a foreign language, to *faire la bouche marcher* (to get your mouth to work). In addition to the language question and the prospect of meeting a legend, I was not at all prepared for my initial encounter.

"It's impossible!" one was tempted to exclaim, seeing Madame

Tagliaferro bound jauntily into the room with the step and mien of a college girl. She answered ingenuously, "*Mais je ne mens pas*" (I don't lie). With total candor, in a charming mix of three-quarters French, one-quarter English, she described her carefully budgeted day of morning practice and early afternoon siesta. "A miracle doesn't happen by itself. You have to help it along. A doctor once told me that the secret to longevity is *couper le jour en deux* (to cut the day in half). After all, a motor that runs from 7 A.M. to 1 A.M. the next day will soon break down, and I am the antithesis of a machine in every way."[1]

She was warm, expressive, alert, and witty, and when she was sharing memories, particularly of her lessons with Cortot, she was rapt.

> He was my Maître. So brilliant, passionate, such temperament. But more than that, you could speak with him about anything. I knew him from when I was fourteen until he died, and yet I never could really say I knew him because he changed so much from day to day. . . . It was droll how all the girls were in love with him. He had splendid eyes and an interesting face. What did he do for me musically? He opened my imagination. Technically, he left me to develop by myself, but he gave me so much more: musical vision.

Imagine my racing thoughts: to transcribe *any* interview from tape requires patience and endless hours. She was chattering on with all these pearls of recollection, and my one tormented fear was that I would lose any single word of it. I could barely get beyond her animation, starting with a blazing head of hair, somewhere between a vermilion and magenta that *The New York Times* described as "a color nature wouldn't dare to imitate."

As we know, artists may be household names on one side of the Atlantic and virtually unknown on the other. Tagliaferro had purposely stayed away from the United States for thirty-nine years after hearing her manager, Arthur Judson, say he would "sell her for such and such number of dollars." She was disturbed and disillusioned by a commercialism that she henceforth associated with this country, and only after Harold Schonberg heard her in recital at the Salle Gaveau in Paris and went home to write a sparkling review did she rethink her decision. At age ninety-one, she returned to the United States for concerts and interviews, apparently no less energetic. Her biography reads like a *Who's Who* in music: with illustrious pianists taking her classes at the Conservatoire Nationale de Musique in Paris where she had been a professor since 1937 and where she had won First Prize in piano at age thirteen. She soloed with Furtwängler, Stokowski, Barbirolli, Monteux, and other great conductors and enjoyed the friendships of pianists such as Claudio Arrau and Arthur Rubinstein, who met her backstage in Paris with a greeting, "Magnifique! Je vous envie," a poignant comment from one veteran who no longer played to one who did.

At the time of that interview my personal life was in flux. I arrived in the vicinity of the townhouse in which she was staying, much too early to ring the bell. Instead I wandered into a nearby shop and was captivated by a large teddy bear that I simply could not "bear" to walk away from. So when I finally rang her bell, I presented a rather unsophisticated figure: attaché case with notes and tape recorder on one arm, shopping bag with teddy peering out on the other! Apparently my teddy bear captivated Madame Tagliaferro as well, and I found I could easily be ingenuous with her and admit that I had bought him for myself. We talked about our preference for teddy bears over ex-husbands, and the conflicts and choices she had had to make for her career. The interview was infused with her *joie* of living and loving and her delightful candor. Yes, we struggled through several language impasses, but her easy laughter and talent for communication made it a sheer pleasure.

In concert at Alice Tully Hall at Lincoln Center in New York, she played the Schumann Piano Concerto and Fauré's Ballade for Piano and Orchestra, Opus 19, with the grandeur and grace of her advanced years and with an intimacy, tenderness, and exquisite tone throughout. She told me in French (Portuguese had been her native tongue in Brazil):

> I believe if I had not become a pianist, I would be a painter. I do not paint, but I know I would have loved it. I would have painted in grand strokes—frescoes, or large canvases. No miniatures. Enormous like my signature. In Portuguese we say "You are either eight or you are eighty," and I am eighty. It has nothing to do with age; it has to do with dimensions: all or nothing, and I do things in a whole-hearted big way. I never played anything I didn't love.

It is easy to remember why I loved her immediately.

. . .

In 1990 I interviewed another nonagenarian, Mieczyslaw Horszowski,[2] who was then ninety-eight. Most of us will be glad to walk at ninety-eight, much less play as he did. To his audiences at Carnegie Hall that year, the vigor of his playing was even more striking after his slow trudge across the great stage to his instrument. If his concert bore no earth-shattering revelations, it did have a clarity, purity, and rightness about everything. Moreover, he was surrounded by a radiance that added to his musical presence, and although he had to sit and rest just behind the curtain before each entrance, he became young every time he touched the piano. Backstage his throng of well-wishers and former students had to be monitored to preserve his stamina.

Formal interviews with Horszowski had already become rare and problematic. Although he had miraculously escaped arthritis, other symptoms of extreme old age had begun to afflict him. Difficulties with hearing and sight led to complete dependence on his wife, Madame Horszowska, about forty years his junior. They met in Italy in 1956, but it was not until 1981 when the artist was ninety that they married, each for the first time. His dependency had two particularly interesting facets. When he wished to re-examine an old work or learn something that had slipped by him during nine decades in music, such as Beethoven's First Piano Concerto, he learned it through dictation, relying on his wife to play it for him.

But it was during my interview with him that I came face to face with the most cumbersome form of dependence on her. I posed a question, presumably to him. She translated it into her native Italian, rephrasing it to him. He answered her in Polish and Italian. She answered me in English. Not one's ideal interviewing circumstances and not too conducive to spontaneity, yet what prevailed was the sense of rare privilege for me to talk, albeit indirectly, with an artist whose close friends included the nineteenth-century violinist Josef Joachim as well as Toscanini, Rubinstein, Ravel, Fauré, Villa-Lobos, de Falla, Granados, and Saint-Saëns, and whose career began with command performances for King Edward VII in 1906.

. . .

The late pianist William Masselos, whose career in the 1940s and '50s was distinguished by his performances of both standard repertoire and contemporary, gave the world premieres of works by Charles Ives, Aaron Copland, John Cage, and Ben Weber. In an interview in 1985 he described that period as

> a special moment in American music. . . .The younger performers and composers were at the end of a truly great push: by this time Satie, Ives, and Varèse had really done their work and contemporary music was starting to be heard and make itself felt. This was also a period when all kinds of things were still new: Debussy's Études, Webern's Varia-

> tions, and Schoenberg's Opus 11, not to mention Ravel's *Gaspard de la nuit*. Those are all classics now, which we tend to take for granted, but they were new music then, and they put tremendous vibrancy into the atmosphere. The younger composers were touched by this and so were the performers: Stokowski, Leonard Bernstein, and Glenn Gould, Merce Cunningham and David Tudor, and so on.[3]

Despite his identification with contemporary literature, Masselos' recording of Schumann's *Davidsbündlertänze* is often considered his definitive performance and possibly *the* definitive performance of that work. His recording is in some ways a microcosm of the man, and conversely, I found him to be like the music—gentle, refined, and witty, yet hesitant, perhaps as a result of a prolonged illness which he described as "Parkinson's-like" that would continue to keep him out of the public eye for many years until his death. From age eleven, Masselos studied with Carl Friedberg, a student of Clara Schumann, and has said that the Schumann pieces are like his musical diary, that this music is his mother tongue, that it gave him a voice. "I guess I have never befriended words," Masselos told me, to explain his reticence and to apologize for the arduous process involved in the several sessions of conversations that comprised the interview. I, in turn, kept reassuring him of my gratitude and sense of rare privilege.

Upon the advice of Arthur Rubinstein, Masselos also studied with David Saperton and Nelly Reuschel, another German with connections to Clara Schumann and ironically the one who introduced him to American music by way of the Griffes sonata. Masselos' retirement recital at Carnegie Hall in 1969 began at 7 P.M. and ended at 11 P.M.: he began with contemporary music, going back in time and ending with Schumann and Chopin. Before that concert, described by critics as a triumph, he had imposed a kind of exile on himself, even though many believed that he could have chosen to pursue and achieve a major career. In fact, he described that event as the retirement of an idea of conventional concertizing, after which he went on to give "exploratory" programs.

As they always do, a collection of memorabilia provided a colorful spark to our meetings: photos of Masselos with eminent composers, conductors, choreographers, painters, and sculptors; letters from colleagues and even from Robert and Clara, programs, and gifts. Perhaps the loveliest treasure was an autograph edition of Erik Satie's *Sports et Divertissements,* short pieces inspired in 1914 by art nouveau plates painted by the French artist Charles Martin, each reproduced adjacent to the work it inspired. From this beautiful album Masselos performed the work in 1958, with Virgil Thomson narrating and slides of each plate projected for the audience. Stacks of old manuscripts, books, and sheet music littered the floor under his piano, evidence of his interesting career. What touched me the most were his philosophical words about the past and the realities of his present condition.

> I believe I had my share of marvelous things happening, and too many folks try to hang on and on to careers. I don't have enough control of my hands to perform, but the teaching is a pretty consuming affair. It's a way of making music, like any other. My life is making music . . . and performing was never more than a part. It is a matter of finding music with your own body. As long as I have a body, I will be musical; I was a musical body long before I ever laid eyes on the piano, and I believe I would go on being one if I never sat at the keyboard again.

. . .

Along with Magda Tagliaferro, Mieczyslaw Horszowski, and William Masselos, I have met and spoken with other pianists who are no longer with us. When I listen to the tapes of these interviews, I feel that their voices and extraordinary thoughts ought to be heard and preserved, and that I am a privileged custodian.

My few hours with Rudolf Firkušny[4] revealed his elegance and warmth, the complete professional commitment that marked his career as a concert pianist, and his passionate identity as a Czech musician. Some pianists decry nationalistic labels—"French" pianist, "Russian" pianist—but Firkušny seemed to revel in his roots, and his walls were virtually papered with the autographs of his mentor, teacher, and spiritual father, Leos Janáček. Those manuscripts were visually beautiful even as calligraphy; the gougings of his pen, where he altered his writing were, for Firkušny, a banner of the fiery Czech national spirit, carrying on the national feelings expressed by Dvořák and Smetana, who wrote music derived from Czech mythology and folklore, even while there was censorship in the other arts. Rudolf Firkušny was born in February of 1912, at the moment when Czechoslovakia began to exist as a nation. Janáček managed to break away from the established traditions and general musical currents dominated by Germany and Austria.

At one point in the interview, Firkušny left the room without an explanation and returned with a much-beloved piano score that Janáček had presented to him when he was only nine. He translated the inscription, "To Rudolf Firkušny to help him in his artistic pilgrimage, with love from Janáček." The score is beautifully embellished with woodcuts, and the name Rudolf Firkušny appears on every single page (for which the young pianist used his deceased father's rubber stamp in a touching little ritual of ownership). The seventy-year-old pianist regarded it with amusement as a "silly" thing, nevertheless proudly displaying it as evidence of a love which no words could better describe.

Firkušny told me that he could use another whole lifetime to accomplish what time had not permitted. Yet even with his concentration on Czech music, he was known for the refinement and good taste that distinguished his performances of the standard solo and chamber literature, particularly Mozart.

. . .

On the occasion of the eightieth birthday of the renowned late pianist Claudio Arrau, I found myself sitting in the semi-dusk of his studio overlooking the water in Douglaston, Long Island, amidst his stunning collection of primitive African sculptures, pre-Columbian terracottas, and ancient icons. On every surface, including his pianos, there were *objets d'art*: mysterious little lacquered boxes, porcelains, oriental rugs upon rugs, contemporary abstract paintings. Certainly the artist had surrounded himself with the things he loved the most. As he told me, "I have lived a long time with every single one of these sculptures and paintings, and they still give me inspiration. I feel fortunate to have been able to collect so many beautiful things throughout my life, and I love having them near me."[5]

Another source of inspiration for Arrau was nature, of course one of my favorite subjects. Both his home on Long Island and his four-hundred-acre estate in Vermont afforded him the opportunity to garden, which he did gloveless (as I do), much to the chagrin of his family and friends. I loved his answer to my request that he try to define the special satisfactions he found in gardening: "A sort of nature mysticism. I have these rather ecstatic moments in nature while communing with the trees, flowers, leaves, and colors which are important to me." In response to my comment that he seemed to have unlimited sources of inspiration, he giggled, "The more the better!"

Arrau's work was distinguished by his punctilious fidelity to the text and dedication to what he intuited as the true meaning of the music. He was always looking for "new clues" to the composer's intent, and he insisted on the courage to express whatever one felt strongly concerning the music, despite any dissension. "Out of such thinking I have taught myself to be independent of everything—of success, of no success, of applause, of no applause, of everything but the music." Many spoke with reverence for his beautiful tone; others said he played as though he had "brains in his fingers."

I found it exciting to hear him remembering the times in Paris, Italy, and even England when critics such as Romain Rolland and George Bernard Shaw were vehemently against German music, selecting Brahms as "the embodiment of all its faults and weaknesses. A performer couldn't even risk putting it on a program because critics would tear it to bits."

Arrau discussed changes in the value system for piano-playing over the years, citing performers such as Edwin Fischer, Alfred Cortot, and Josef Hofmann whose wrong notes were overlooked and viewed as signs of genius, as compared with the current ethic of technical perfection. His opinion was that a trade-off was made between the poetry of "the good old days" and the technical wizardry of today. He spoke of the times when programs were lengthier without any regard for the attention span of the audience; he recalled the atmosphere of artistic ferment in Berlin during the Weimar Republic, and pianists like Artur Schnabel and Edwin Fischer personifying the union between artistic freedom and fidelity to the text, which, in turn, became Arrau's guiding principles.

In our conversation he would stop nothing short of the meaning of life itself: "I think the highest goal any human being can have is to develop all his gifts and fulfill himself." Yet as rich as the interview turned out to be, I remember coming away from the meeting feeling as though I had not truly connected, personally, with Mr. Arrau, as I have done in almost every other encounter. The artist rarely made eye contact with me, speaking as though to some spirit out in space, and I think the answer lay in a character trait which he defined as an element in the nature of a great artist: "It is the capacity to work alone and to be alone to reflect and dream. I, myself, love to be alone. I am never bored. I like people, too, but many times I feel the urge, like Thoreau, to just retire and meditate, and I do it often."

Arrau was an artist whose piano-playing I respected more than loved, yet I saw elements in his lifestyle that strangely echoed my own—the inspiration coming from art and nature, and a love of solitude and meditation for their restorative powers.

~ 32 ~

Away From Home

EVER since I won a trip to Europe on the television quiz show "Concentration" when I was twenty, I have had occasional attacks of wanderlust; mine is not the variety that manifests itself to explore the vast unknown. I prefer to revisit the few countries we have enjoyed most—Italy, France, and England. Any time we go anywhere else, I have the distinct impression of being in the wrong place.

My husband and I honeymooned in England and Scotland, wanting especially to spend a bit of time in the Lakes region at an inn called Sharrow Bay in Ullswater. We wrote for reservations and were informed that they were fully booked. Undaunted, I wrote back to say that I was a pianist and watercolorist (at that time I was painting a lot) and that my husband was a poet. (My husband's main field of expertise is certainly literature, but he is one of the world's unknown, unpublished poets, which is perfectly fine with him.) Apparently this all sounded sufficiently romantic to the proprietors, who wrote us back at once, describing their charming gatehouse with a room called Maria that they hoped we would find suitable. "Suitable" was hardly the word. The leaded glass windows opened onto fragrant meadows with cows lowing almost under our windows. The lavender-scented, Swiss-cotton linens, potpourried drawers, wildflower and birdwatching manuals at our bedside, sherry decanter on the bureau, fresh fruit, and cabbage-rose upholstery and draperies created an enchanted atmosphere way beyond our expectations. The dining experience was strictly gourmet, and in the drawing-room of the main house, which had massive windows opening right onto Lake Ullswater, was a Bösendorfer piano. On several evenings I was invited to play for the guests, which I did with pleasure. We spent our days walking and stopping to write and paint. Each of us came back with a journal, mine with pages and pages of ecstatic entries alternating with my watercolor sketches, including one of Ernest writing a poem at the water's edge. His diary was laced with poetry. Friends who have perused our respective journals have suggested we try to publish them together, but their value is as personal chronicles of a lovely trip, documented more intimately than photos could do.

There is a special delight in being in an enchanting place, having no particular responsibilities, temporarily losing one's identity and then resurfacing momentarily as a pianist in a somewhat exotic milieu. It is altogether different from going to a place as a pianist to give a concert because the impulse to play is pure and unfettered by expectation or anxiety. The Chopin I played in that beautiful parlor in the twilight of those May evenings took on the intimacy of the rooms for which his music was meant. It was like a nineteenth-century salon fantasy: I could step aside and see myself as a character out of the past, as I did upstairs in the gatehouse against the backdrop of quaint floral wallpaper in our lovely room.

. . .

Years later our travels in Italy were artistically nourishing wherever we went. Built by a civilization that worshipped beauty as a value unto itself, Italy, with its avenues of cypresses, fields of sunflowers, narrow, winding streets, rosy-hued ancient stone buildings, delights the eye before one even steps into the museums, churches, and gallerias. As a believer in the symbiosis between music and art, I did not have to go on a pilgrimage for the beauty to feed right into my musical life. The environment was conducive and things just happened.

We stayed with friends in the gently rolling Tuscan hills outside of Siena. The watercolor pigments I have so often used—burnt sienna, raw sienna, and the umbers—came to life around us. We visited the Accademia Musicale Chigiana, a remarkable music festival and conservatory housed in a former palazzo right in the middle of Siena, where I had another experience that bordered on fantasy. The palazzo, a two-story stone structure from the fourteenth century, is filled with great paintings, frescoes, and gorgeous rare instruments, including Liszt's own Bechstein. The students take their lessons surrounded by the Renaissance works of Botticelli, Sassetta, Donatello, Perugino, and Matteo di Giovanni.

During a tour of the rooms I played wonderful harpsichords and pianos, but the jewel of the palazzo is surely the recital hall, the *salone dei concerti*. This room evokes visions of the salons wherein Mozart or Beethoven might have performed. There are painted portraits of Palestrina, Frescobaldi, and Monteverdi, and a vast fresco across the ceiling depicting the triumphal return of the Sienese from battle against the Florentines. The little hall is so aesthetically and acoustically perfect that I believe I played better there than I had ever played before. This great salone, host to Rubinstein, Casals, Pollini, and so many other illustrious artists, became my dream hall. It was as though I had donned the red shoes of ballet myth; I couldn't stop and could have played forever. Later I jokingly told the conservatory's director that I would play there any time, with or without fee, even in the middle of the night; and though the idea of performing there will always haunt me, my guess is that I enjoyed it more purely and thoroughly than I would have if I had been engaged to give a formal concert in the hall.

Our friends, the Palladinos, were living in a villa owned by an Italian contessa whose Scottish husband was bedridden. The day after our visit to the palace we were invited into his room, which had a magnificent view of his adopted country's landscape. He had an upright piano there, and hearing that I was a pianist, he requested some Scottish folk songs. That I managed to come up with "Annie Laurie," "Flow Gently Sweet Afton," and "The Minstrel Boy" I chalk up to the rare and warm hospitality of our hosts, my own elevated state of awareness, and good luck. The gentleman was moved to tears. Later that evening on our friends' adequate and ripe old upright, tuned especially for my visit, I played Scarlatti, Chopin's Barcarolle (after all we were headed for Venice), and much to our host's pleasure, some Neopolitan folk songs. Thank goodness we had the old *Fireside Book of Folk Songs* at home when I was growing up.

Then there was the jolly friar in the tiny chapel at the San Franscesco monastery atop a mountain in Fiesole, overlooking Florence; he allowed me to play the organ in response to my poor Italian: *Scusa, posso suonare il organo per favore?* Not only do I not speak Italian, I do not play the organ. Yet what a thrill it was to sit in a little eleventh-century church, imbued with a sense of solitude and isolation from the outside world, and break the absolute silence with Bach. We could all benefit from a stay in a monastery; whatever may be given up is more than gained back in peace and perspective. We were able to partake of that thanks to the nuns who run a little pensione in Fiesole. A ring of the bell is answered by one of the gracious sisters, and the visitor is thus embraced and enclosed within their safe refuge, the better to reflect and work. One evening while I was reading, I was amazed to hear the serene E major Prelude from Book I of Bach's *Well-Tempered Clavier* played with utter refinement in the adjacent music room. A young law student taking exams in Florence had sat down at the piano, and naturally we ended up playing for each other, grateful for the encounter. That's what I mean when I say that things just happened.

In Venice we rode on all manner of water craft, from tiny gondolas in narrow canals to large *vaporetti* cruising to the outer islands. We lived the Barcarolle from the gently rocking motion of the opening bars to the grandeur of the final pages. Just as Chopin seemed to chalk the whole thing off as only a dream in one sweeping scale, punctuating it with two sets of octaves as though to say, "That's that," so I too, regrettably, left Italy behind for a while.

~ 33 ~

Home Again: Some Final Thoughts

IT IS springtime again, and my husband and I are cleaning up the garden beds, transplanting, pruning, and generally rejoicing in the most exquisite moment of the year. We sauntered into the woods and found that a tremendous oak tree had fallen; the earth must have shook but we were probably out when it happened. Woodland plants and vines are already entwining themselves around it, and there's a good chance a raccoon or fox has made a den in the hollowed out trunk. In my herb garden the mint, parsley, oregano, lavender, thyme, and chives made it through the winter. I will have to replant some rosemary and sage. This is the first day we can open the bedroom window wide and smell the freshness of the soil mixed with the scent of herbs. From now into the summer, we will listen each morning from the bed to hear which songsters have arrived. We will keep the birdbaths filled and watch silently from the porch as a cosmos arches and dips with the weight of a tiny goldfinch. We have traveled and visited gardens from Giverny to Boboli, but there is no garden I love better than our own; I am certain every gardener feels that way. This is as far into the field as I want to be.

. . .

The city is a mecca and an energizer. It is close enough so that we can always fill ourselves to the brim with music and art any time we want. I will never weary of hearing great artists in live performance and marveling at their individuality. In years past, we would stand for hours in the cold in lines that wrapped around a city block, bucked up by the promise of a beautiful concert or museum exhibition. We have paid our share of scalpers' prices for seats for the opera, and in our student days, we sat high in the alpine regions at Carnegie, hanging on every note that wafted up to us. No studio recording can come close to that excitement.

Yet during the past few years, even with the luxury of excellent press seats, I have sometimes wondered about staying home, listening to choice recordings in silence and comfort rather than driving in bumper-to-bumper traffic to try to listen to a great performance in the midst of what sounds like a tuberculosis sanitarium. At a recent concert of Richard Strauss' great tone poem for cello and orchestra, *Don Quixote*, a hacking cougher pretty much ruined the final wrenching moment where the cello's descending glissando signifies Don Quixote's death. Just at the point in my life when I think I have unlocked the secret to concentration as a performer on stage, I am losing the ability to tolerate distractions as a listener. When I go backstage and find my friends and colleagues in distress after dealing with a disrespectful audience, I feel this all the more.

But then I remind myself that we must keep on sacrificing both as artists and as appreciators. The mere fact that musicians will continue to mount the stages of the world to express their gifts and to hope that in some way they have changed the world by doing so is as basic an indicator of the health and survival of our planet as any spotted owl, certainly.

I probably have enough fodder for years to come from all my encounters in the field—formal interviews may be a thing of the past. The arduous process of persuading someone to share ideas, scheduling, selecting provocative questions and inducing response, coping with technical difficulties, transcribing conversations from tape, crafting the article, and then sparring about tinkering by editors all used to seem more romantic to me than they do now. It will be sheer bliss to engage in similar conversations but with a freedom of spirit and repose, without future ramifications. I am always amused when folks tell me how glamorous they think the life of a music journalist must be or, for that matter, how glamorous it must be to get up on a stage and receive all that applause (as though none of it is hard work). None of it is glamorous. Yes, there are great rewards, and oddly, they are in the most private moments.

As there is no piano I love more than my own, nor any audience better educated and more appreciative than those I could gather in our own living room, the thought of limiting my playing to home base becomes ever more attractive.

I have never been ambitious. If I have followed any path, it has been out of love or curiosity, and the result of an abundance of creative energy. I am deep into the habit of playing the piano and writing. There will always be a stack of new music at the left of my piano and the odd biography or book of letters on the right. I will always want to jot things down, and probably there will be the occasional essay, maybe even more books.

Any time I think about cutting down on my teaching, I realize how involved I am with each of my students; the moment one of them leaves, another irresistible one comes along. I would love more time for gardening, painting, and cooking. Beethoven once said, "Only the pure of heart can make a good soup." I used to make some pretty good soups according to my husband; now I wouldn't mind being judged by my soups rather than my sonatas!

My life in music has been quite wonderful so far, even charmed. By some miracle, I have been able to maintain its equilibrium without sacrificing any of the other things I love, and for that reason I feel blessed. After my interview with clarinetist Richard Stoltzman, he commanded me to "Stay right there!" and ran out to get me a copy of his Mozart concertos recording. We had had a particularly joyful exchange about keeping the "dance" element alive in our music and our lives. On the record jacket, he scribbled, "To Carol, With love to a great 'dancer.'" And what are we dancing to? I feel there is a continuous song of life and that we must all keep listening to it. And then some day I want to haunt this house we live in, nestled in its verdant landscape, with its clean light, aromatic gardens, and the music of thrushes, Bach, Carolina wrens, Beethoven, robins, Mozart, goldfinches, Chopin, cardinals, Brahms, whitethroats, Ravel, catbirds, Schumann.

Notes

Preface

1. Carol Montparker, The Anatomy of a New York Debut Recital: A Chronicle (Evanston, Illinois: The Instrumentalist Company, 1984; reprint, New York: Pro-Am Music, 1989). Portions first appeared under the title "Chronicle" in The Piano Quarterly, summer 1976.

Chapter 1

1. Robert Browning, "Home Thoughts From Abroad," *Robert Browning's Selected Poems* (New York and Boston: Thos. Crowell and Company, 1896), 113.
2. Beethoven to Louis Schlosser, a young musician and friend, 1822–23, in *Beethoven: The Man and the Artist, as Revealed in His Own Words*, ed. Friedrich Kerst and Henry Edward Krehbiel (New York: Dover Publications, 1964), 29.
3. Eugène Delacroix, 1842, quoted in Ates Orga, *Chopin*, The Illustrated Lives of the Great Composers (London, New York: Omnibus Press, 1976), 103.
4. Olivier Messiaen, *Technique de mon langage musical*, 1942, quoted in Paula Hutchinson, "Performing Messiaen's *Le Merle Noir*," *Flute Talk*, October 1993.

Chapter 3

1. Quoted in Carol Montparker, "The Painter and the Pianist," *Clavier*, January 1993.
2. Quoted in Carol Montparker, "Jerome Lowenthal, Artist at Large," *Clavier*, January 1992.

3. Soetsu Yanagi, *The Unknown Craftsman: A Japanese Insight Into Beauty,* trans. and ed. Bernard Leach (Tokyo Kodansha International, Ltd., 1972.)

Chapter 5

1. Quoted in Dulcie Leimbach, "Making Music and Turning Heads," *The New York Times*, 1 June 1997.

Chapter 6

1. Carol Montparker, "Chopin's Barcarolle," *Clavier,* April 1983 and May/June 1983 (interviews with David Bar-Illan, Claude Frank, Byron Janis, Nadia Reisenberg, Gary Graffman, Rudolf Firkušny, and James Tocco); and "Interpretations of Chopin's Ballade #4," *Clavier,* December 1994 and January 1995 (interviews with Paul Schenly, Ruth Laredo, Jerome Lowenthal, Garrick Ohlsson, and Harris Goldsmith).
2. Carol Montparker, "Max Wilcox: Rubinstein's Alter Ego," *Clavier,* January 1987.
3. Yanagi, *The Unknown Craftsman.*

Chapter 7

1. Quoted in Erika Duncan, "After Years of Illness, Pianist Reunites with Chopin," *The New York Times*, Long Island Section, 27 October 1996.

Chapter 8

1. Mont Parker was changed legally to Montparker in 1982.
2. Mr. Henahan referred to a concert at Yale University, where I played Mendelssohn and Chopin cello and piano sonatas with my son, Dennis Parker.
3. Mr. Gould's midnight-owl phone habits are well-documented in biographies and film.
4. Quoted in Carol Montparker, "The Indomitable Leon Fleisher," *Clavier,* October 1986.

Chapter 11

1. Quoted in Carol Montparker, "Jerome Lowenthal, Artist at Large," *Clavier,* January 1992.
2. Carol Montparker, "A Pianist For All Seasons," *Clavier,* November 1989.

3. Quoted in Carol Montparker, "Conversation With Peter Frankl," *Clavier,* October 1981.
4. Quoted in Carol Montparker, "Krystian Zimerman," *Clavier*, April 1988.

Chapter 12

1. Robert to Clara Schumann, in Nancy B. Reich, *Clara Schumann: The Artist and the Woman* (Ithaca: Cornell University Press, 1985), 86, 91–92, 95.

Chapter 13

1. Will Crutchfield, "The Merits of Playing From Memory," *The New York Times*, 16 October 1986; Bernard Holland, "Remembering is Child's Play (Yeah, Right!)," *The New York Times*, 19 March 1995.
2. Holland, "Remembering."

Chapter 14

1. Bernard Holland, "Appeals to the Heart From the Unknown, Failed, and Forgotten," *The New York Times*, 13 February 1994.
2. Quoted in Carol Montparker, "Words and Music," *Clavier*, March 1986.

Chapter 15

1. Quoted in Carol Montparker, "The Lieder Pianist: Partner or Accompanist?" *Keynote*, April 1981.
2. Quoted in Carol Montparker, "Partner, Not Accompanist," *Clavier*, November 1982.

Chapter 17

1. Quoted in Carol Montparker, "Practicing With Claude Frank," *Clavier*, January 1983.
2. Ibid.
3. Ibid.

Chapter 19

1. Alfred Brendel, *Music Sounded Out* (New York: Farrar, Straus & Giroux, 1990).
2. James Huneker, *The Man and His Music* (New York: Charles Scribner's Sons, 1901).

Chapter 20

1. Alfred Brendel, *Music Sounded Out*.

Chapter 21

1. Clifford Curzon quoted by Lydia Seifter in "Remembering Clifford Curzon, A Great English Pianist," *Clavier*, January 1997.

Chapter 22

1. Quoted in Carol Montparker, "Krystian Zimerman," *Clavier*, April 1988.

Chapter 27

1. Wolfgang Amadeus Mozart to his father, 23 January 1782, Vienna, autograph Mozarteum, Salzburg.

Chapter 28

1. Felix Mendelssohn to Marc-André Souchay, 15 October 1842, in *The Musician's World: Letters of the Great Composers*, ed. Hans Gal (London: Thames and Hudson, 1965), 170.
2. Quoted in Carol Montparker, "Radu Lupu: Acclaim in Spite of Himself," *Clavier*, May/June 1981.
3. Carol Montparker, "Alfred Brendel: The Search for Truth," *Clavier*, April 1989.

Chapter 29

1. Carol Montparker, "Krystian Zimerman," *Clavier*, April 1988.
2. Carol Montparker, "Shura Cherkassky: Sprightly Sage of the Piano," *Clavier*, November 1990.

Chapter 30

1. Quoted in Carol Montparker, "Jazzing It Up With George Shearing," *Clavier*, July/August 1980.
2. Quoted in Carol Montparker, "Taking Five With Dave Brubeck," *Clavier*, February 1987.
3. Quoted in Carol Montparker, "Dick Hyman and All That Jazz," *Clavier*, October 1988.

Chapter 31

1. Quoted in Carol Montparker, "The Legendary Magda Tagliaferro," *Clavier*, March 1982.

2. Carol Montparker, "Mieczyslaw Horszowski: Musical Fountain of Youth," *Clavier*, September 1990.
3. Quoted in Carol Montparker, "A Few Rare Hours With William Masselos," *Clavier*, January 1985.
4. Carol Montparker, "Rudolf Firkušny: Aristocrat With a Folk Tradition," *Clavier*, February 1984.
5. Quoted in Carol Montparker, "Claudio Arrau: Portrait of the Artist at Eighty," *Clavier*, March 1983.

Bibliography

Brendel, Alfred. *Music Sounded Out*. New York: Farrar, Straus & Giroux, 1990.

———. *Musical Thoughts and Afterthoughts*. Princeton, New Jersey: Princeton University Press, 1976.

Carmi, Avner and Hannah. *The Immortal Piano*. New York: Crown Publishers, 1960.

Chase, Mildred Portney. *Just Being at the Piano*. Berkeley: Creative Arts Book Company, 1985.

Kerst, Friedrich, and Henry Edward Krehbiel, editors. *Beethoven: The Man and the Artist, as Revealed in His Own Words*. New York: Dover Publications, 1964.

Moore, Gerald. *Furthermoore*. London: Hamish Hamilton Ltd., 1983.

Orga, Altes. *Chopin*. The Illustrated Lives of the Great Composers. Sydney: Omnibus Press, 1983.

Reich, Nancy B. *Clara Schumann: The Artist and the Woman*. Ithaca: Cornell University Press, 1985.

Sadie, Stanley, editor. *The Norton/Grove Concise Encyclopedia of Music*. New York: W. W. Norton and Company, 1988.

Shuter-Dyson, Rosamund, and Clive Gabriel. *The Psychology of Musical Ability*. London and New York: Methuen, 1981.

Ulrich, Homer. *Chamber Music*. New York: Columbia University Press, 1948.

Walter, Bruno. *Of Music and Music-making*. New York: W. W. Norton and Company, 1957.

Yanagi, Soetsu. *The Unknown Craftsman: A Japanese Insight Into Beauty*. Trans. and ed. Bernard Leach. Tokyo: Kodansha International, Ltd., 1972.

Index

Abrams, Mary, 38
Albéniz, Isaac, 53
Albright, Madeleine, 177
Allen, Woody, 125, 264
Amir, Ronit, 148
Arden, David, 153
Argerich, Martha, 99, 108, 121, 247
Arrau, Claudio, 53, 269, 275–277
Arron, Judith, 126
Ashkenazy, Vladimir, 77, 179, 194, 246, 254

Bach, Johann Sebastian, 20, 29, 53, 60, 80, 118, 159, 160, 214, 217, 262, 263, 266, 281; *Goldberg Variations*, 67, 81; partitas, No. 1, 64, 258; No. 2, 209; *St. John Passion*, 154; *St. Matthew Passion*, 61, 154; Two-Part Inventions, 84; *Well-Tempered Clavier*, 28, 161, 228
Barber, Samuel, 138
Barbirolli, Sir John, 269
Bar-Illan, David, 90
Barrett, Elizabeth, 71
Bartók, Béla, 23, 28, 160
Baryshnikov, Mikhail, 152
Beethoven, Ludwig van, 19, 20–21, 53, 60, 61, 72, 77, 91, 93, 116, 121, 143, 150, 162, 197, 260, 266, 280, 285; "An die ferne Geliebte," 39; *Egmont* Overture, 131; piano concertos, No. 1, 145, 196, 265, 271; Nos. 3 and 4, 145; piano sonatas, Op. 27, No. 1, 64; Op. 78, 161; Op. 109, 29; Op. 111, 160–161; Septet, Op. 20, 61; Sonata for Cello and Piano, Op. 69, 42; string quartets, Op. 18, 62, 144; Opp. 133 and 135, 144; Violin Concerto, 261
Bellow, Saul, 26
Berg, Alban, 160, 161
Berkowitz, Sol, 36, 61, 155
Berlin, Irving, 61
Bernstein, Esther R., 84, 231
Bernstein, Leonard, 216, 263, 272
Bisceglie, Joe, 86–88
Bonnard, Pierre, 223
Borge, Victor, 258, 259
Bouboulidi, Rita, 108, 126
Brahms, Johannes, 19, 48, 111, 112, 113, 117, 119, 136, 139, 144–145, 161, 199, 276; Ballade, Op. 118, No. 3, 214; Fantasies, Op. 116, 64, 162; Intermezzo, Op. 116, No. 6, 262; *Klavierstücke*, Opp. 116–119, 166; piano concertos, No. 1, 63, 145, 166, 194, 221, 230; No. 2, 102; Requiem, 154; Sonata, Op. 120, No. 2, 166–167; Trio, Op. 114, 166; Waltzes, Op. 39, 138

Brendel, Alfred, 33, 79, 80, 151, 159–160, 162, 171, 249, 250
Brodsky, Stan, 34
Brown, Frederick, 191
Browning, Robert, 18, 38, 71
Brubeck, Dave, 263–264
Busoni, Ferrucio, 159

Cage, John, 271
Calder, Alexander, 40
Carmi, Avner, 52–53
Casals, Pablo, 267, 280
Castellini, John, 61, 154, 155
Cather, Willa, 45
Charles, Prince of Wales, 83
Chase, Mildred Portney, 72
Cherkassky, Shura, 255–257
Chopin, Frédéric, 21–22, 28,53, 64, 67, 77, 91, 92, 93, 104, 152, 164–166, 187, 195, 223, 235, 265, 272, 279, 282; Ballade No. 4, Op. 52, 89, 197; Barcarolle, Op. 60, 58, 89, 90, 161, 165, 281; Fantaisie, Op. 49, 64, 162; Mazurka, Op. 59, No. 2, 165–166; Nocturne, Op. 15, No. 2, 165; Polonaise, Op. 53, 55; Sonata No. 3, Op. 58, 34; waltzes, "Minute," 85; "2/4," Op. 42, 190
Clementi, Muzio, 116
Clinton, Hillary, 131
Copland, Aaron, 263, 271
Cortot, Alfred, 93, 267, 268, 276
Couperin, François, 23
Crutchfield, Will, 119, 120
Cunningham, Merce, 272
Curzon, Sir Clifford, 184

da Vinci, Leonardo, 35
Dash, Robert , 35–37, 254, 255
Debussy, Claude, 22, 92, 93, 159, 181, 215, 224, 271
Delacroix, Eugène, 22
Demus, Jörg, 135
Diebboll, John, 51
Dukas, Paul, 23
Dvořák, Antonin, 274

Edward VII, King, 271
Eliot, T. S., 67
Ellington, Duke, 263
Elman, Mischa, 137, 223

Faddis, Sylvia, 69
Falla, Manuel de, 271
Fauré, Gabriel, 267, 270, 271
Feltsman, Vladimir, 79
Fidelman, Josef, 31, 49, 59, 156, 180, 196, 210, 214, 222, 225, 226, 230–231
Firkušny, Rudolf, 78, 90, 274–275
Fischer, Edwin, 276
Fischer-Dieskau, Dietrich, 76, 135
Fleisher, Leon, 82
Fontrier, Gabriel, 155
Franck, César, 195
Frank, Claude, 79, 90, 149–151
Frank, Pamela, 149
Frankl, Peter, 78, 99, 195
Friedberg, Carl, 272
Furetïare, Antoine, 216

Galuppi, Baldassare, 38
Gershwin, George, 59, 216, 263
Gilbert, Sir William, 61
Gilels, Emil, 81
Gillock, William, 83
Godowsky, Leopold, 198
Goethe, Johann Wolfgang von, 222
Gould, Glenn, 43, 71, 80, 81, 82, 98, 118, 272
Gould, Morton, 257
Graffman, Gary, 79, 90

Graffman, Naomi, 109
Granados, Enrique, 271
Grieg, Edvard, 84
Griffes, Charles Tomlinson, 272
Gulda, Friedrich, 260
Gutiérrez, Horacio, 78, 79, 147

Hammerstein, Oscar, 227
Handel, George Frideric, 154, 155
Hanks, Tom, 194
Hardy, Thomas, 18
Haydn, Joseph, 84, 154, 159, 160
Helfgott, David, 130–131
Henahan, Donal, 74–76
Henry, Harold, 231
Hillel, 170
Hofmann, Josef, 276
Holland, Bernard, 119, 120
Hollander, Lorin, 90–91
Hopper, Edward, 245
Horn, Joan, 62
Horszowski, Mieczyslaw, 270–271, 273
Huneker, James, 164, 165
Hyman, Dick, 264–266

d'Indy, Vincent, 267
Ives, Charles, 263, 271

Janáček, Leos, 274
Janis, Byron, 69, 90
Jarrett, Keith, 260
Joachim, Joseph, 271
Johnston, Brent, 73
Joseffy, Rafael, 53
Judson, Arthur, 269

Kallir, Lilian, 149
Keats, John, 18
Kennedy, Nigel, 261
Keyes, Gene, 101, 167
Kissin, Evgeny, 79
Klee, Paul, 35
Kleinsinger, George, 84
Kraus, Lili, 122

Laredo, Ruth, 79, 108
Larrocha, Alicia de, 59, 107–108
Leschetizky, Theodor, 198
Levine, James, 135
Liszt, Franz, 21, 23, 50, 52, 53, 62, 91, 92, 149, 159, 165, 198, 217
Lowenthal, Jerome, 38, 39, 78, 148–149, 151
Lupu, Radu, 27, 62, 77, 98, 121, 129, 130, 132, 138, 151, 166, 172, 191, 248, 249

MacDowell, Edward, 67, 84
Mack, Ted, 85
MacLaine, Shirley, 83
Mahler, Gustav, 136
Maimone, Margarethe, 103
Mandyczewski, Eusebius, 167
Martin, Charles, 78, 273
Masselos, William, 78, 271–273
Mendelssohn, Felix, 21, 112, 145, 154, 165, 195, 245, 263, 266
Messiaen, Olivier, 23
Michailowski, Alexander, 164, 223
Mikuli, Carl, 164
Milhaud, Darius, 263
Milnes, Sherrill, 105
Milstein, Nathan, 137, 223
Miner, Laura Lynn, 78
Mittman, Leopold, 57, 58, 61, 63, 137, 164, 180, 183, 184, 194, 195, 210, 218–226
Mocsanyi, Paul, 50
Monet, Claude, 22, 67
Monsaigneon, Bruno, 81
Monteux, Pierre, 269

Moore, Gerald, 76–77, 135, 136, 139
Moore, George, 22
Morgenthau, Henry, Jr., 84
Morris, William, 18
Moskowski, Moritz, 198
Mozart, Wolfgang Amadeus, 19, 20, 41, 79, 80, 91, 116, 237, 260, 263, 266, 275, 280, 286; Double Concerto, K. 365, 146; Piano Concerto, K. 488, 145–146; Requiem, 154; Sonata for Two Pianos, K. 448, 138
Mussorgsky, Modest, 58, 214

Neuhaus, Heinrich, 230
Newman, Barnett, 33

Orenstein, Arbie, 24
Orga, Altes, 287

Parisot, Aldo, 224
Parker, Dennis, 42, 166, 224
Parker, Kim, 18, 42, 47, 261
Perahia, Murray, 138
Piatigorsky, Gregor, 223
Picasso, Pablo, 182
Pollini, Maurizio, 247–248, 280
Poulenc, Francis, 262
Prokofiev, Sergei, 54, 153
Pythagoras, 20

Rachmaninoff, Sergei, 61, 138, 195
Rampal, Jean-Pierre, 47
Ravel, Maurice, 23, 24, 58, 92, 117, 182, 271
Reich, Nancy B., 111
Reisenberg, Nadia, 90
Repin, Ilya, 58
Respighi, Ottorino, 154
Reuschel, Nelly, 272
Rolland, Romain, 218, 223, 276
Roosevelt, Franklin Delano, 84
Rosenthal, Moritz, 53
Rösler, Gustav, 62
Rovinsky, Anton, 265
Rubinstein, Aniela, 74
Rubinstein, Arthur, 27, 63, 72, 73, 84, 99, 121, 141, 151, 171, 172, 253, 257, 269, 271, 272, 280
Rubinstein, John, 74
Ryder, Craig, 86, 88

Saint-Saëns, Camille, 271
Sand, George, 21, 22
Saperton, David, 272
Sargent, John Singer, 35
Satie, Erik, 78, 271, 273
Scarlatti, Domenico, 159, 281
Schiff, Andras, 20, 160, 167
Schickele, Peter, 79, 245
Schnabel, Artur, 265, 276
Schneider, Larry, 254
Schoenberg, Arnold, 35, 117, 154, 160, 272
Schonberg, Harold C., 129, 231, 269
Schreiber, Howard, 229–230
Schreiber, Walter, 86, 229
Schubert, Franz, 20, 21, 62, 67, 84, 122, 136, 138, 149, 152, 154, 160, 162–164
Schumann, Clara, 111–115, 116, 272, 273
Schumann, Robert, 38, 80, 111–114, 136, 161, 166, 272–273; *Aufschwung*, 214; *Carnaval*, 165; *Davidsbündlertänze*, 160, 272; Fantasy, Op. 17, 39, 160; *Kinderscenen*, 203; *Kreisleriana*, 28; Piano Concerto, Op. 54, 145, 147, 230, 270; *Waldscenen*, 24; *Warum?*, 67
Segovia, Andrés, 122
Serkin, Peter, 99
Serkin, Rudolf, 74, 129

Shakespeare, William, 18, 150
Shaw, George Bernard, 71, 276
Shearing, George, 262–263
Shostakovich, Dmitri, 153
Silverman, Robert, 80
Simon, Abbey, 85
Slonimsky, Nicolas, 265
Smetana, Bedrich, 274
Solti, Georg, 110
Sondheim, Stephen, 227
Starker, János, 80, 118, 133, 138, 139–140, 183
Stern, Isaac, 125
Stevenson, Robert Louis, 54, 169
Stokowski, Leopold, 269, 272
Stoltzman, Richard, 285
Strauss, Richard, 136, 284
Stravinsky, Igor, 61, 155
Sullivan, Sir Arthur, 61

Tagliaferro, Magda, 79, 267–270, 273
Takemitsu, Toru, 19
Tatum, Art, 263
Tchaikovsky, Piotr Ilyich, 59, 62
Tennyson, Alfred, Lord, 18
Terry, Ellen, 71
Thibaud, Jacques, 267
Thomson, Virgil, 273
Torra, Juan, 108
Toscanini, Arturo, 154, 271
Tovey, Donald Francis, 61
Tudor, David, 272

Uchida, Mitsuko, 29, 108, 160–161
Utrillo, Maurice, 220

Varèse, Edgard, 271
Velasquez, Diego, 182
Verdi, Giuseppe, 154
Villa-Lobos, Heitor, 271
Vuillard, Edouard, 219, 223

Walter, Bruno, 20
Watts, André, 49, 62, 64, 77, 78, 97, 125, 132, 149, 151, 173, 191, 195, 245, 246, 247
Weber, Ben, 271
Weber, Carl Maria von, 79
Weber, Max, 220, 221
Webern, Anton, 91, 271
Welty, Eudora, 25
White, E. B., 31
Wieck, Friedrich, 111
Wieniawski, Henryk, 41
Wilcox, Max, 63, 64
Wolfensohn, Joseph B., 125
Woolf, Virginia, 32
Wordsworth, William, 18

Yanagi, Soetsu, 39, 64
Yeats, William Butler, 19

Zimerman, Krystian, 20, 102, 186, 253